PRODUCTIVITY

IS POWER

PRODUCTIVITY IS POWER

Five Liberating Practices for Undergraduates

Second Edition

HILLARY RETTIG

Author of *The 7 Secrets of the Prolific*
and *The Lifelong Activist*

Foreword by James Wilkinson, Ph.D.
Emeritus Director
Derek Bok Center for Teaching and Learning, Harvard University

Infinite Art Press

Productivity Is Power
Five Liberating Practices for Undergraduates
second edition
by Hillary Rettig
Foreword by James Wilkinson, Ph.D.

ISBN 979-8-9896387-1-0 paperback
ISBN 979-8-9896387-2-7 ebook

Cover by Lee Busch/LBDesign, www.lbdesign.com
Formatting and interior design by Woven Red Author Services, www.wovenred.ca

Publisher's Cataloging-in-Publication data
Names: Rettig, Hillary, author. | Wilkinson, James, 1943-, foreword author.
Title: Productivity is Power : 5 Liberating Practices for Undergraduates, second edition / Hillary Rettig; foreword by James Wilkinson.
Description: Includes bibliographical references and index. | Kalamazoo, MI: Hillary Rettig dba Infinite Art, 2024.
Identifiers: LCCN: 2024901338 | ISBN: 979-8-9896387-1-0 (paperback) | 979-8-9896387-2-7 (ebook)
Subjects: LCSH College students--Time management. | Study skills. | Academic achievement. | BISAC STUDY AIDS / General | STUDY AIDS / Study & Test-Taking Skills | SELF-HELP / Personal Growth / Success | SELF-HELP / Self-Management / Time Management | YOUNG ADULT NONFICTION / Study Aids / General
Classification: LCC LB2395.4 .R48 2024 | DDC 378.1/7--dc23

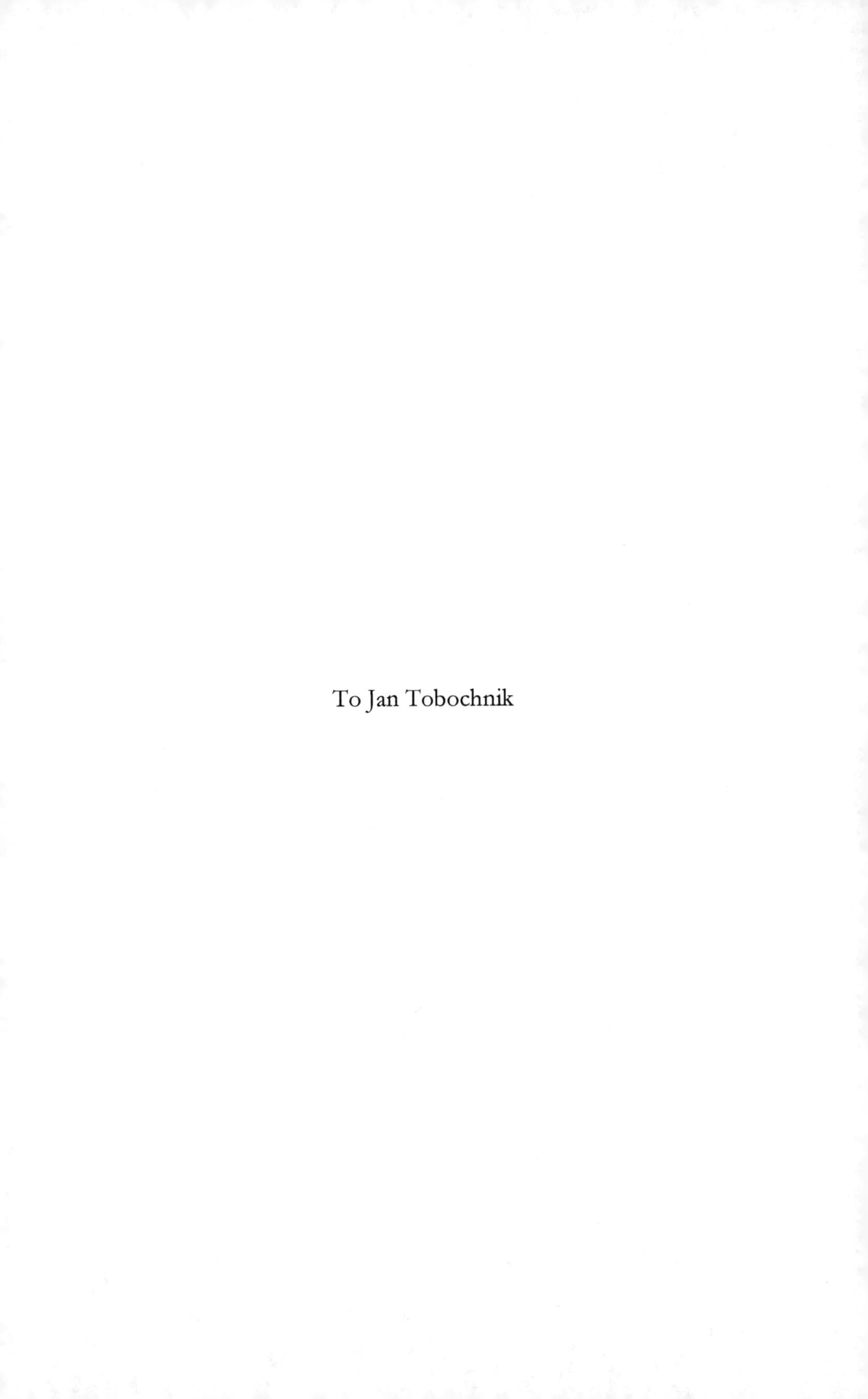

To Jan Tobochnik

Contents

Vocabulary/Text Notes

Except where indicated, I use the words "professor" and "teacher" interchangeably, and also use those terms to refer to all educators, including tenure-track professors, adjunct professors, graduate student instructors, teaching assistants, coaches, tutors, advisors, and others.

I also use the words "college" and "university" interchangeably.

I define "procrastination" as the problem of not being able to reliably do your work as planned. And a "block"—as in "writer's block" or "creative block"—is a severe, prolonged bout of procrastination. When I need a verb form, I generally use "procrastinate," and my preferred adjective is "underproductive." In both cases, I'm referring to the entire spectrum of underproductivity, from slight procrastination to a severe block.

For reasons that will become clear, I avoid using labels like "procrastinator" and "perfectionist" in conversation or when teaching, but I do use them in this book for brevity and clarity.

I use descriptors like "productive" and "prolific" not to indicate some arbitrary standard of productivity, but someone working at their own comfortable-but-focused capacity. Ditto for "successful": I always use that to mean you got a good result relative to your situation and efforts.

I frequently distinguish between a job you do entirely, or primarily, for money, and a "vocation" or "mission" you do out of interest or passion. (Of course, some are lucky enough to be able to earn a living from their vocation, and if that's your goal this book will help.)

I don't distinguish between "creative" and "uncreative" work: it's all creative.

I use the term "mentor" as a catch-all for any kind of advisor, be they a teacher, coach, family member, coworker, colleague, supervisor, therapist, or friend.

I use gender neutral pronouns (singular they/them) except when a person's pronouns are gendered or when gendered pronouns are useful for clarity.

The case studies in this book are composites that reflect real-life situations. Many of the shorter anecdotes and examples, however, are true stories that happened pretty much as told, although I do change the names and other identifying details of those involved.

On Using the Correct Toolset

The techniques in this book have helped many, but no technique helps everyone, so feel free to skip any that aren't working for you. I'm unable to guarantee a positive result when using any of the techniques in this book.

Underproductivity often occurs alongside physical health problems (e.g., fatigue), mental health problems (e.g., anxiety or depression), a learning difference (e.g., dyslexia or ADHD), and/or neurodivergence. In these situations, my techniques can be useful adjuncts to medical or therapeutic treatment, but should not replace it. If you are dealing with one of these types of conditions, or think you might be, please consult a specialist.

Foreword

This book could be a lifesaver. Addressed to students struggling with the demands of college work and prey to procrastination, it offers a detailed and practical set of strategies for realizing their potential. As such, it should appeal to a broad audience. How many students today feel stressed by college workloads? Far too many. How many blame themselves for performing poorly? Again, far too many. But their distress is not inevitable. *Productivity Is Power* offers them a lifeline.

The reasons for student stress vary. Coping mechanisms that served well enough in high school may fail when confronted by the greater demands of college-level work. The cohort of friends that gave emotional support may have dispersed. Many students are living away from home for the first time, with the attendant temptations of life without parental supervision. Added to this mix is the fact that asking for help can be hard, especially if you have never needed help before.

But the main enemy, the author argues here, is perfectionism. Students want to do well, know they are underperforming, and then blame themselves, procrastinate, or both. Procrastination postpones what may seem an inevitable failure, yet also triggers a cascade of self-blame and further diminished performance. Simply put, self-punishment is a terrible motivator. There has to be a better way to succeed.

As this book makes clear, college support services and concerned faculty do offer counsel and guidance toward this goal. But their efforts are constrained by a lack of resources and time. Sadly, student demands for services often exceed the capacities of those equipped to offer them. No one on campus, least of all faculty, can do everything expected of them in the time available. Teaching, research, family obligations, committee service, and (one hopes) self-care all claim a part of faculty's daily schedule. Students can at best secure a sliver of adult attention when they need a generous slice, and are most often left to cope on their own.

Enter *Productivity Is Power*. The book offers both a nuanced set of diagnostics, enabling readers to discover where the root of their performance problems lies, and a wealth of practical solutions to set matters right. And whereas it offers students the tools and help they need, it does so without feeding their guilt for needing help in the first place. Instead, *Productivity Is Power* models the attitude the author wishes her readers to cultivate—kindness and understanding toward oneself, a sober analysis of poor academic performance, and confidence that one can improve.

Of course, validating students for who they are while still motivating them to change requires a delicate balance between acceptance and incitement. Students' self-criticism, feelings of unworthiness, or suspicion that they are perhaps the "admissions committee's big mistake" can easily rob them of the confidence and energy needed to address flagging productivity. Theirs is a problem that can be solved only if they believe that it's open to solution. As Hillary Rettig herself insists, guilt is disempowering. Encountering *Productivity Is Power* feels like entering a guilt-free zone.

It should be added that overcoming the syndrome of self-disempowerment and procrastination is a skill whose usefulness extends well beyond the college years. If the transition from high school to college tests students' coping skills, then the transition from college to postgraduate employment tests them all the more. Jobs in the "real world" come with deadlines and expectations of on-time performance. So do living with a partner and pursuing personal projects. Becoming reliably productive is in fact a life skill, and mastering it early pays dividends. This wise and timely book shows the way.

James Wilkinson
Senior Associate and Director Emeritus
Derek Bok Center for Teaching and Learning, Harvard University

Introduction: A New Kind of Productivity Book for a New Generation of College Student

If you've picked up this book, I assume it's because you're a college student who would like to do great work as easily and effectively as possible. (Or, perhaps you're someone who cares about such a student.) Maybe you'd like to get better at sticking to a schedule—and especially at starting your work on time. Or, at working steadily and with good focus for hours at a time. Or, at handing in your work on time or a bit early.

Perhaps you'd even like to have fun while doing it all. That's not too much to ask! Maybe you remember a time when you were younger and did art, math, science, history, or some other creative or intellectual endeavor just for the fun of it.

This book will help you reclaim that glory.

More specifically, it will teach you how to recognize, understand, and remove your barriers to joyful productivity, including procrastination, perfectionism, ineffective work processes, unhealed rejections, and unmanaged time.

Of course, there are plenty of generic productivity books that address these kinds of topics, some of them excellent. But I wrote this book specifically for undergraduates, for these reasons:

First, the undergraduate years are pivotal. Stay mostly on course during them and you can accelerate your progress and growth in college and beyond. But spend a lot of time lost in the weeds, as some of us do (see below), and you can struggle for a long time, perhaps missing out on some valuable opportunities.

Second, the undergraduate years are uniquely challenging, productivity-wise. There's a lot going on, starting at the neurological and developmental levels. Our frontal cortex, which is responsible for much of our judgment and decision-making, doesn't even finish developing until we're twenty-five. Then there's the sudden transition from constant parental and teacher supervision to a more independent lifestyle with many more opportunities—academic, extracurricular, and social—and distractions. Finally, add in the fact that you're in a new community, surrounded (hopefully) by different people and situations from those you grew up with.

It's a lot to handle.

In fact, I think today's college students have it rougher than previous generations. The combination of soaring tuition, exploitative student loan programs, and a terrible job market has put enormous pressure on you. Meanwhile, your professors and the other school professionals whom you would turn to for help are themselves under pressure from budget cuts and other factors.

As if all this weren't enough, you also have to contend with some terrible political and social crises, including rampant inequality, rising authoritarianism, the unfolding climate catastrophe, and pandemics. If you're distracted or upset by all of that, by the way, that just means you're a caring person who's been paying attention. Don't worry: I'll show you some techniques for staying focused even during difficult and distracting times.

Finally, let's not forget social media, a complex subject from productivity and other standpoints. On the one hand, it's a fun and liberating technology that's an essential part of many people's personal and work lives. (And it can be especially liberating for those with disabilities or who belong to marginalized groups.) On the other hand, it's been linked to some serious productivity, health, and other problems; and the fact that it is both ubiquitous and constantly "on" only adds to those concerns. Throughout this book, I'll be discussing ways to keep your social media use in balance.

You do have one excellent thing working in your favor, however, and that's *you*. I have a lot of respect for today's college students and other young people. Generally speaking, I think you're far more astute—politically, socially, and emotionally—than previous generations. Many of you also have a very healthy (for you and the planet) global and systems outlook. And many of you are also far more attuned to issues of identity, equality, justice, and inclusiveness than previous generations. These are all great things that will strengthen and enrich not just you, but society as a whole.

One Student's Story

A long time ago, at a university far, far away, a young woman graduated without a plan.

Actually, that was me! I was the one without a plan.

I had been an "accelerated" student, starting elementary school a year early and also skipping a grade. And so, I entered college at sixteen, full of accomplishments and confidence, ready to conquer the world. Instead, college wound up conquering me. I was clueless as to how to succeed and hit so many roadblocks, both academic and personal, that it's a miracle I managed to graduate at all. Many stemmed from ignorance—I was the first person in my family to go to college, although at the time being a "first gen" wasn't yet recognized as a barrier to success—but I also had a bunch of personal and interpersonal issues I hadn't even yet recognized, much less begun to work on.

My grades were all over the map and I also switched majors a lot, including in my senior year. It was pure chaos, and I felt, often, like pure chaos. Sure, some of my professors tried to help, but it was a large school and I was one of thousands. So "help" mostly consisted of a once-a-semester meeting with my advisor, plus meetings with my professors (or teaching assistants) whenever I reached out with questions. But what do you do if you don't even know what questions to ask?

What I don't remember is anyone ever sitting down with me and saying, "You look confused. Here's how this all works." I sure could have used that talk.

After college, I lacked a plan (as you already know), and so I spent the next few years hanging around my pleasant college town, taking easy secretarial and administrative jobs on campus. I then spent a couple of years traveling around Europe before returning to my native New York City to write fiction ("the dream"). This was in the 1980s, and financially, at least, I was in the right place at the right time since I could support myself by working a few nights a week in the word processing department of a financial services firm in Rockefeller Center. Sitting in a large, brightly lit, windowless room alongside a couple dozen other typist-dreamers—including many would-be actors, writers, artists, opera singers, etc.—I spent twelve hours typing and correcting memos, contracts, reports, and other capitalist ephemera. The work was easy, my coworkers fun, and the pay outstanding: around $16 an hour, which would be around $38 an hour today. And because it was an overnight shift, the firm also paid for a luxurious Town Car to take me home in the morning. (I loved that Town Car.)

It was an easy and fun existence—but still, I was avoiding all forms of professional accomplishment. My fiction writing was going nowhere, mostly because, for years, I wrote and rewrote the same opening of a novel over and over. (Despite my confusions and disappointments, I must acknowledge my significant generational and other privileges at that time in my life. Meandering confusedly through life is a lot pleasanter when you can do it on those good 1980s wages versus the starvation wages most employers pay today. Also, white privilege, able-bodied privilege, and perhaps some other privileges played a role in my ability to survive on relatively easy part-time work.)

Things finally started to gel for me in my thirties when I started doing freelance articles for computer magazines. This led to a job as an editor at a computer trade magazine where I wrote business profiles and case studies. It wasn't the most glamorous writing job but I loved it—largely because it offered the opportunity to interview many top-achieving people on their success. As a perennial underachiever, I especially wanted to know how my interviewees had overcome their barriers to success, and many were remarkably candid on that.

After many of these interviews, let's just say I got a clue.

In 2000, the technology sector crashed and I also got an obnoxious new boss. I quit my job and, in the absence of other publishing options, took one as a business teacher and coach at a nonprofit entrepreneurship program in Boston. That's when things really got interesting, because, even though I hadn't planned it that way, I was now seeing the flip side of the entrepreneurial story, the ones who hadn't yet succeeded—and who, in some cases, probably never would, because they couldn't manage their time or get motivated to do their work (write business plans, contact mentors, etc.). To be fair, most of our clients were busy adults with jobs, kids, and other responsibilities, so their path was never going to be easy. But the goal, in many cases, was achievable.

Our clients were cool people, and it saddened me to watch them get in their own way. (Just as I'm sure it saddened some of my professors to watch me get in my own way.) And so, based on my knowledge of productivity, creativity, time management, and a few other disciplines, I created two new modules for our business curriculum: one on time management and another on overcoming procrastination and other internal barriers to success. I worried that some students would find the "barriers" module, especially, to be too "touchy-feely," but everyone loved it. (I think it helped that I shared my own story and struggles so that I was engaging with them on terms of equality.) I knew, after the very first time I taught it, that I was onto something.

One of the memorable pieces of advice I had gotten, back in my interviewing days, was to "focus relentlessly on your key value-add"—meaning, the thing you do that is most valuable to the customer. (The guy who told it to me had grown a $250 million business from scratch, which was probably why it was memorable.) That was clearly my productivity work—and so, I followed his advice and that's how I wound up with a career focused on helping people get productive. For more than twenty years, I've been writing, thinking, teaching, and coaching on that topic: it's been a hugely rewarding path, and I'm especially pleased that my work seems to speak, in particular, to people seeking to make a positive contribution.

Which brings us back to this book....

Why Productivity Is Power

A few words about my approach. People come to productivity work from different backgrounds, including psychology, education, management, and creativity. There's also an academic field of "procrastination studies." However, as Andrew Santella notes in his book *Soon*, a historical overview of procrastination, there's a lot of debate among the field's experts even on the fundamentals: "If you want to start a heated argument among a group of procrastination researchers, ask whether chronic deferral has more to do with our inability to manage time or with a failure to regulate our emotions." (To which I would reply, echoing the little girl in the popular Internet meme, "Why not both?")

As for me, I've come to the field, as discussed above, from the perspectives of entrepreneurship, education, social work, and creativity (from all those years studying writing). Crucially, however, also from the perspective of social justice. From a young age, I've cared about injustice and have sought to do my share in creating a fairer world. My activism has centered, over the years, on feminism, economic justice, free software/free culture, and veganism/animal rights; and my very first book, *The Lifelong Activist*, was a self-help guide for progressive and Left activists.[1] It was, in fact, my social justice perspective that helped me to zero in on disempowerment as the primary cause of underproductivity—something I don't think any other general-audience book has done. (Some works in critical pedagogy and related fields do discuss this, but their treatment tends to be much more theoretical, and much less nuts-and-bolts, than what I'm offering here.) This perspective has also helped me to recognize that perfectionism is a much broader and more systemic problem than it's often presented as.

Some progressives are skeptical of self-help books such as this one, mostly because the field has tended to minimize, or ignore entirely, the role of societal forces in people's struggles. Progressives can be even more skeptical of productivity and time management books—like this one!—because those techniques have sometimes been used exploitatively to extract the maximum amount of labor from workers. Happily, this antipathy appears

---

[1] www.lanternpm.org/books/the-lifelong-activist/

to be softening, with more people recognizing that it is possible to both acknowledge the societal roots of many of our so-called "personal" problems *and* to focus on improving our individual condition and coping strategies where we can.[2]

In this book, I'm committed to acknowledging the societal contributions to the problems I discuss. This commitment starts with my definition of **productivity**, which is: the ability to work as easily, effectively, and joyfully as possible on your schoolwork and other priorities, within the limits of whatever constraints you may be facing. You'll notice that this definition focuses on the *process* of doing your work, versus quantified goals (e.g., to be able to write X pages or do Y math problems per hour) or desired outcomes (e.g., to get great grades or a great job). We can't use quantified goals because everyone's different, every project is different, and our work capacities vary depending on the situation. We can't specify outcomes for the same reasons, and also because overfocusing on outcomes triggers perfectionism and procrastination. (I'll explain why later.) This doesn't mean that you shouldn't go for the great goals and outcomes. Of course you should! But you should hold onto those goals lightly, as opposed to with an iron grip the way many perfectionists do. Besides, it's by focusing on process that you'll (somewhat paradoxically) have your best shot at attaining those great goals and outcomes. (Again, I'll explain why later.)

Also note the inclusion, in the definition, of those "other priorities." I want you to be "productive"—again meaning easy, effective, and joyful—in your self-care, relationships, recreation, and whatever other non-school activities are important to you. That's primarily because you're a human being whose needs deserve to be met, but also because our success usually rests on the foundation of a balanced and healthy life.

Now for the second big word in my book's title, **power**, which I define as the ability to use your strengths, skills, talents, energy, focus, and other capacities to achieve meaningful outcomes in your schoolwork and other priorities. In college, these "meaningful outcomes" often come in the form of grades, but learning and growth are even more important, if harder to quantify.

Power also consists of the ability to influence and lead others without robbing them of their own productivity and power. Power *with* others, in other words, not *over* them.

---

[2] See, for instance, *You Are Your Best Thing: Vulnerability, Shame Resilience, and the Black Experience*, co-edited by activist Tarana Burke and self-help author Brené Brown.

Implicit in both definitions is that, as much as possible, you're doing stuff you really want to be doing—i.e., working and living as authentically as possible.

We might as well tackle the third word in my title, that "is." Yes, I'm saying that productivity (as defined above) is the same as power (ditto). The more productive you are, the more empowered you'll be, and *vice versa*. I'll also be explaining this later on; for now, just know that, whenever you see someone who is underproductive, you can be sure that that person is also disempowered. As some immediate proof, I'll point out that many people procrastinate only on one or two key projects, like their schoolwork or exercise, but are productive the rest of the time. So it's clear they're not lazy or undisciplined, but that something is preventing them from using their "power" (energy, focus, discipline, etc.) in the service of the projects in question.

So how does an underproductive, disempowered person get their power and productivity back? That's the life- and world-changing question this book answers.

What to Do If You've Got an Urgent Deadline

This discussion is for those who, right now, are facing an urgent deadline. If that's you, keep reading. If not, feel free to skip to Chapter 1. (I'll be covering all the points in more detail throughout the rest of the book.)

Here's what you should do if you're facing an urgent deadline:

Clear Your Schedule

Your most urgent needs right now are for time and energy, so make a list of everything you're supposed to be doing, including schoolwork, extracurricular projects, your job (if you have one), and personal chores and errands. Then, take a serious look at each item and ask yourself: "Is it essential I do this *now*?"

If the answer is "no," postpone it. (Or, if you don't have to do it at all, cancel it.)

What about self-care? (Sleep, grooming, exercise, medical and therapy appointments, etc.) Don't cut that: your health and well-being are important, and not just because they aid your productivity. However, if you're doing an intensive athletic or other practice, you might want to skip a few sessions.

Your social life and recreation? Postpone or cancel most of your engagements, keeping just two or three of the most fun. (We don't want you to get all cranky and isolated.)

After you've finished, repeat the entire process and see if you can cut some more. (You often can.)

This process should liberate lots of time for your urgent project. Use two-thirds of it for the project, and the remaining third for some additional self-care and recreation.

Ask Your Professor for a Deadline Extension

They might grant you one, especially if you're late for reasons beyond your control, like an illness. Ask sooner rather than later, however, because waiting till the last minute makes you look bad, and also leaves you working under unnecessary pressure and stress.

Reduce Your Project's Scope

Meaning: figure out which parts you don't have to do, and eliminate them. Be ruthless! Instead of writing your paper on all the causes of World War I, for instance, maybe focus on just one or two. Or, if you're writing up a science project, maybe just discuss your key experimental finding in detail and summarize the rest.

After you've eliminated all the unnecessary chunks from your project, start trimming bits and pieces. (They add up.) Do all this cutting sooner rather than later so you don't waste time working on stuff you cut later. (If you're afraid of "overcutting," check with your professor. Chances are you'll be fine, because novice scholars—that's you!—tend to overstuff their projects.) Finally:

Read—or at least Skim—Part III

It's loaded with techniques that will help you accelerate your work.
Good luck! See you after you're done.

PART I

EFFECTIVENESS

1. The Problem Isn't Laziness

You've probably noticed how people don't like talking about it when things aren't going well. "How are you doing?" you ask. If the answer isn't "Great!" it's usually "Good." Or, at worst, "Okay."

Sometimes a friend will tell you about their relationship, job, health, or even, if you're really close, money problems. But there's one thing people have trouble opening up about to even their closest friends, and that's their problems getting their work done. There seems to be something uniquely shameful about underproductivity. And yet, so many of us have been there:

1. The endless days and nights when you know you should be working but are doing anything and everything but.
2. The more-or-less constant feelings of guilt, shame, and fear.
3. The lies. Such as telling yourself, "I'll work on it tonight," when you know you won't. And telling your friends, "I work best under pressure" when you know you don't. And telling your professor, "It's almost done" when you know it isn't.
4. The frantic couple of days before—or after—your deadline, when your fear finally builds to the point where you start working. Being fear-driven, however, you feel no real attachment to the work and are super distracted and inefficient.
5. The death-march all-nighters when every second feels like you're dragging a heavy weight.
6. The feeling of defeat when you hand the work in knowing it could have been so much better.

7. And finally: the humiliation of getting a mediocre grade and maybe a comment from your professor like, "Great idea, weak execution" or, "Were you rushed?"

The problem is procrastination. Everyone does it, at one time or another, so why all the secrecy and shame? It's because we misidentify the causes. Many people think they procrastinate because they're lazy or undisciplined but that's wrong: we procrastinate because we haven't been taught the attitudes and habits of productive work. Even worse, we've been taught some antiproductive attitudes and habits, like perfectionism.

And college can sure catalyze the problem. Get a group of smart people living and working together, set higher expectations for them than they've ever had to meet before, and grade them competitively, and you've created one heck of a pressure cooker. The pressure often leads to procrastination, as Sarah's story illustrates:

For Sarah, college had always been more than just "the next step": it was the place where she would finally get to be herself and find her community. Raised by a conservative family in a Midwestern suburb, she hadn't fit in at either home or school. She was too artsy, too introspective, and too willing to question the status quo. She was grateful for her small circle of high school friends but was hoping that, in college, she would fit in better with the broader campus culture.

She also differed from many of classmates in not having a clearly defined career goal. Many intended to go into medicine, engineering, or business, but none of those appealed to her. This was yet another source of friction between her and her parents, and it also made it hard for her to figure out which college to go to. Eventually, however, a wise guidance counselor suggested she do a double major in biology and anthropology/sociology, subjects she found interesting and that would prepare her for a career in many fields. (She could always change her majors later if she wanted.) The guidance counselor also suggested she attend a small liberal arts college (often referred to by the acronym "SLAC") where the emphasis would be on teaching as opposed to research or sports, and where she'd get more individual attention.

Sarah followed all this great advice and was thrilled when she got accepted into one of her desired schools. And for the first few weeks, at least, college was everything she had dreamed of. She loved her classes, the political and cultural scene, and her dorm, a lively place where there was always an interesting conversation going on.

There were only two problems. The first was that she had more work than ever before—mountains of it, it seemed, every week. The pressure was relentless and she was in constant danger of falling behind.

The second was her grades, which were lower than she had expected. She had always been one of the top students back in high school, and had assumed she would maintain that status in college. But now she was surrounded by, and in constant competition with, students who were just as smart and well-prepared as she was, if not more so. It was a shock.

Worst of all, the only solution she could come up with was, "Just work harder!" And she couldn't even figure out how to do that. Along with the sheer quantity of work she had to get through, an old procrastination problem she had struggled with during high school had returned.

Things came to a head when she got a D on her chemistry midterm: the first D she had ever gotten. As she stared at the grade in disbelief and horror, she knew something had to change. Her advisor had been urging her to get some help at the Study Skills Center but Sarah had resisted this advice. Now she knew she had no choice.

Sarah's meetings with her Study Skills Center coach were revelatory. She learned that, like many students from even supposedly good high schools, she hadn't ever been taught how to study. Even worse, she had developed some unhelpful habits, like relentlessly focusing on grades (instead of the work itself), relentlessly comparing herself to others, trying to study in distracting settings (like her dorm's commons areas), and doing her work at the last minute. These were humbling revelations, but they pointed the way to solutions that actually worked—and that did, in fact, work for Sarah.

When you're stuck the way Sarah was stuck, the situation can seem hopeless. But it isn't. The first step to solving the problem is understanding the true nature of that complicated phenomenon we call procrastination.

Sticking (or Not) to the Plan

Procrastination is when you get derailed from your plan.[3] So instead of getting up at, say, 8:00 a.m., you get up at 9:00 (or 10:00 or 11:00).

Or instead of studying, you play video games.

Or instead of eating a healthy lunch or dinner, you eat a bunch of junk food.

The key question is: what's derailing you? Often, we have a quick answer to that: "Me! I'm derailing myself because I'm lazy, undisciplined, etc." Not so fast! If you're like many people, you would do anything not to procrastinate, and have been trying for years to break the habit. So it's pretty clear you're not really in charge.

I'll tell you who the "derailer" is in Chapter 11. For now, though, let's take a closer look at the phenomenon of procrastination, starting with five crucial points:

1. **Procrastination always has a cause, and it's not us.** We know this because many people who procrastinate do so mostly in one or two crucial areas, like schoolwork or exercise. Meanwhile, they're dynamos everywhere else. It's clear, therefore, that they're not lazy or undisciplined, but are facing additional barriers in those particular areas.

2. **Our reasons for procrastinating are always valid.** There are many reasons you might not feel like doing your work, including fatigue, illness, boredom, confusion, overwhelm, and distraction. These are all 100% legitimate—meaning, understandable, forgivable, and human—motivations, and so are the more frivolous-seeming ones, like that it's nice out and you want to spend the day outdoors, or that you're lonely and want to hang out with a friend. The problem, in other words, isn't that you don't feel like working, but how you respond to that feeling. Which brings us to…

3. **Procrastination isn't a sin or character flaw, but a suboptimal response to our obstacles and barriers to doing our work.**[4] We

---

[3] And a "block," as in "writer's block" or "creative block," is a serious and sustained bout of procrastination. In this book, I mostly use the words "procrastination" and "block" interchangeably.

[4] I mostly use the words "obstacle" and "barrier" interchangeably. However, when such a

all procrastinate sometimes, and a little procrastination probably isn't going to hurt you. But if our reflexive response to every obstacle is to procrastinate, then we've got a problem, because most of us encounter dozens of obstacles every day. (More on obstacles in Chapter 9.)

4.   **You can't punish yourself out of a procrastination problem.** Think about it: if punishments—like shame, guilt, and deprivation—worked, wouldn't we all be super-achievers by now? Most procrastinators have been punishing themselves, or been punished by others, for years, with zero effect except that the problem got worse.

5.   **You can solve it, though!** In fact, I'm going to give you a whole bunch of effective solutions. Use them and you can achieve the central goal of productivity work, which is to be able to work as easily, effectively, and joyfully as possible on your schoolwork and other priorities, within the limits of whatever constraints you may be facing. This goal encompasses two others: (a) the ability to optimize your use of your time, skills, energy, and other resources; and (b) the ability to show up on time and do whatever work you're supposed to be doing with a high degree of clarity, engagement, focus, and fun. (Because we all need fun, and fun is motivating.)

First, however, let's discuss the true cause of procrastination.

---

distinction is useful, I use "obstacle" to refer to "mostly-internal" constraints like perfectionism, and "barrier" to "mostly-external" ones like a lack of financial or other resources.

2. The Problem Is Disempowerment

Why would someone who works productively at almost everything else be unable to do their schoolwork?

Why would a student who has never had any trouble doing their schoolwork find themselves blocked on their senior project?

Why do you get excited over a project when you happen to think about it while doing something else, but then that excitement is gone when you sit down to do your work?

And why, when you sit down to watch television or play a video game "for a few minutes," do you often wind up doing it for hours?

The answer, in all cases, is disempowerment: the state of being unable to use your strengths, skills, talents, knowledge, energy, enthusiasm, and other capacities. Some people exist in a state of general disempowerment, which means they aren't able to get much of anything important done, while others are mostly disempowered in one or two key areas or around one or two key projects.

As you will see, there are many circumstances that can disempower us. But how, exactly, does disempowerment cause procrastination? And how can the situation be remedied? To answer these important questions, you first need to understand that every creative and intellectual act, including those you do as part of your schoolwork, is an act of self-expression, self-assertion, and self-advocacy. And whenever you share your work with others, you're revealing yourself at a pretty deep level. (Your thoughts, ideas, values, vision, voice, etc.) Self-expression and sharing almost always carry some risk because you're exposing your ideas—and sometimes yourself—

to criticism, judgment, and rejection. Even when delivered sensitively, that criticism, etc., can hurt. But if it's delivered cruelly or unjustly, as it often is, it can hurt a lot more. (More on this in Chapter 34.)

We procrastinate, in large part, to avoid that hurt. If you don't hand your work in, after all, it—and, by extension, you—can't be criticized or rejected. And even if you do manage to hand it in, procrastination provides a built-in justification for any bad grades or other disappointing outcomes you receive: "I was rushed." The problem is that, at the same time procrastination is keeping you safe from potential critics, it's also isolating you from, and thus rendering you invisible to, your essential audiences, including not just your professors, scholarship committees, and potential employers, but helpers, mentors, collaborators, and appreciators of all sorts. At its core, procrastination is a form of self-silencing and, sometimes, self-censorship (if you're silencing ideas you think will offend, or be rejected by, others). It can also be a form of hiding—and sadly, because your rushed work almost never reflects your best efforts, what you're often hiding is the best part of you, and your best ideas.

Finally, procrastination is also often hoarding. "I'll hand in my work when it's ready," the procrastinator thinks—only, it never is. Or, "I'll hand it in after this last set of changes"—only, the "last set" leads to another, and another, and another. Or, worse, "I know I need help with this project, but I need to get it into better shape before I show it to someone." But the need to "get it into better shape" never ends. (More on hoarding in Chapter 14.)

Isolation, invisibility, self-silencing, self-censorship, hiding, and hoarding are all highly disempowered responses to the risks of self-expression, and the "safety" they offer comes at a very high price: self-sabotage. Fortunately, there are more empowering responses to the risks, which I'll be discussing throughout this book.

Where the Disempowerment Comes From

Generally speaking, there are three main sources of disempowerment-based procrastination: your family, society, and certain life events. I discuss each below.

Family Disempowerments

Research has linked procrastination in teenagers to "untreated traumatic experiences"[5] and authoritarian—i.e., harsh and controlling—parenting. In the latter case, psychologist Timothy Pychyl notes that procrastination, "may become one of the few means available to rebel against this [parental] control, a form of passive aggression."[6] We'll be revisiting this idea of procrastination as rebellion in Chapter 11.

In her book *Adult Children of Emotionally Immature Parents*, psychologist Lindsay Gibson notes how insecure and controlling parents discourage their children's self-expression, including their abilities to speak their truth and ask for help. At the same time, these parents encourage "uncertainty and self-doubt," "guilt and shame over imperfections," and "stereotyped gender roles." Make no mistake: these children are being taught to silence themselves and hide their true selves—and absent some corrective therapy or mentoring, the need to do so will likely persist into adulthood, often resulting in a procrastination problem.

Societal Disempowerments

You don't have to have had a difficult childhood to be disempowered, however. Perfectionism, which I discuss in the next chapter and extensively in Part II, is highly disempowering, and rampant throughout our culture. You can also be disempowered by an ineffective work process (Part III), unhealed traumatic rejections (Part IV), unmanaged time (Part V), and a lack of planning and support (Appendices). And yeah: it's usually several of those happening at once.

On top of all this, many groups—including women, people of color, queer people, disabled people, poor people, and immigrants—experience systemic oppression and implicit bias. The former is when an organization's policies intentionally or unintentionally lead to unequal outcomes for mem-

---

[5] www.hazeldenbettyford.org/articles/teen-mental-health

[6] www.psychologytoday.com/us/blog/dont-delay/200903/parenting-style-and-procrastination. Psychologists recognize four parenting styles: authoritarian (lots of rules and control, little affection and support), indulgent (few rules, lots of affection), neglectful (few rules, little affection), and authoritative (lots of rules, lots of affection). Authoritative is considered best.

bers of marginalized groups, while the latter is when the organization's policies aren't explicitly biased, but its members' attitudes and behaviors are. Many universities have worked hard to eliminate the former problem, but the latter remains prevalent (perhaps because policies are easier to change than people's attitudes). If you're a member of a targeted group, you unfortunately have the added, unjust burden of learning how to recognize and cope with barriers such as discrimination, harassment, stereotype threat, tokenization, and microaggressions. Your college hopefully has a multicultural center, LGBTQ+ center, and other resources that can help, and you should also check out online resources such as www.apiascholars.org, www.campuspride.org, www.hsf.net, www.nationalequityproject.org, www.nccsdonline.org, www.niea.org, and www.firstgen.naspa.org.[7] It's a shame that you might have to do such extra work, especially at an educational institution. But coping always beats non-coping, a.k.a., procrastination.

Our final source of disempowerment is...

Life Events Disempowerments

Some life events can also be disempowering. Obviously, the "bad" ones, such as an illness, job loss, or relationship breakup, can be, but even some "good" ones can be, at least temporarily. Transitions are disempowering, and the transitions from high school to college, and between each year of college, are some of life's biggest. (See Table I.) True, these particular "transitional disempowerments" are made intentionally, with the goal of spurring your intellectual, creative, social, and emotional growth. But you still have to be able to cope with them.

---

[7] This article offers a great overview of the barriers faced by first-generation students and those from economically-disadvantaged or otherwise marginalized backgrounds, plus solutions: http://www.harvardmagazine.com\2017\11\mastering-the-hidden-curriculum.

Table I: Common Productivity Obstacles Caused by College Transitions

Transition	Common Productivity Obstacles
From High School to Freshman Year of College	You've got a new home, role (college student), friends, community, etc. (Possibly all very different from what you grew up with.)
	You've gone from having lots of supervision (from parents, teachers, guidance counselors, etc.) to very little.
	The work is harder than in high school.
	You're surrounded by high achievers: the competition is probably tougher than what you're used to.
	You have more opportunities—academic, extracurricular, personal—but also more distractions.
From Freshman to Sophomore Year	You're re-entering after summer break. Re-entries are tricky, and it can take more time than expected to regain your productivity after one.
	You're under more pressure now than you were in your freshman year. (E.g., the feeling that, "I should have school all figured out by now.")
	If you're living off campus, you've got a more complicated housing and dining situation.
	"Sophomore Slump," a kind of malaise often caused by being past the excitement of freshman year but still miles away from graduation.
	The work is harder.
	You're now taking upper-level classes with juniors and seniors, which can be intimidating.
	You're under pressure to choose a major (and career).
	You may also be under pressure to get a summer internship, even though sophomore-year internships can be hard to get.
	You've got yet more opportunities and distractions.
From Sophomore to Junior Year	You're re-entering after a summer break or internship.
	The work is harder.

Transition	Common Productivity Obstacles
	Possibility of disillusionment if an internship was disappointing or your major isn't working out the way you'd hoped. (Please talk to your advisor about this.)
	Possible pressure to get a summer internship.
	The need to start thinking about, and planning for, your life after graduation. (This can take a lot of time, and be scary.)
	You've got yet more opportunities and distractions.
From Junior to Senior Year	You're re-entering after a summer break, internship, or a semester or year abroad. (Re-entry after time abroad can be an especially big challenge.)
	Continued possibility of disillusionment.
	The work is harder. In particular, your senior project or capstone is probably the biggest and most complicated project you've ever done.
	The need to start detailed planning for your post-college career and life. (Time-consuming and stressful.)
	You're anticipating post-graduation challenges (e.g., finding a job, housing, etc.) and losses (of friends, community, support systems, etc.).
	"Senioritis," a decrease in motivation as graduation approaches. It's very common, and usually not a problem in small doses.

To make matters worse, many of your friends will be facing the exact same challenges, and so you all won't be as helpful to each other as you'd like. Hopefully, however, you'll all be able to work together on the exercises in this book, starting with Exercise 1, below.

Exercise 1

Make a list of any transitional obstacles you're currently facing, and journal* about how each is affecting you and your ability to do your work. While writing, take some time to appreciate how you've persevered—including by reading this book—in the face of all those obstacles.

*Whenever in this book I talk about journaling, I mean "free writing," also known as "stream of consciousness writing." Start with a question like, "How has the transition from freshman to sophomore year affected me and my work?" Then take your time writing out as complete an answer as you can. Let the words flow and don't worry about spelling, punctuation, or grammar: you're not showing this to anyone. The goal is introspection: a better, clearer, more comprehensive introspection than you can achieve just by thinking about the problem. Just remember to always write in a problem-solving way (e.g., "I can see three ways the transition is affecting me...") and never in a shaming or blaming way ("I'm lazy, that's all!"). Always be your own best coach.

Please do this exercise, and every exercise in this book, with as much energy, focus, and dedication as you can. In the realm of personal growth, halfway measures don't get us far. (In fact, they're likely to be counterproductive, yielding all the pains of the effort with few or none of the rewards.) But putting your heart and soul into the quest can be transformational.

3. Procrastination and Perfectionism

In the last chapter, I discussed how a disempowering desire to self-silence or hide is often at the root of procrastination; also how our disempowerment can arise from our family, society, or life events. But how is it that some who have experienced significant disempowerment can still manage to be productive? And why do so many who haven't experienced it still wind up procrastinating? Great questions! Let's answer them one at a time.

On the question of why some people are productive despite having had a disempowering childhood, or having endured other disempowering circumstances, please keep in mind that, just as procrastination always has a cause (or causes), so does productivity. Maybe the person had the resources—like money and family connections—to overcome their barriers. Or maybe they had one or two key people who supported and mentored them. Or maybe they had excellent skills in one or two key areas—technical, interpersonal, strategic, or otherwise—that helped them break through. Or maybe they were lucky in some other way. (Most likely, they were lucky in several ways.)

As to the question of why so many who haven't experienced serious personal disempowerment still procrastinate, there are three answers. First, procrastination is strongly habit-forming. Every time you do it, you become more disempowered and fearful around your work, thus making it harder to do that work in the future. In some cases, procrastination probably crosses the line into addiction, generally defined as a self-reinforcing or compulsive behavior with negative consequences. Hard as it is to overcome a habit, it's even harder to overcome an addiction.[8]

Second—and recalling that procrastination is often used as a way of hiding from possible negative reactions to our ideas—even many seemingly neutral or benign tasks actually do have a scary, self-revealing component. Having to memorize a list of Italian irregular verbs may seem like a routine task, for instance, but if your studying Italian is expressive of a deeper desire to, say, travel or live in Italy, or to have an art history career, then any fears you have around that goal could manifest themselves in procrastination.

Please note that even a small amount of disempowerment can trigger procrastination, especially if it happens around an activity that's also challenging in other ways. Worse still, if we happen to confide in someone about our challenges, we're often told to, "Stop whining!" or "Toughen up!" This mentality is deeply perfectionist, which brings us to the third reason why even people who haven't faced serious personal disempowerment can have trouble working: perfectionism. It's a hugely disempowering force in many people's lives, not just because it's ubiquitous in our culture and media (more on this in Chapter 15), but because, along with being a barrier in its own right, it also blocks your ability to solve your other problems. It does that not just by making you think you're lazy or otherwise "the problem" (as discussed earlier), but by swamping you with guilt and shame: emotions that aren't conducive to problem-solving.

To sum up: perfectionism can cause you to procrastinate even in the absence of an authoritarian childhood or other barriers. Conversely, if someone is lucky enough to not be too perfectionist, they'll have an easier time coping with any barriers they might be facing.

I discuss perfectionism in detail in Part II. For now, all you need to know is that it creates not just a fear of failure, but a terror of it. Many perfectionist characteristics, including the tendencies to: (a) **define success narrowly and unrealistically**, and (b) **try to use punishment (e.g., harsh self-talk and deprivation) as a corrective or motivator**, contribute to that terror. But the biggest contributor is that perfectionists (c) **overidentify with their work**. To a perfectionist, every "success" is a source of personal validation and every "failure" a devastating indictment. (I frequently put

---

[8] Experts say procrastination has much in common with "classic" addictions like alcoholism. See, for instance, www.cambridge.org/core/journals/behavioral-and-brain-sciences/article/abs/addiction-procrastination-and-failure-points-in-decisionmaking-systems/2255C0E5BE4D6A86ED9BE92646EE5819#.

quotation marks around words like "success" and "failure" to indicate that these concepts are relative, and also that perfectionists often misuse them. See below and also Chapters 22 and 23.) This overidentification can lead you to be constantly judging, evaluating, and critiquing both your work and yourself, all in a desperate and exhausting effort to stave off the inevitable "failures."

But wait! It can get worse because perfectionists also incline towards negativity. They constantly see themselves as failing, even at times when they've succeeded. (E.g., "An A- is okay, I guess, but I'm bummed I didn't get an A.") That means that, because of their constant overidentification, they are also constantly in despair.

Overidentification can also manifest itself as:

- Pathologizing, meaning that you interpret ordinary work obstacles and setbacks as a sign you're incapable of doing the work. Example: "I missed a couple of bugs in my program so I guess I'm a bad programmer."

- An overemphasis on external recognition and rewards—so that, for instance, a good grade or a compliment from your professor (or a friend or stranger) can put you over the moon. (And the obverse: an even slightly critical one can ruin your day.)

- Using your work as a source of self-worth or legitimacy. "If I could only achieve X then I would finally be Y" is a common perfectionist formulation. Example: "If I could only get on the Dean's List then I would finally justify my parents' sacrifices in sending me to college." Let's be clear: the goal (in this case, the Dean's List) is often fine and admirable. The problem is when your sense of self-worth or legitimacy hinges on it.

When you encounter someone who is generally productive but is procrastinating on one or two key projects, it's a sure bet they're overidentified with those projects.

The Disempowerment Cascade

Perfectionism triggers procrastination in a five-step process I call the Disempowerment Cascade. Here are the steps:
1. While working, you encounter one or (usually) more obstacles (confusion, boredom, distraction, overwhelm, fatigue, etc.).

2. You have a presentiment of failure. "Oh no!" you think. "My work's not going well! I'm going to fail!" Note that, for reasons I'll be discussing in Chapters 13 and 14 (catastrophizing, negativity, shortsightedness, etc.), you're often afraid of failing not just at the current work session, but the entire project—and also at your class, college career, post-college career, life, etc. That's a lot of fear! So, naturally...

3. You panic. Which leads you to...

4. Urgently attempt to get yourself back on track. Unfortunately, most procrastinators know only one way to do this, a harsh and shaming inner monologue that goes something like this:

5. "What's wrong with you? Why are you so lazy? This stuff isn't hard! Anyone could do it! Anna's already finished! Why can't you be disciplined like her? C'mon! If you don't get to work, you're gonna fail and everyone will know you're a loser...and did I mention that the stuff you've already done sucks?" All this monologue does is add fear on top of fear. And so, eventually, your panic rises to the point where you must...

6. Escape ("derail") via procrastination. You start scrolling on your phone, or bust out a video game, or do some tedious chores. (Because anything's better than facing your work and that terrifying prospect of failure.)

Those are the steps—and it's important to note that they can happen at any point while you're working or even before you start working. (In which case, you probably won't even start.) All five steps can, and usually do, happen in a flash, so you might not even be aware of them. All you know is you have a sudden, irresistible urge to do something—anything—other than your work.

The Disempowerment Cascade model shows that it's not the obstacles (confusion, boredom, overwhelm, etc.) that are the barrier to productivity, but our terrorized reaction to them. When we're terrified, we lose capacity—which happens to be the definition of disempowerment, remember? That's why the only "solution" we can come up with to our predicament is the unsatisfactory one of procrastination.

The Disempowerment Cascade model suggests two key differences between productive and underproductive people:

1. **Productive people learn to interrupt the Disempowerment Cascade.** Specifically, they replace the "panicking" step with

problem-solving, with the goal of eliminating, or at least minimizing, the obstacle causing the derailment. This enables them to return to work as soon as possible, as discussed in the next chapter and also Chapters 9 and 10.

2. **Productive people learn to minimize occurrences of the Disempowerment Cascade.** They do this by promptly dealing with their obstacles. If a productive person's workspace is noisy or uncomfortable, for instance, they'll quickly find a better one and be more selective in the future. If they get derailed after receiving an upsetting text message, they'll decide that, from then on, they won't check their phone until after they've done their work. **To outsiders, it looks like these people have phenomenal willpower but what they're really doing is constantly removing obstacles to their productivity.**

Meanwhile, the underproductive people—who, let's not forget, are convinced that they themselves are the problem—tend not to recognize their true obstacles. This means, of course, that they are unlikely to solve them.

And so those obstacles keep reoccurring, and often get worse over time.

Exercise 2

Think back on a recent incident of procrastination and describe the roles that disempowerment and perfectionism played. Then describe how disempowerment, procrastination, and perfectionism are all mutually reinforcing.

4. A Quick Solution to Procrastination: Reclaiming Your "Lost" Options and Outcomes

Disempowerment often misleads us into thinking we have fewer and worse options than we really have. Maybe you think, for instance, that your only options for a class are to "get an A" or "be a failure." Even if you have a decent shot at getting that A, you're still putting huge pressure on yourself.

Here are some other examples of perceived poor options:

- Marci feels stuck having to choose between a college major (and career) she loves but that doesn't pay well (music) and one she is less enthusiastic about but that does pay well (engineering).
- Chris feels that, because their laboratory partner is slacking off, they're stuck either having to do more than their fair share of the work or getting a bad grade.
- A non-school example: Oliver feels like he must either stay in a bad romantic relationship or be doomed to loneliness.

Disempowered people also often perceive themselves as having only poor potential outcomes: meaning that, no matter how hard they work on a project or how carefully they navigate a situation, they are doomed to failure. This often leads to feelings of hopelessness and futility, arguably the most disempowering emotions of all. (As the Star Trek Borg—who are constantly telling their victims that, "Resistance is futile."—surely know.) Psychologists call the act of anticipating terrible outcomes catastrophizing, and many underproductive people do it a lot. They may think they're being realistic or preparing for the worst but they're really disempowering themselves.

Even though I've been talking a lot about feelings and perceptions, I'm not saying the actual obstacles—poor musician pay, a slacking lab partner, and a bad relationship—aren't real and serious. Of course they are. The perceptual problem lies in believing you have worse options and outcomes than you actually have. Catastrophizing can lead you to do this and so can dichotomizing, a common perfectionist behavior in which you see the world in either/or terms. Notice how all of the above examples are dichotomized, with Marci feeling like she must choose between a career she loves and one that pays well, Chris feeling like they must choose between either doing more than their fair share of the work or getting a bad grade, and Oliver feeling like he's stuck between staying in a bad relationship or being lonely.

Like all perfectionism, dichotomization can shut your motivation right down. And so, whenever you're feeling unmotivated take a break from whatever it is you're trying to do and either journal about the problem or talk it over with someone, with the goal of creating better options and outcomes for yourself. Once you do that, your motivation should return.

Back to our examples:

Instead of feeling stuck having to choose between a major she loves (music) and one that pays well (engineering), Marci could: (1) do a double major, (2) choose projects spanning both fields, such as audio engineering or computer-generated music, (3) pursue a musical career ultra-professionally so as to have the best chance of success, and/or, (4) pursue an engineering career in a way that supports her music. (For instance, getting a job in a "music town" like New Orleans, Seattle, or Chicago.)

Instead of feeling stuck between having to do more than their fair share of the work or getting a low grade, Chris could, (1) talk with their lab partner. (The partner might be unaware of the problem, or doing more than Chris realizes, or have a valid or easily correctable reason for underproducing.) Or, Chris could, (2) ask their professor to assign them another partner. Or, they could cut their losses and: (3) settle for the lower grade (if the project isn't important) or (4) go ahead and do the extra work (if it is).

Instead of feeling stuck between a bad relationship or a life of loneliness, Oliver could: (1) spend more time with friends, (2) join a club or other organization where he'll meet new people, and/or (3) do some online dating.

Or, if he feels the relationship is salvageable, he could, (4) get some relationship counseling.

In each case, we've gone from two bad options (and the associated bad outcomes) to four better ones—and whenever you use this technique, you should achieve a similar result. What you're really doing, when you use this technique, is re-empowering yourself. If disempowerment is the state of being unable to access your strengths, skills, talents, knowledge, and other capacities, empowerment is the ability to access and use all of those.

I am *not* saying the above solutions are easy, perfect, or fair—only that they are all better than procrastinating, which solves nothing and usually makes things worse. Besides, life can, and often does, surprise you. Once you've used this book's techniques to free yourself from perfectionism, ineffective work processes, traumatic rejections, and unmanaged time, your options may, in fact, turn out to be much better than anticipated. As writer adrienne maree brown says in her book *Emergent Strategy*, "Creating more possibilities is...where we shape tomorrow towards abundance."

5. "Unproductive" Versus "Quasiproductive" Procrastination, and Other Distractions

People procrastinate in two main ways: unproductively and quasiproductively.

Unproductive Procrastination (UP) is when, instead of your scheduled work, you do a low-value activity like gaming, social media, or television. (Yeah, they can sometimes be high value, but often they're not, especially if you're using them to procrastinate.)

Quasiproductive Procrastination (QP) is when, instead of your scheduled work, you do an activity that has some value. It could be other, less urgent schoolwork. Or you could go for a run, do some chores, or do a favor for a friend.

QP is sneakier than UP because it gives you the illusion of being productive. "I didn't get any studying done today, but at least I got in a run," you tell yourself. Or, "at least I cleaned up the place." Or, "at least I helped a friend." Also, others will encourage your QP. The other runners will give you props for your dedication, your suitemates will be glad you cleaned up, and your friend will be grateful for the help.

A common, and extra-sneaky, form of QP is when you procrastinate on one part of your project by overworking another. Examples include researching your paper to death but never writing it, and endlessly revising it but never handing it in. (See Chapters 31 and 32 for solutions to those problems.) And there are lots of other forms of QP, including overoptimizing (a.k.a., "letting the perfect be the enemy of the good enough"), ambivalence (which I discuss in Chapter 24), indecision, and "overthinking the problem" a.k.a., "analysis paralysis."[9]

As the humorist Robert Benchley put it, "Anyone can do any amount of work, provided it isn't the work he is supposed to be doing at that moment."

So how do you know when you're doing QP? First, remember that, as discussed in Chapter 1, the goal of productivity work is to be able to stick to your plan. So, if you had planned to do X, but are now doing Y, and Y is somewhat useful, there's a good chance you're doing QP.

Also, we usually do know, deep down, when we're procrastinating. So, learn to listen for, and to, that small voice in your head that's saying, "I ought to be doing something else."

Finally, overdo a QP activity enough and it will become UP—and then you'll really know you're wasting time.

Debunking the Productivity Myths: "Good Procrastination," Multitasking, etc.[10]

Every once in a while, some expert claims that procrastination is "thinking time" and therefore useful. Or that you can "productively procrastinate" on a big, scary task by doing lots of little, unscary ones instead. (Yup, they're actually recommending QP.) Or they offer some other rationale or justification for procrastination.

---

[9] Like this cat: www.youtu.be/p_17nvsuFFA.

[10] Citations for this discussion: Can't concentrate on more than one complicated task: sloanreview.mit.edu/article/the-impossibility-of-focusing-on-two-things-at-once/. Interruptions are expensive: www.npr.org/2015/09/22/442582422/the-cost-of-interruptions-they-waste-more-time-than-you-think. Social media degrades cognitive capacity of those around you: www.en.wikipedia.org/wiki/Cognitive_load; cellphones degrade cognitive capacity even when not used: https://hbr.org/2018/03/having-your-smartphone-nearby-takes-a-toll-on-your-thinking; cell phone use lowers your final grade: www.rutgers.edu/news/cellphone-distraction-classroom-can-lead-lower-grades-rutgers-study-finds.

Repeat after me: there's no such thing as "good procrastination." (Or "positive" or "productive" procrastination.) Procrastination is always grounded in disempowerment, and disempowerment is never good.

Similarly, every few years, multitasking (working on more than one thing at a time) gets hyped as a productivity technique. But it's a sham for three reasons: (1) most of us can't concentrate on more than one complicated task at a time—and when we try, our efficiency goes way down; (2) it takes way longer to get back up to speed after an interruption than most people realize; and (3) multitasking can lead to QP by encouraging you to focus on your easier tasks at the expense of your harder ones.

So don't multitask.

While I'm at it: don't mix work and social media. Research has shown you can't work effectively while keeping one eye on your feed—which shouldn't be surprising, since social media apps are designed to hijack your attention. In fact, the social media designers are so very good at their jobs that using social media degrades not just your own cognitive capacity (more on this in Chapter 45), but that of those around you. Research has also shown that just having your cellphone near you, even if you're not using it, can distract you; and that using your phone or tablet during classes can cost you up to a full letter grade on your final.

So, either shut off your phone while studying or leave it in a locker or other inaccessible location.

Another way to put all of the above is: don't be what Cal Newport, in his book *How to Become a Straight-A Student*, calls a "pseudo-worker." "The pseudo-worker looks and feels like someone who is working hard—he or she spends a long time in the library and is not afraid to push on late into the night—but, because of a lack of focus and concentration, doesn't actually accomplish that much."

You may be the cosmic exception to all this: the rare person who can multitask or work effectively while also using social media. But you're probably not—and if you get this wrong, you're at risk for some serious self-sabotage.

Disconnecting Shouldn't Be Radical

One of productivity work's big divides is between those who try to work while connected to the Internet (and its many distractions) and those who have figured out that that's a really bad idea. The second group understands the benefits of disconnecting, including not just increased productivity but less stress, better health, and more enjoyment of life.[11]

Yes, I know you need to be on the Internet sometimes. But you probably don't need to be on it as much as you think. You can, for instance, organize your work so that you do all your online tasks together in a batch, thus freeing yourself to disconnect after they're done. And you can also train yourself to save minor online tasks—like looking up a date or writing a quick email—for your next online session, instead of constantly letting them interrupt your flow.

Another great technique is to download lectures and other videos so you can listen to them offline. Doing this also gives you more flexibility, such as the ability to listen to lectures while driving or on the bus.

Even many people who think they must be online constantly for their work can cut back some—and often a lot. After writer and consultant Gregory Ferenstein started using timers to limit his social media use, for instance, he realized that:

> [T]here was hardly ever a time when I needed to constantly monitor social media. Even when I posted something that was popular, I rarely needed to spend more time than a few minutes on the app to meaningfully engage. The marginal utility [meaning, the additional value] from minutes 5 to 60 on Facebook and Twitter wasn't much more than the first 5 minutes.[12]

You don't hear much about it, but many people do disconnect regularly. (See the citations in Footnote 12.) Some only go online in the afternoons or evenings after finishing their creative work, while others limit online work to a specified time and duration each day, while still others abstain on weekends or do multiday "digital detoxes." Novelists Zadie Smith, Isabel Allende, and Jonathan Franzen are famous "disconnecters," and so is Cal Newport, who's written two books on the topic: *Digital Minimalism* and *A World Without Email.* Way back in 1990, programming legend Donald Knuth explained his decision to almost entirely dispense with email this way: "Email is a wonderful thing for people whose role in life is to be on top of

---

[11] See, for instance: www.insidehighered.com/blogs/gradhacker/how-killing-your-home-internet-can-boost-your-productivity, www.theminimalists.com/internet/, and blogs.publishersweekly.com/blogs/shelftalker/?p=5127.

[12] www.forbes.com/sites/gregoryferenstein/2019/01/31/how-i-cut-my-social-media-use-with-app-limits/

things. But not for me; my role is to be on the bottom of things. What I do takes long hours of studying and uninterruptible concentration."[13]

Let's be clear, however, that even many who need to "be on top of things"—like, say, many activists or entrepreneurs—benefit from limiting their online time, both because their work does have an intellectual or creative component, and because a lot of our online time is spent on low-value activities. It's okay to do some of that escapism. (And I allocate time for it in Chapter 49's sample time budget and schedule.) But too much is problematic not just from a productivity standpoint, but a health one.[14]

If all this sounds extreme, please remember that the choice isn't a dichotomized "always online" versus "always offline" one: it's about recognizing that the Internet is a tool and figuring out how best to use it. It's especially about recognizing that the apps are designed by experts to suck you in, and that being sucked in is a form of disempowerment. By the way, that "sucked in" feeling has a name: a **ludic loop**. The classic ludic-loop-generating technology is the slot machine, which uses fun and flashy displays—plus the lure of the occasional small win, and the possibility of an extremely rare big win—to "hook" people and extract their time and money from them. But many social media apps, television shows, games, and other escapist diversions are also designed to generate ludic loops. (In social media, the feeling that you're winning often comes from people following you or responding to your posts.)

Once you do decide to limit your online time, you've got three main choices:

First, you can **try a WiFi /social media blocking app**, like Forest, Freedom, or Cold Turkey. If one of these works for you, that's great. But it's easy to get sucked into procrastination before and while using them, and also easy to "cheat" and restore your access. (No, I'm not going to say how.)

A better solution, in my view, is to **work in a space without WiFi**. Some of the top artist residency programs, including Yaddo and MacDowell, now limit Internet access to a library or other common area, leaving the

---

[13] www.calnewport.com/blog/2008/07/17/bonus-post-how-the-worlds-most-famous-computer-scientist-checks-e-mail-only-once-every-three-months/

[14] Mental health: penntoday.upenn.edu/news/social-media-use-increases-depression-and-loneliness. Also see Chapter 17 and Footnote #35. Physical health: See, for example: www.mayoclinic.org/healthy-lifestyle/adult-health/expert-answers/sitting/faq-20058005, www.ncbi.nlm.nih.gov/pmc/articles/PMC5574844/, academic.oup.com/ije/article/41/5/1338/709862, and Footnote 23.

rest of the campus, including the artists' studios, disconnected. Similarly, you can probably find a WiFi-free library, café, or other study space where, like those pampered artists, you can work in luxurious disconnected peace and freedom. As a bonus, you'll find yourself working alongside some highly productive others who have also discovered the benefits of disconnecting. (Which should further boost your own productivity.)

The best solution to online distraction is to do the bulk of your work on a computer from which you've deleted not just Internet connectivity, but (obviously) all games and other distractions. In practice, this usually means using two computers: the disconnected one, on which you do your writing, programming, problem sets, and other work that requires sustained focus and concentration, and the connected one, on which you do your research, social media, gaming, etc. (In many cases, the disconnected computer can be an old one you repurpose.) This two-computer system can not only boost your ability to concentrate, it can also help you create some empowering new options for yourself. One of my most effective productivity tricks, for instance, is this: every night, before going to bed, I shut down my "connected" computer while leaving my "disconnected" one on. That way, when I return to my office the next morning, it's the disconnected one that's "alive" and beckoning to me. This simple-but-powerful ritual almost always ensures I start right in on my work in the mornings instead of getting waylaid by social media.[15]

If you do most of your work at home—or at an office, assigned library carrel, or other fixed location—working with two computers is pretty straightforward: you leave your disconnected computer at that location and carry around your connected one (swapping files between them using thumb drives). True, the juggling gets more complicated if you're moving around a lot or working at multiple locations. Still, try to use a disconnected computer whenever you can.

Again, we're talking about a big divide here. Some people, when I suggest they disconnect, understand why. But others are aghast, as if I had suggested they disconnect an arm or leg. A college-aged reader of the manuscript for this book called the advice "peak Boomer," not realizing that many Boomers hate it too! People of all ages have come to find the idea of disconnecting, even briefly, unthinkable. But ask yourself why that's so, and

---

[15] Productivity expert Nick Wolny came up with a similar system involving the use of two smart phones—one optimized for work and the other for personal use: see debugger.medium.com/how-to-use-your-old-iphone-to-set-better-work-boundaries-741f3b00fcf8.

who is benefiting from your spending long periods online in corporate-engineered ludic loops.

Especially if disconnecting seems unthinkable, that's reason enough to give it a try. Few habits have as much potential to improve your productivity and life.

6. Building Your *Sitzfleisch*

Humans are social creatures but studying is often a solitary activity—and so feelings of loneliness or isolation are a common obstacle to productivity. Happily, however, all it often takes to neutralize those feelings is a study buddy working quietly alongside you. They don't need to be working on the same thing you're working on: just having the company is enough to keep you going.[16]

Not all study buddies are alike, however. I learned early on that the most helpful ones show up on time, or a bit early, and work steadily through the interval. The less helpful ones show up late and get up from their desks a time or two—each time interrupting my concentration and, I'm sure, their own. And the least helpful often leaving their desks.

The Germans have a handy word for the ability to sit still and stay focused on a task, *sitzfleisch.* (It translates roughly to "having a good sitting butt.") Probably the world champion of it was the 4th century philosopher Didymus of Alexandria, who wrote 3,500 books (actually, papyrus scrolls), and whose nickname, according to historian Stephen Greenblatt in his book *The Swerve*, was "Bronze Ass." Didymus probably wasn't a fan of what we now call "life balance," so you don't want to emulate him. Like all qualities, *sitzfleisch* is a double-edged sword: useful for some things (e.g., schoolwork

---

[16] Good study buddies can be hard to find, so here's an article on apps that can pair you with some: www.bbc.com/worklife/article/20200812-the-online-work-gyms-that-help-spur-productivity. I've used www.focusmate.com and found it useful.

and competitive chess) and not so much for others (e.g., staying healthy and fit).

Neurodivergence, disability, and other factors can also play a role in determining how much *sitzfleisch* a person has. Still, for many people, the ability to sit still and stay focused for thirty, forty, or sixty minutes at a stretch is both achievable and a good thing, productivity-wise.

Whatever your current amount of *sitzfleisch* is, you can increase it by using the below Timed Work Intervals technique.

First, some preliminaries:

1. **Do all your preparation before starting your work session.** This includes gathering your materials, refreshing your drink, adjusting the temperature (or your clothing), and using the bathroom.

2. Next, **study in a space without clocks**. Yeah, that includes removing the clock from your computer desktop. (I cover mine with some black electrical tape.) You'll stop counting the minutes and your sense of time will, somewhat magically, simultaneously seem to both expand (so you get more done) and go more quickly (so you get less bored and impatient). You know that daydream where time stands still and so you finally have enough time to do everything you want? Working without a clock is probably the closest most of us can get to that in real life. (And yes, the technique also works for exercise and other activities where we're tempted to count the minutes.)[17]

3. Next, **grab a kitchen timer**—not your phone, which is distracting. (And has a clock.) Kitchen timers are cheap and come in many fun colors and styles; I recommend using them and other props whenever you can because doing so adds interest and variety to your work.

Now you're ready to start your Timed Work Interval:

1. Pick a part of your project to work on. Pick one you truly want to work on, not one you think you should be working on. That feeling of wanting to work on something is called "inspiration" and you shouldn't waste it. (More on inspiration in Chapter 29.)

---

[17] This "no clock" technique is also used by many stores, casinos, and other commercial spaces that want you to lose your sense of time so you'll hang around longer and spend more money.

2. Set the timer to count down from three minutes. Or two minutes, or one minute, or thirty seconds: it's important to choose an interval you can easily complete.

3. Start the timer and start working. Work steadily but without stress or pressure. Focus on the bit of work right in front of you, ignoring, for the moment, the rest of the project, and especially any concerns or expectations you have about the outcome. (And, obviously, any outside concerns, like your relationship or what you're having for lunch.) , during your interval, you feel yourself getting scared, stressed, distracted, judgmental, impatient, anticipatory, etc., gently talk yourself back to the work that's right in front of you. That fear and stress, by the way, is perfectionism—and so what you're also doing here is practicing nonperfectionism while working. Good stuff! If you finish the bit you're working on or find yourself getting bored or stuck, no problem. Immediately—and without fuss or drama—switch to another part of the project and keep working. (Repeat as necessary.)

4. When the timer goes off, take a break. (See Chapter 33 for tips on taking effective breaks.)

5. When you're ready, repeat Steps 1 – 4 either with the same or a different bit of work. (And keep repeating until you're done with your work session.

After you can reliably complete three minutes of stress-free (nonperfectionist) work, you can increase the timer to five or ten minutes. Then, fifteen, twenty, thirty, forty minutes, etc., until you reach your desired interval length. If, during an interval, you accidentally glance at a clock and are disappointed at how much time there is remaining in your interval, try reframing your situation more positively. Not, in other words, "Thirty more minutes! The time is crawling. I hate this!" But, "Wow, I still have thirty minutes left. What a gift of abundance! Okay, back to work...no rush...let's have fun and see what I can do with these math problems."

If you ever find yourself having trouble completing your intervals, either because you're distracted or because the current project is difficult, don't hesitate to return to shorter ones. Remember, the important things are to: (a) finish your interval while (b) working nonperfectionistically throughout. (Eventually, you'll regain your "lost" *sitzfleisch*.)

Probably the biggest barrier to this exercise will be your Inner Perfectionist stepping in and saying something like, "Three minutes is nothing! We should go for three hours!" Feel free to ignore this misguided advice. (I'll discuss how to deal with your Inner Perfectionist in Chapter 19.)

7. The Secret to Quantity and Quality

The goal of timed work intervals is not to get a lot of work done or to do great work: it's to complete your interval while remaining nonperfectionist throughout. As Steven Pressfield says of his own work sessions in his book, *The War of Art*: "How many pages have I produced? I don't care. Are they any good? I don't even think about it. All that matters is I've put in my time and hit it with all I've got."

But wait! I hear you object. I actually do want to get a lot of work done! And I also want to do great work!

Fair enough—and the secret to achieving both goals is nonperfectionism.

Let's start with quantity. While it may seem sensible to set an ambitious page count or other quantity goal, doing so creates a perfectionist overfocus on product over process. (More on this in Chapter 13.) Think about it: if quantity goals worked, wouldn't we all be super-productive by now? Most of us have been setting, and missing, such goals for years. But by setting a process goal of putting in your time while maintaining a focused but non-perfectionist mindset, you free yourself to do as much work as possible.

But don't many professionals use quantity goals? And what about my deadlines? If I don't set a quantity goal, I'll miss them all!

You're right: many professionals do set quantity goals—and you can too, after you've overcome your perfectionism. To set such a goal while perfectionism is still holding you back, however, is likely only to backfire. (And as the Pressfield quote illustrates, many professionals—including me, by the way—continue to stick with process goals.)

As for deadlines, yeah, we do have a bit of a problem. We're aiming not for a quick fix, but growth, and growth takes time. And so, for a while, your output might be lower than you'd like or even lower than it is now. (Because you're no longer using punishment as a motivator.) That will be scary, but stay the course and things should soon start to improve.

Now onto quality. In their book Art & Fear, David Bayles and Ted Orland tell a story of two groups of ceramics students, one of which was told they would be graded based on the quality of their pots, and the other on the quantity. (The more pots, the higher the grade.) I'll let them tell you what happened:

> Came grading time and a curious fact emerged: the works of highest quality were all produced by the group being graded for quantity. It seems that while the "quantity" group was busily churning out piles of work—and learning from their mistakes—the "quality" group had sat theorizing about *perfection*, and in the end had little more to show for their efforts than *grandiose* theories and a pile of dead clay. [Italics mine—and I'll have more to say about grandiose theories in Chapter 13.]

Quantity creates quality, in other words. Not only does aiming for quantity give you more practice, it defuses perfectionism by puncturing the illusion that you can do a perfect job. Even the most committed perfectionist must relax their standards when given just fifteen minutes to throw a pot or write a paragraph.

The above anecdote also illustrates another productivity truism: that most of the time—and almost certainly within the context of a well-run college course—you have everything you need to succeed. Enough ideas, skills, help, talent, etc. This is crucial to understand because many perfectionists suffer from a scarcity mentality that convinces them they don't, in fact, have enough. (More on this in Chapter 13.)

When I say you should aim for quantity over quality, I am not suggesting you hand in sloppy work. What I mean is that you shouldn't overwork your projects in a perfectionist quest to eliminate every single possible error. "Excellence doesn't require perfection," as the novelist Henry James noted. Even in the few situations where the goal truly is "zero errors," like your resume and cover letter, you achieve that not by going over your work a zillion times (which doesn't even work, since we all tend to miss our own mistakes), but by working with others (e.g., a career coach and proofreader).

The above story also illustrates how even reasonable-sounding goals, such as "to do good work" or "get a great grade," are perfectionist, reflecting an overfocus on outcomes and external recognition, shortsightedness, grandiosity, etc. These goals also often trigger a controlling (a.k.a., perfectionist) mindset where, consciously or subconsciously, you're trying to force the work in a certain direction. Creativity, however, is an organic, nonlinear, and liberated process: try to control it, even a little, and you'll shut it right down. (More on this in Chapters 25 and 29.)

The only ways to maximize your quality creative output are to:

1. **Become radically nonperfectionist** so that your ideas and inspiration flow freely.
2. **Do your time management** (Part V) to ensure that you have plenty of time not just to do your work, but to think, read, watch, listen, experience, experiment, play, etc.

One final tip for your intervals: don't judge your experience of them. Many perfectionists have such a strong habit of judging that, once they stop judging their work, they start judging their feelings around doing their work. "I did my work today but I didn't enjoy it," they'll grumble at me—to which I'll reply: "Fantastic! You did your work! That's the important thing." True: the goal is joyful productivity. But no one is joyful all the time, and not all projects are equally fun. (And, as I'll discuss in Chapter 31, even fun projects typically have a "yuck" stage in the middle.) Your job is to continue working, while noting—but not giving too much attention to—any negative feelings that may arise. Do that and the negative feelings will likely dissipate, leaving you free to more fully experience the positive ones.

8. Working on the Right Stuff

Effectiveness means both doing the right stuff, and doing lots—or, at least, enough—of it. In this book, I mostly focus on the "doing lots" part, since it's your professor's job to teach you what the right stuff is for their particular subject. But here are a few guidelines for making sure that you are getting the most out of the time you're putting into your schoolwork:

Remember that the goal isn't to study, it's to learn. Memorization and knowing how to look stuff up are important parts of learning, but not the whole thing. True learning only occurs when you engage deeply with the material. As Paulo Freire noted in his classic *Pedagogy of the Oppressed*, "Reading is not walking on the words; it's grasping the soul of them."

Think of your favorite book, film, album, etc. Probably you've read or seen or listened to it many times and know parts of it by heart. Perhaps you've thought about its various meanings and how they relate to your situation and life experiences. Maybe you've even read the artist's biography, researched their techniques and influences, and thought about why they made the choices they did.

And maybe you've even created your own work in response to theirs.

That's engagement, and you should seek to engage similarly with the people, places, times, ideas, principles, practices, and methods you're encountering in your classes.

Seek out the best teachers. Especially for difficult classes. A great teacher can not only help you learn, they can open your mind and transform your life. Now, some teachers are natural performers: their classes are always lively and fun and filled with all kinds of intellectual razzle-dazzle. Go ahead and take their classes. But don't overlook the less-flashy ones who show their caring and commitment via well-prepared lectures and course materials, homework that's returned on time and with substantive comments, and a willingness to go the extra mile for a student.

Read (and reread) the syllabus. It's an important document that should not only provide you with a helpful overview of the class, but other information that will help you to study more effectively.[18]

Resource yourself as abundantly as possible. Excellent supplies make the job easier and more fun. Obviously, many students don't have a lot of cash, but to the extent that you do, you should invest it in tools (like ergonomic furniture, see Chapter 9), supplies (like timers or those fancy colored markers you've been coveting), and services (like tutoring, see Chapter 47) that help you learn.

Learn the subject's best practices. Meaning, the best ways to do the work, including how to avoid or overcome common obstacles. Ask your professor, and also do a Web search on, "how to study [subject name]."

Read critically. In their book, *How to Study in College*, Walter Pauk and Ross Owens suggest that, when reading for an assignment, you first skim the assigned section, and then go back and read it closely—and maybe more than once. While reading, stop frequently to restate things in your own words, and to ask and answer questions. (E.g., "Why did it happen this way and not that way?" and "How does this reflect what we've been discussing in class?" and "How does [specific example] fit into this analysis?")

Pay attention in class. Shut your phone and laptop off[19] and focus on the professor. If you want to take extensive notes, record the lecture and take

---

[18] Snoop Dogg agrees! See
https://www.youtube.com/watch?v=aL_fP5axQV4&ab_channel=sallypotter .
[19] See, for example: www.nytimes.com/2017/11/22/business/laptops-not-during-lecture-or-meeting.html.

them later from the recording. (But always ask your professor's permission before recording.) Listen actively and critically, really thinking about (and questioning) what the professor is saying, while also working to connect the information with what you already know.

Have a learning goal for each study session. Not, for instance, "to do my reading," but "to understand the causes of the Cold War." And not, "to do my problem set," but "to learn how to solve complex differential equations."

Team up. Motivated study buddies will not only help you learn, they'll inspire you with their ideas and enthusiasm. (And you'll do the same for them.)

When asking for help, be specific. Don't hide behind generalities: tell your professor exactly what you're having trouble with.

Get visual. Create flow charts, diagrams, timelines, bubble maps, and other visual aids that convey the material in fresh and useful ways. (Just be careful not to overdo this, so that it becomes a form of Quasiproductive Procrastination.)

Teach someone else. Even your dog, cat, fish, or ferret! Or, if no one's around, pretend that you're explaining the topic to a five-year-old. It's when we try teaching others that we truly understand what we know and don't know.

Write it out. Another sure-fire way of finding out what you know and don't know.

During tests, first calculate how much time you have for each problem; then do the easiest ones first. If they're easy enough, you might wind up with some extra time for the harder ones. Stay mindful of the time and watch out for Beginning Bias (Chapter 32).

And a few other tips for solving math, science, engineering, and other technical problems:

Read the entire problem, and think for a moment about it, before trying to solve it. Some students jump right into solving without having fully read or thought about the information presented. (Needless to say, some homework and test questions are worded in such a way as to trick you into doing just that.) A good preventive against doing that is to underline everything in the problem's text that you think you'll need to use in the solution. (See, also, Chapter 26's discussion of "slow work.")

Write out the solution's basic steps or logic without doing any of the research or calculations. Be sure, however, to include the units (e.g., kg, mol, m/sec^2), since making sure that your answer includes the correct ones is an important way of checking your work. This technique will help you figure out which approach makes the most sense, thus helping you avoid false starts and other wasted time.

After you've solved a problem, try explaining your solution in non-technical language. Again, try teaching that hypothetical five-year-old. (Bonus points if you also explain what doesn't work.)

This has been a tiny overview of a vast topic. For follow-up reading, I recommend Walter Pauk and Ross Owens's *How to Study in College*.

9. The Re-Empowerment Process I: Overcoming Your Obstacles

Creating options, as we did in Chapter 4, is a quick and easy way to re-empower yourself; and it's particularly useful when you're in a rush. To get maximally productive, however, you should take the time to identify and resolve all your obstacles to doing your work. I discuss the first part of this process, obstacle identification, in this chapter and the second part, obstacle resolution, in the next.

Obstacles fall into six categories:

- **Project-Related.** Your project is difficult, confusing, boring, overwhelming, etc. Or your teammates aren't doing their job.
- **Course-Related.** There's a mismatch between you and the course. Maybe you lack the right skills or preparation for it. Or maybe it's badly organized or taught.
- **Resource-Related.** Your workspace is uncomfortable, inconvenient, noisy, or ill-equipped. Or you lack a well-functioning computer or other necessary piece of equipment.
- **Time-Related.** You don't have enough time.
- **Personal Issues.** You have physical or mental health challenges or a learning difference.[20] Or you're dealing with perfectionism or one

---

[20] As per the "On Using the Correct Toolset" note at the beginning of this book, if you're dealing with a physical or mental health issue, or a learning difference, please consult a specialist.

of the other barriers to productivity I discuss in this book. Or you're dealing with serious relationship, financial, or other problems. (Or are worried about someone else who is.)

- **Societal Issues.** You're distracted by events in your community or the larger world. (And perhaps also anxious, depressed, or grief-stricken about them.)

A word about that "Resource-Related" category: it's more important than it might seem because **a lot of procrastination begins in the body**. (You feel a bit uncomfortable, and that feeling builds until you have to get up from your chair.) There's also a safety issue, because a bad setup can cause an injury. (Once, after working on a slightly-too-high desk for just a few weeks, I got an elbow injury that took two years to heal.) So, to the extent you can, always use an ergonomic setup.[21] Many dorms and study spaces now offer ergonomic desks and chairs, but if you need to get your own, there are many cheap sources, like Ikea or craigslist.com. Some colleges also have periodic sales of used furniture, which you can learn about by contacting the facilities department.

I know many students don't have a lot of money, but to the extent you have it, investing in furniture and supplies that make studying easier, safer, and pleasanter is an excellent choice.

Returning to the entire list, that's a lot of potential obstacles! Picture each as a string, and all of those strings snarled up in a giant ball; then, picture that giant snarly ball blocking—as in "writer's block" or "creative block," get it?—your work. Some people visualize their block as a boulder or wall, but I think a snarl is a much more useful representation because it reflects the fact that your block is made up of multiple "strands" (obstacles) that you can "untangle" (resolve) one at a time. Even better, the more untangling you do, the easier the rest of the snarl becomes to deal with.

The next time you feel tempted to procrastinate, therefore, don't waste time with negative self-talk. Instead, grab your computer or notebook and make a list of all the obstacles that are blocking your ability to do your work. Be sure to include any "small" ones, such as that your chair is uncomfortable and your lighting poor. They add up—and, like icebergs, are often bigger than they seem.

---

[21] Here are two good, quick ergonomics primers: www.youtu.be/i1wIcVRP9xQ and www.youtu.be/9mJDs2CGZRI. And for a deep dive: www.ergo.human.cornell.edu/ergoguide.html.

Table II shows a sample Obstacle List for a student stuck on an art project.

Table II: Sample Obstacle List

Category	Obstacles
Project-Related	• I've got a whole bunch of pieces and don't know how to put them together (a.k.a., confusion or overwhelm). • No matter how hard I work, this project is destined to fail (a.k.a., futility). • I'm so bored with this thing!
Course-Related	• The instructions were confusing. I don't know what I'm supposed to be doing. • My professor can be hard to reach so I can't ask questions. • They can also be harsh so I'm afraid to ask. • Also, I don't want to let them know how little I've gotten done.
Resource-Related	• The art studio is way on the other side of campus. It's hard to get to, especially during winter. • It's also cold and uncomfortable. • There aren't enough paints and other supplies.
Time-Related	• Not enough time! I've got a ton of other stuff to do.
Personal Issues	• I'm exhausted. I never get enough sleep. • My brother is going through a hard time and I'm worried about him. • I'm also worried about whether my scholarship will be renewed for next year.
Societal Issues	• The current political situation really upsets me. • I'm also worried about the ecological crisis.

Sixteen obstacles may sound like a lot, but it isn't: most people come in at anywhere between ten and forty. (Yes, forty.) In fact, many people are shocked at the number of obstacles they come up with, because much of the time we're often only half-aware of many of our obstacles…

…which is why you should do Exercise 3!

Exercise 3

Make an Obstacle List for a project you've been procrastinating on. After you've finished, take a moment to reflect on it, and especially to feel some compassion and respect for yourself. Maybe at times you've bashed yourself for your supposed laziness or lack of discipline. (Or others have.) Now it turns out you've worked honorably to do your work in the face of many obstacles.

What's better than doing an Obstacle List while doing your work? Doing one before you get started, so that you can identify potential barriers and nip them in the bud! Get in the habit of doing such a preemptive list, especially before difficult projects.

Obstacle Resolution

After you've created your Obstacle List, list possible solutions to each obstacle, and then start implementing the best. Table III shows the beginning of our art student's solutions list.

Table III: Sample Solutions List

Category	Obstacle	Possible Solutions
Project-Related	1. I've got a whole bunch of pieces and don't know how to put them together (a.k.a., confusion or overwhelm).	1. Use journaling to clarify what the confusions are. 2. Ask your professor for help. (Or another professor or a teaching assistant, if that's easier.) 3. Ask a classmate or an artistic friend for help. 4. Make a to-do list; tackle one item at a time.

Category	Obstacle	Possible Solutions
		5. Use the solutions in Parts II and III of this book to help defuse perfectionism.
	2. No matter how hard I work, this project is destined to fail (a.k.a., futility).	1. Journal for clarity: are there reasons you feel this way and can they be addressed? (And how, exactly, are you defining "failure?") 2. Are you being perfectionist? (See Part II.) 3. Discuss with your professor or another advisor.
	3. I'm so bored with this thing!	1. See solutions in Chapter 32.
Etc.		

Two very cool things happen when you start coming up with solutions:

You empower yourself. Every problem-solving step you take—from identifying the problem, to journaling about it, discussing it with others, listing possible solutions, trying out a solution, improving that solution, and implementing the improved solution—empowers you some, thus making it easier for you to take the next step. It's a virtuous cycle! (The opposite of a vicious cycle.) And the more empowered problem-solving you do, the more empowered you become.

You become less afraid and more optimistic. That's partly because of the empowerment and partly because the solutions often turn out to be easier than we expect. You write, "ask a classmate for help," for instance, and immediately think of a nice person you can ask. Or, "get more sleep," and immediately think of some evening events you can cancel so you can do that. However, even with the solutions that take more work, or years of work (e.g., learning to cope with a chronic physical or mental health condition), and even for those problems that may never be fully solvable (e.g., a difficult family situation) or are largely out of your control (e.g., bias), you're still way better off problem-solving than procrastinating.

Some of your solutions, especially for problems in the Personal category, may involve seeing a counselor or therapist. Most colleges do offer such services but limit you to a few appointments, which usually isn't enough. See if your insurance will cover additional appointments with a therapist in the local community. If not, see whether there's a therapist who offers a sliding scale fee structure. If you have to pay out of pocket and are in a position to do so, then do it: good therapy is one of the best investments around. (I speak from experience, by the way.)

Your therapist should not only offer services congruent with your needs—trauma work, eating disorder work, relationship counseling, addiction recovery, etc.—but be a good fit in terms of personality and communications style. And after the first couple of getting-to-know-each-other sessions, your work together should yield at least some meaningful change. If your first therapist isn't doing all this for you, keep looking until you find one who does.

Exercise 4

Come up with solutions for the obstacles you listed in Exercise 3 and start implementing the best ones.

10. The Re-Empowerment Process II. Getting Help and Resolving Conflicts

Got a problem?

Someone you know has a solution.

Oh, I know: you don't want to ask for help. You're afraid you'll look "dumb"—although asking for help is the opposite of that. Or, you don't want to "impose" on anyone—even though, in college, you are literally surrounded by people whose job it is to help you. Or, you think it's somehow more admirable to go it alone. Sure: try that for a while, anyway. But if you really do need help—and why wouldn't you? We all do.—it's best to accept that, because: (a) as discussed in Chapter 2, the desire to go it alone, no matter how well-rationalized, is often rooted in deeper issues; and (b) a failure to ask can lead to some spectacularly time-wasting forms of Quasiproductive Procrastination (QP), such as:

- Trying to figure out which direction to take your project, when your professor can tell you in a flash.

- Struggling with a computer problem, when the friendly gurus at your college computer center know how to fix it.

- Wasting time, and risking failure, doing a difficult project from scratch when a more-experienced person can tell you what works and doesn't work. (Otherwise known as "reinventing the wheel.")

- Having both halves of a conversation in your head when you should be talking to the other person. (A common form of QP.)

The bottom line is that isolation, no matter how tempting or well rationalized, is not your friend—and asking for help is one of the most empowering things you can do. The latter is why, often, after someone emails me for help, I'll get a second email from them a few minutes later saying, "Never mind! I figured it out for myself!"

You'll also be empowered by the actual help you get, as well as by your strengthened relationship with your helper. (Who will themselves be further empowered by having helped.) So many great outcomes from the simple act of asking for help! And so, you should ask early and often—and even before you start a project. (Example: "Hi! I'm planning to do X. Can you tell me the best way to do it? Also, what problems do people typically encounter and how can I avoid those?") Do this not just for your schoolwork, but all your important endeavors.

Unfortunately, there can be barriers to asking for help, especially for students from disadvantaged and nontraditional backgrounds. In his book *The Privileged Poor*, Anthony Abraham Jack notes that college students from poor backgrounds who had attended elite public or (via scholarship) private high schools were, like their more affluent classmates, "at ease and proactive in connecting with faculty, building support networks, and asking for help." But those from poor backgrounds who had attended overcrowded and under-funded non-elite public high schools often weren't. "Faculty and administrators, for them, remain authority figures who should be treated with deference and left unburdened by their questions and needs."

There can be other reasons why a student from any background would be reluctant to reach out, including shyness and overwhelm. But Jack is clear that a reluctance to interact with faculty and administrators comes at a great cost:

> Developing rapport with key faculty and administrators was the road not just to assignment extensions, but also letters of recommendation, on-campus jobs, and off-campus internships. And these connections also meant so much more: having a faculty member or dean in your corner often meant getting the benefit of the doubt when in a bind; or the single in the dorm with the nice

windows; or introductions to corporate recruiters and help with negotiating job offers.

You should also be connecting with your peers. Along with the social benefits, a recent study shows that having a "peer social network" can increase your chances of succeeding in tough STEM (science, technology, engineering, and math) fields.[22]

Resolving Conflicts

Sooner or later, one of your solutions will conflict with someone else's needs. When that happens, I recommend a conflict resolution technique I call Cooperative Problem-Solving. It's based on one in Adele Faber and Elaine Mazlish's famous parenting book, *How to Talk so Kids Will Listen & Listen so Kids Will Talk*, which I recommend to everyone, whether or not they have kids, because it's an excellent and fun communications guide.

Cooperative Problem-Solving consists of eight steps:

1. **State the problem** and how it makes you feel.
2. **Listen** with patience, care, and respect to the other person's response. That's not only kind, it motivates them to work with you, and also provides you with the information you need to craft a mutually acceptable solution.
3. **Restate the other person's points.** This shows that you've been listening and also helps ensure that you're on the right track in terms of coming up with a solution. Please note that you want to "restate" and not "repeat." Verbatim repetition can not only be annoying—kids often do it to tease each other—it can convey the impression that you haven't actually been listening. (Think of a classroom full of kids being forced to repeat what their teacher says and droning away mechanically at it.)
4. **Get their agreement that you've restated their views accurately.** You do this by asking, after restating, "Did I get that right?" or something similar. If they reply, "Yes," then good work! If they say, "no," however, ask them to repeat what they said and try restating again. (And again, if necessary, until you get your "yes.") By the way, a "no" oesn't necessarily mean that you weren't listening well: it could be that the other person didn't express themselves

---

[22] www.advances.sciencemag.org/content/6/45/eaba9221

clearly or were clarifying their thoughts as they spoke with you. After you get your "yes," you can move on to...

5. **Brainstorm solutions.** You and the other person each list possible solutions without judging or evaluating them.

6. **Negotiate.** It's interesting how late in the process this step occurs. (Conflict resolution really is mostly about listening.) You negotiate by vetoing the solutions each of you finds wholly unacceptable, and then figuring out a good compromise among the rest.

7. **Restate** the agreed-upon solution and get the other person's "yes." And if you don't get a "yes" the first time around, repeat Steps 6 and 7 (and 5, if necessary) until you do.

8. **Express sincere gratitude.**

Here's how the steps work in action:

Hector has become increasingly frustrated that his suite has become "Gaming Central." Practically every night, one of his suitemates, Lou, has friends over; and they spend all night gaming in the common living room. The noise makes it impossible to study and sometimes to sleep. Also, Hector would sometimes like to sit in his own living room and watch TV!

He's tried dropping hints but that hasn't worked, so he knows he has to discuss the problem with Lou. And so, one afternoon he knocks on Lou's door and asks if he has time to talk. Here's how the conversation goes:

Hector (Stating the Problem): I'm wondering if we could do something about the constant gaming in our suite. It's keeping me from studying and sleeping, and it's really stressing me out, especially with finals coming.

> **Note:** It would be great, at this point, if Lou responds with something like: "Sorry! I didn't know there was a problem. Please tell me what I can do to make the situation better." And you know what? People often do respond with that kind of helpfulness and consideration. For the sake of this example, however, let's assume that Lou doesn't.

Lou: Really? It's bothering you? No one else has complained.

Hector: I can't speak for anyone else. But the situation isn't working for me—and another problem is that sometimes I want to watch TV but you guys are monopolizing it.

Lou (defensively): Well, what do you want me to do?

Hector: I appreciate your willingness to talk it over and I know it's not the easiest conversation to have. But why don't you tell me your take on the situation? (Now he *listens* with patience, care, and respect.)

Lou: It's supposed to be a commons area, isn't it? I've got as much right to use it as anyone. We've also got the best gaming system in the dorm so everyone wants to play here. Last week, we tried playing on Kevin's system and it froze. But it works fine on ours.

Hector (Restating and Getting the Yes): Okay, I heard that: the living room is everyone's area to use and we also have the best system. Is that right?

Lou: Yup.

Hector (Brainstorming): Can we come up with any solutions?

Lou: You could always study in the library. That's what it's there for.

Hector: Okay, that's one. Any others?

Lou: You could wear noise-canceling headphones.

Hector: Okay. Any others?

Lou (thinks for a moment, then shrugs): Not really.

Hector (Negotiation): Okay. The headphones idea isn't bad. Still, I feel like I should be able to study in my own room if I want. And I also need to be able to sleep without you guys waking me up all night. Isn't that reasonable?

Lou: Yeah, I guess so.

Hector: So how about this: your friends can hang out in our living room until 9:00 p.m. After that, you all go somewhere else.

Lou: How about midnight?

Hector: How about 9:00 p.m. on weeknights, and midnight on Fridays and Saturdays?

Lou: And Sundays?

Hector: It's gotta be 9:00 p.m. Sundays are study nights.

Lou (sighs): Okay. But how about 1:00 a.m. on Fridays and Saturdays?

Hector (after some consideration): Sure. I'll also go ahead and buy some earplugs, but could you guys lower the volume?

Lou: Okay.

Hector: And no gaming at all during midterms and finals weeks, okay?

Lou: How about just in the afternoons?

Hector: I guess afternoons are okay—I can always go to the library. But nothing after dinner, okay?

Lou: Okay.

Hector (moves onto Restating and Getting the Yes): Okay, so we agree that you guys will shut off all the games at 9:00, except on Fridays and Saturdays, when you'll go till 1:00. I'll get some earplugs, you'll lower the volume, and no gaming after dinner on test weeks. Is that all okay?

Lou: Yup.

Hector (Gratitude): Thanks a lot for working with me on this. I really appreciate it.

If the other person won't engage in this process, or won't compromise at all, that's too bad. Do your best to create some acceptable options for yourself. Or ask a mutual friend, or someone in authority—in the case of housing disputes, maybe a resident advisor—to mediate. There's no guarantee that that will work, but even if it doesn't you'll be glad you advocated for yourself.

11. The Best Solution to Procrastination

The best solution to procrastination is, obviously, to not need to do it in the first place—and you can achieve this. To see how, let's take a closer look at our friend the Disempowerment Cascade. Turns out, it's an interaction among three internal personae (or "voices"). They are:

The Fragile Creator. The persona who's trying to work. They're fragile not because you're weak, but because the work is challenging and you're facing many obstacles.

The Terrified and Terrorizing Perfectionist. (Also sometimes known as the Inner Critic or Inner Bully.) This persona is both hyper-self-critical and terrified of failure, which isn't a great combination. They're also almost certainly suffering from some other problems that I'll be discussing in Part II, including shortsightedness, negativity, and a fixation on supposed personal flaws. They are, in fact, the persona responsible for Chapter 3's disempowering inner monologue: "'What's wrong with you?,' 'Why are you so lazy?,'" etc. And when the pain they cause becomes intolerable, the third persona is invoked...

The Rebellious or Helpless Procrastinator. Contrary to what you might guess, your Inner Procrastinator is not your enemy. Their job is to rescue the fragile Creator from the bullying Perfectionist and in some ways they represent the best part of you: the part willing to fight for freedom, authenticity, and self-expression, and against bullying, coercion, and injustice. The problem is that they are invoked in circumstances of panic and stress, and are therefore disempowered and not great at problem solving. In fact, the only "solutions" they can come up with to address the perfectionist bullying are:

Rebellion. As in, "Why am I stuck inside doing this stupid work when everyone else is outside having a great time? It's not fair! Screw it, I'm going out!" (Recall Timothy Pychyl's point, from Chapter 2, about how procrastination often originates as a rebellion against authoritarian parenting.) And,

Helplessness. As in, "I can't even try to get started on my work."

Here's the tricky part: although your Inner Procrastinator can only come up with those two bad solutions, they can come up with infinite ways to sell them to you. So if it's not, "It's nice out and dammit I deserve a break!" it's "I should do all these less-important tasks first so that tomorrow I can focus better on my big project." Or, "A little TV won't hurt." Or, "[Insert your favorite rationalization for procrastination here.]"

Always remember that the fundamental goal of productivity work is to be able to show up on time and do what you had planned to do. Maybe not every single time—we all have emergencies and "off" days. But most of the time. When you accept that foundational truth and stay mindful of it while working, you will become much less susceptible to your Inner Procrastinator's manipulations.

The best solution would be to retire your Inner Perfectionist persona because it's in response to them, and as a protection from them, that you invoke your Inner Procrastinator in the first place. I'll discuss ways to do that in Part II.

PART II

COMPASSION

12. Perfectionist Myths and Realities

Note: Chapters 12 – 15 provide an overview of perfectionist attitudes and behaviors. Then, Chapters 16 – 24 discuss solutions. To remind you: I use labeling, dichotomizing, and generalizing to keep the prose concise. So you'll see a lot of "Perfectionists do this..." and "Nonperfectionists do that..." In real life, however, I would avoid doing that. (It's okay to label a behavior, but not a person— and anyhow, no one is entirely perfectionist or nonperfectionist.)

Perfectionism is a set of attitudes and behaviors that make it hard, or impossible, to do your work. Unfortunately, many people confuse it with having high standards (see Chapter 21) or think that, "It's good to be a little perfectionist." That can make it hard to identify the problem, much less solve it.

Let's, then, be clear: perfectionism is *never* a good thing. It never helps, and always hinders, your creativity and productivity. It can also hinder you in other areas of your life, including your relationships and health. After you've finished this section, I hope you will commit to rejecting perfectionism in all its forms, and in all areas of your life.

Beth's story, below, shows us how perfectionism can create serious problems for a student—but also how, with the right support, that student can overcome her perfectionism and resolve those problems.

Procrastination had never been a big problem for Beth, a creative writing major. Her fiction had always come easily and had always been well received by professors, classmates, editors, award committees, and others.

And so, she hadn't expected to run into any problems with her senior project, an interconnected series of short stories based on her family history and centering on the small farming community where she had grown up.

But she was running into problems. She was determined to create as true and nuanced a portrait of her family as she could, including both the positives (the close family ties, hard work, and perseverance in the face of obstacles) and negatives (poverty, addiction, and loss), but she was finding it hard to balance all those elements. At the same time, she worried about how her family would react to the stories when they read them. Would they see her as "airing dirty laundry" or, worse, holding them all up for public judgment and ridicule? There had already been grumblings from home about some of her other autobiographical works.

Beth felt trapped, in other words, between telling the stories she wanted to tell and the knowledge that doing so was liable to upset those she loved. And that wasn't the only thing blocking her: last year, a semi-famous writer who had been a visiting instructor in the creative writing program had harshly critiqued one of her stories, calling it "clichéd" and "derivative." Beth still cringed to recall his comments, and she was also now constantly on the alert lest any other bit of her writing be clichéd.

Beth also faced another source of pressure, which was that this was the project she was hoping would launch her literary career. If her stories turned out well, her plan was to get them published in literary magazines and then later expand them into a novel. It was important that she have some early success with her writing, both because a writing career had always been her dream and because an early success would vindicate her choice to major in creative writing, as opposed to a more "practical" field, like teaching or nursing, as her parents had wanted. Besides, nearly every time she read a literary blog or listened to a literary podcast, she learned about yet another 20-something writer who had gotten a book contract: why shouldn't she be one of the young successes?

Beth knew she should be setting all of these concerns aside while writing but was having trouble doing that. Her worries kept crowding into her thoughts and crowding out the stories she was trying to tell. Her writing pace had slowed to a crawl and she was also unhappy with the quality of what little she managed to produce. Whenever she compared her prose to that of one of her idols, like the short story master Alice Munro, she felt like crying.

Eventually, things got to the point where she couldn't even bring herself to go near her computer.

Finally, in desperation, she consulted her school's writing center. (She had previously ignored it, thinking that a "serious writer" like herself shouldn't need it.) Fortunately, the writing coach they assigned her—let's call him "Muse"—happened to have a lot of experience helping people overcome their procrastination, perfectionism, and other barriers. Along with helping Beth to recognize how those barriers were blocking her ability to write, Muse also showed her how to do Timed Work Intervals (Chapter 6), Quickdrafts (Chapter 30), and other techniques that supported and encouraged her creativity and productivity. Beth embraced those methods and was able to start writing again.

In a follow-up meeting, Beth summoned the courage to tell Muse what the visiting instructor had said about her work. When she finished, Muse shook his head angrily. "We heard a lot of complaints about him," he said. "Apparently, he critiqued all the students' work very harshly. We told the Creative Writing Program that he shouldn't be invited back." Beth was incredibly relieved to hear all this and readily agreed to Muse's suggestions that she: (a) do her best to ignore the harsh instructor's comments, and (b) show her story to the professor supervising her senior project for some more balanced and useful feedback.

As for Beth's concerns about offending her family, Muse told her that that was a very common concern among writers of autobiographical fiction and nonfiction. His advice was that Beth, "write the stories you want to write and that want to be written. Then, later on, you can decide whether to show them to your family or anyone else." Beth found that advice liberating.[23]

Muse then raised a concern of his own: Beth's unrealistic career strategy. "The fiction world is really competitive," he said. "Contrary to all the media hype, almost no one gets a book published soon after college. You need a more realistic plan." This was hard for Beth to hear, but it also came as a relief because, underneath it all, she had known her plan was unrealistic. Muse aided her in coming up with a more realistic one whereby she would build up a meaningful body of work over time, while at the same time supporting herself by working at publishing jobs that would facilitate her success.

---

[23] Note how the advice helped her to create more options (Chapter 4).

With all this great help, Beth was able to regroup, have more realistic expectations, and get more relaxed about her writing—all of which meant that she could be more productive, and…

…finish her senior project on time.

13. How Perfectionists Think

In this chapter, I discuss the most common perfectionist attitudes; and in the next, some common perfectionist behaviors. Obviously, there's a lot of overlap between attitudes and behaviors, with the attitudes often causing the behaviors. But the attitudes discussed in this chapter can cause many types of antiproductive behaviors and so it's useful to discuss them separately.

Perfectionists devalue process and overvalue product/outcome. For them, it's all about the grade. (Or getting the scholarship, landing the job, etc.) Nothing else matters, including how hard they worked, what they actually accomplished (in terms of learning, performance, etc.), what internal or external barriers they overcame, and any courage, kindness, integrity, or other admirable qualities they displayed along the way. This viewpoint isn't just inhumane, it creates vast pressure and sucks all the joy out of your work.

Also, reducing the actual work you're doing to a mere means to an end makes it hard to stay motivated on big projects in particular.

Overfocusing on outcomes is actually dangerous because you're never guaranteed a good one. You could be well-prepared for a test, for instance, and still do disappointingly because it was poorly designed or happened to focus on your weakest area. Or you could prepare like mad for a job interview and still not do well because you got nervous or the interviewer was inept. Or you could ace the interview and still not get the job because of nepotism, discrimination, or (more benignly) a budget cut. True: most of the time your grades and other outcomes should be commensurate with your efforts. If they're not, something's wrong and you should consult your mentors. It's also okay to hope for a good outcome, so long as you don't get too attached to that hope. But for the most part, you want to avoid expectations.

Perfectionists define success narrowly and often unrealistically. To them, only an A—or, better yet, A+— is acceptable.

A professor says your paper was "very good"? Big deal! If it wasn't "excellent" or "outstanding," you've failed.

You're a runner-up in a tough academic, athletic, arts, performing, or other competition? Who cares? You didn't win.

Obviously, this attitude also creates vast pressure. It also redefines your successes as failures, which is one of the most demotivating and pointless things you can do. (This perfectionist tendency to confuse "success" and "failure" is why I frequently put those words in quotation marks.)

Perfectionists are grandiose. Grandiosity is when you think the normal rules of productivity don't apply to you, or—put somewhat differently—that things that are difficult or even impossible for others should be easy for you. This can lead to:

1. Unrealistic goal setting. ("I can handle four classes, a research project, a serious extracurricular commitment, and a job.")
2. Underestimating the difficulty of challenges. ("This will be a piece of cake!")
3. Unwillingness to research and plan ("Boring!") or ask for help. ("I'll figure it out myself.")
4. Expecting yourself to succeed despite being under-resourced. ("Last year it took five people and $500 to do this community project, but this year we should be able to do it with three people and $300.")
5. Tendency to take shortcuts. ("I'll do the bare minimum for this class and then make it all up on the final.")
6. Tendency to think you or your project are special or unique. ("My project is so cutting-edge that there are no role models and no one I can turn to for help.")
7. Lack of respect for experience and expertise. ("I know my professor wants us to do the problems this way but I'm going to do them that other way because it's faster.")

8. Pointless rebellions. ("I won't bother getting a haircut for my job interview because my resume says it all.")
9. Stinting on self-care. ("I only need four hours of sleep a night." Or, "I don't need to see a counselor for my depression.")
10. Trivialization of your pain or suffering. ("Who cares if I'm unhappy? It's my work that matters.")

Grandiosity can also cause you to take on overly ambitious projects, often out of a misplaced desire to impress yourself or others. I can usually tell if someone's fallen into this trap because: (a) the project in question is too huge a leap from their previous work, (b) they lack the training or preparation to do it, (c) they're isolated (no mentors, collaborators, etc.), and/or (d) their plan has an overintellectualized or overcomplicated quality. (Out of all of those, I would say that the lack of mentors is the biggest red flag.) Don't get me wrong: ambition is great. But taking on an overly ambitious project is, like all perfectionism, a dead end. Overly ambitious projects tend to bog down in Quasiproductive Procrastination (QP) because the person has no real idea of how to proceed—and so, they wind up burying themselves in pointless, and often repetitive, busy work. Then, when they can no longer sustain the illusion that they're making progress, the QP devolves into full-blown Unproductive Procrastination (UP), at which point it's only a matter of time before they give up.

To be clear, this particular problem should never happen in college, since your professors should be assigning projects at the appropriate level of difficulty. But sometimes they screw up or (gasp!) students don't follow instructions. And sometimes projects mushroom out of control.

Perfectionists usually have a compelling-sounding (to them) rationalization for their grandiose ideas. Point out that a perfectionist is overscheduling themselves and they'll reply that they are well-organized. Or that they need to plan their big project and they'll say they're good at "winging it." But the rationales fall apart at the slightest scrutiny. No one, no matter how well-organized, can cram ten hours of work into five hours. And while you may be able to wing a small or unimportant project, winging a big or important one is a recipe for disaster.

Perfectionists overidentify with their work. As discussed in Chapter 3.

Perfectionists are shortsighted. They live in one big, hyperjudgmental "now," in which every project (or task) is of the utmost importance. Even worse, every *moment* of every project is of the utmost importance. Shortsightedness results in a pressured and miserable work experience, and is therefore one of the main reasons perfectionists quit projects. (And classes, schools, careers, etc.) Whenever a perfectionist hits a "bump"—even a small or ordinary one—they can't see their way past it, and get so discouraged they quit. (Pathologizing, which I discussed in Chapter 3, only adds to this problem.)

And how does a perfectionist quit a project? Often by glomming onto a shiny new one they hope will be, "the one that keeps me interested enough to finish." But it never is, for the simple reason that the problem isn't the projects, it's the perfectionism. (And if you're thinking some people do the same thing with their romantic relationships—perpetually ending them when they get challenging and moving onto others they hope will magically go better—yeah, you're right.)

Perfectionists are impatient. Because of their overfocus on product, overidentification, and shortsightedness, they need—no, crave—their success *now*. This impatience doesn't just make for a miserable work process, it compromises the quality of your work and is a barrier to learning (Chapter 26) and health and happiness (Chapter 42).

Perfectionists are also impatient in their careers, craving youthful success. Many constantly compare their progress to that of their friends, acquaintances, siblings, and others, including celebrities. The ubiquitous "30 Successful People Under 30"-type articles feed this impatience and, worse, favor the privileged. As podcaster Kristen Meinzer put it: "What would happen if [those types of articles] excluded people whose parents paid for their college, paid the down payment on their first place, or paid the bills while they worked unpaid or low-wage internships?"[24] (More on comparisons in the next chapter.)

Perfectionists are negative. As noted in Chapter 4, they underestimate and devalue their available options and outcomes. Even worse, they devalue their accomplishments, others' accomplishments, and others' willingness and ability to help them. They also mentally filter out positive results and

---

[24] www.twitter.com/kristenmeinzer/status/1281287686662377476

outcomes, seeing only their perceived "mistakes" and "failures." Tell a perfectionist you think their work is excellent except for one tiny thing and they'll only hear the tiny thing—and inflate it into a great big thing.

This negativity can lead to a **scarcity mentality**, where you think you either "aren't enough" (e.g., not smart, disciplined, or attractive enough) or "don't have enough" (money, time, talent, etc.) to succeed. Negativity and scarcity can also contribute to hoarding (Chapter 14), since they can convince you your work is lacking—research, polish, originality, etc.—and so you hold onto it hoping to improve it. (See, also, Chapter 14's discussion of fixations, and note how this scarcity mentality aligns with Chapter 4's idea of not having enough good options or potential outcomes.)

A scarcity mentality can also manifest itself in the belief that it is somehow nobler or more impressive to succeed in the absence of adequate resources. Examples range from the centuries-old "starving artist in the garret" stereotype to the more recent "I ate ramen for five years before my big break" media profiles of successful artists and entrepreneurs. Please note that what I'm objecting to is not scarcity itself—scarcity is neither a virtue nor a vice, just an unfortunate circumstance that some must deal with—but a romanticizing of scarcity. It's vital you not buy into this romanticizing because, perfectionist myths aside, it's hard to succeed when you're under-resourced.

Perfectionists distrust success and often reframe their successes as failures. If a perfectionist gets a good grade, they'll come up with five reasons the achievement should be dismissed. (E.g., "the project was easy" or "the teacher's an easy grader.") And if their work is going easily, they'll worry they're not challenging themselves enough. They might even add unnecessary work just to make it harder!

There can be a cultural component to this problem. You may have been taught, for instance, that talking about your successes is boasting. There's a difference, however, between taking pride in your achievements and boasting about them. Pride is based on an objective assessment of yourself and your work. It's an emotion you primarily communicate to yourself, although others can sense and respond to it. It is also incredibly motivating so you don't want to cheat yourself of it.

Boasting, in contrast, is grounded in insecurity, and primarily aimed at others. (Who aren't fooled.) I'll discuss it some more in the next chapter.

Remember that the word "humble" derives from the same Latin root as "humus," meaning earth or ground. The classical virtue of humility isn't about being self-effacing or overly modest: it's about being grounded. It's been my experience that successful people from all backgrounds are able to "own" their achievements. Speaking of which...

Perfectionists can also suffer from **impostor syndrome**, the belief that you haven't earned your success or don't belong in the professional or other communities you wish to be a part of. Those from marginalized or under-represented communities can be vulnerable to this, as can those who have experienced a harsh criticism or rejection (see Part IV).

Perfectionists are rigid. This shows up, especially, in a tendency to stick with a solution long after it's clear it's not working. If a perfectionist keeps getting distracted by their phone, for example, they'll, "keep trying till I can concentrate, dammit!" Or, if they're in a contentious relationship, they'll keep using the same ineffective coping strategies over and over again.

Perfectionists can also be rigid about their career choices. For them, it's "medical school or bust!" or "Employer X or bust!," with no backup plan. It's fine to work hard toward a cherished dream. (The Appendices offer some tips.) But it's always dangerous to not have a backup.

I've saved the worst for last:

Perfectionists try to use punishment as a motivator. It usually takes the form of either a shaming label (e.g., "I'm such a loser!"), a threat ("If I don't do well, I'm going to be in trouble."), or deprivation (e.g., "I'm going to sit here until I get it right. No breaks!"). What's confusing is that these tactics sometimes work in the short term. But punishment always leaves you more disempowered around your work and, thus, less able to do it in the future. (Which is why I say perfectionists "try to" use it as a motivator.) We also become habituated to punishment, so that it eventually stops working even in the short term. The first time we call ourselves, or someone else calls us, "lazy," for example, it feels terrible, and might shame us into doing our work. But the fifth or tenth time? Yawn.

Because perfectionists are constantly feeling like they failed, they are also constantly punishing themselves—which, needless to say, is a terrible way to live. Punishment also provokes opposition. That's easy to spot when the "punished person" and "punisher" are different people—think of a teenager rebelling against their domineering parents. But it also happens within us, when we respond to our bullying Inner Perfectionist by calling up our rebellious Inner Procrastinator. (As discussed in Chapter 11.)

The biggest problem with punishment, however, has nothing to do with whether it works: it's that it's inhumane and immoral. You should never do it to yourself or anyone else.

So those are the main perfectionist attitudes. See how they can all work together to create a trap? Overfocus on outcomes and define success narrowly and grandiosely, and you're pretty much guaranteed to "fail," especially if you're both impatient for your success and mistrustful of any successes you happen to achieve. Overidentify with that "failure," and you'll feel even worse, especially if you shortsightedly can't see past it. And respond to all that by punishing yourself and you're guaranteed to feel not just miserable, but hopeless—especially if you rigidly refuse to consider any other way of approaching your work.

And procrastination will soon start to seem like your only way out.

14. How Perfectionists Behave

Below are some common perfectionist behaviors, all of which derive from one or more of the attitudes discussed in Chapter 13.

Labeling. By now, I hope you understand why you shouldn't use punishing or shaming labels like "lazy" or "undisciplined." But even positive labels can be problematic. Being labeled as "gifted" or "talented" can put a lot of pressure on you, leading to perfectionism and procrastination. (Also see Chapter 16's discussion of "model minority.")

Some people get into trouble by overidentifying with a professional label such as "artist" or "engineer." It's okay to use those labels, only don't do so in a way that pressures you or limits your options. Beliefs such as "an artist should be willing to sacrifice everything for their art" and "an engineer should only be concerned with data and never feelings" are both incorrect and unhelpful. (Also notice both statements' dichotomization and grandiosity.)

Be careful, also, with descriptive labels. You might see yourself, for instance, as "pragmatic," "idealistic," or "caring." That's wonderful—until you take things too far, and your pragmatism becomes stodginess, your idealism becomes shallow fantasy, and your caring becomes overgiving (Chapter 48). As it turns out, many of our vices are our virtues taken a bit too far.

You also want to avoid labeling your work. A professor once told a friend of mine that her paper was "brilliant": she spent the rest of the semester terrified of not living up to that high standard. Perfectionists also often label their projects as "hard" or "easy," then dichotomize those labels so that "hard" becomes, in their mind, impossible, and "easy" trivial. This leads to a lot of fear (in anticipation of your supposedly hard stuff) and discouragement (when your supposedly easy stuff turns out to be harder than anticipated). Better to let those labels go and let your work just be your work. And when praising someone else's work, it's a good idea to follow psychologist Carol Dweck's advice from her book *Mindset*, and praise not their outcome or talents, but their "growth-oriented *process*—what they accomplished through practice, study, persistence, and good strategies." (Italics mine.)

The worst labels are hyperbolic. Statements like "my paper is garbage" and "my workout is hell" do nothing but increase your fear and disempowerment around the activity in question. And while we're on the topic of word choice, be aware that there are a few seemingly benign words that, all by themselves, are enough to make a statement or thought perfectionist. One is "just," as in the statement, "It's just ten math problems." The implication—and dangerous expectation—is that your work should go easily. Ditto for "only," which is often used the same way. Another stealth-perfectionist word is "should," as in, "I should be able to do it all."

In my writing productivity classes, we often do an exercise entitled "Perfectionism Test" where students identify the perfectionist elements in a group of sentences. After we're done, I say, "There's one more perfectionist thing on the page—can you find it?" Most students can't. "It's the title!" I point out. "Why call this a 'test?' Why not call it an 'exercise' or a 'game?'" The simple act of swapping in "exercise" for "test" causes everyone in the room, including me, to relax.

These kinds of perfectionist word traps are everywhere, so please watch your words and keep things as light and playful as possible.

Comparisons. Perfectionists constantly compare themselves to anyone and everyone, including family members, friends, strangers, and famous people both living and dead. They'll compare themselves on their grades, wealth, and other outcomes, on personal attributes such as looks and popularity, and on personal qualities such as talent or discipline. They'll even compare themselves to *themselves* at a higher level of performance. A perfectionist who was once able to write an "A" paper overnight, run a four-and-a-half-minute mile, or perform a near-flawless Brahms piano sonata will constantly expect themselves to repeat that exceptional achievement, and constantly bash themselves for failing.

Speaking of Brahms, he was relentlessly compared to Beethoven, to the point where people joked that his First Symphony would be, "Beethoven's 10th." And you know what? It took him *21 years* to produce that symphony. The miracle was that he was able to produce it at all, given the enormous pressure and public scrutiny he labored under. "You can't have any idea what it's like always to hear such a giant marching behind you," he bemoaned in a letter to a friend.

The situation is even worse on social media, where many platforms encourage constant comparisons, both with your friends and with the carefully curated and photo-edited feeds of celebrities and influencers. Psychologist Melissa G. Hunt, whom I quoted in Chapter 5, says these constant comparisons are among social media's most harmful aspects.

Perfectionists also often forget that even many fair-seeming comparisons really aren't. (Recall Kristen Meinzer's comment about the "30 Under 30" articles, cited in the last chapter.)

As if all this weren't bad enough, **many perfectionists also constantly compare themselves to—and constantly bash themselves for falling short of—an idealized version of an identity or role that's important to them**, such as the "good student," "dedicated artist [or activist]," or "dutiful child of immigrant parents." Philosophers call this the "Nirvana Fallacy," and it is an especially demoralizing and exhausting habit. Many perfectionists also compare their work sessions to an idealization and bash themselves for falling short in terms of quantity or quality. They'll even compare themselves to some mythical creator for whom the work is always easy and joyful, and bash themselves for falling short of that ideal as well.

Comparisons can be a useful analytical tool. A perfectionist comparison rarely is, however, because the goal of a perfectionist comparison isn't objective analysis but to shame yourself into doing better. One sign your comparison is perfectionist is that it leaves you feeling bad; another is that it omits crucial information. A perfectionist poetry student, for instance, might bash themselves because their poems aren't as good as the ones in their textbook, ignoring the crucial points that the latter: (a) are considered, by the book's editor at least, to be "the best of the best," and (b) were probably written when the poets were more experienced than our student. Post-college, our poet might obsess over the fact that they are making less money in their editorial job than a friend is making in finance, omitting the crucial points that they love their work and would hate finance.

Whenever you feel bad about yourself or your work, there's usually a perfectionist comparison involved.

Competitiveness. Often goes hand in hand with comparisons. Sure, competition can be fun and help you excel. But perfectionists often focus just on winning, and they'll also try to compete in situations that shouldn't be competitive. In response to a Quora.com query, "What's it like to be a straight-A student?", a self-described perfectionist student posted this:

> I am constantly comparing myself to my best friend (she is also my academic competitor). I find myself hating others when they score higher than me and smiling when they do not do as well as me. This is completely awful of me, and I am trying to slowly change, but my academic pressures prevent me from going back to my old, relaxed self.[25]

Boasting and Misplaced Pride. Perfectionists often feel the need to boast about how hard they're working or the massive sacrifices they're making. "Yeah, I shouldn't have pulled three all-nighters last week," they'll say, sounding all rueful and abashed. But you can hear the pride underneath.

Another common perfectionist boast is about how tough their class or major is. Examples: "[Insert name of major]: only the strong survive," "This class is designed to weed out the weak," And, "You can't learn this stuff—you've either got the talent or you haven't." Along with being tedious and rude, this kind of boasting can discourage students from under-represented groups and those who haven't had the privilege of an elite high school education,[26] and it also lets bad teachers off the hook. (So perhaps it's not surprising that some academic professionals, who ought to know better, also repeat these boasts.)

Hoarding. As noted earlier, perfectionists hoard their work. Unfortunately, the more you do that, the more scared and disempowered around your work you become, and the more you need to do it. (A vicious cycle!) Another way to visualize this is that the hoarding creates a wall between you (and your work) and those with whom you should be interacting, including not just

---

[25] www.quora.com/What-is-it-like-to-be-a-straight-A-student/answer/Cathy-Tran-5
[26] www.nytimes.com/2020/11/16/science/weed-out-classes-stem.html

your professors but potential collaborators, mentors, employers, and audiences. To be clear, you're not just keeping your work behind the wall, but advice, support, and opportunities outside it. And the more you hoard, the bigger, taller, and more impenetrable that wall gets. (Solutions to hoarding in Chapter 32.)

Fixating. Perfectionists are generally self-critical but they also often have one or two areas where they are especially so. These fixations often start when someone harshly criticizes you or your work and that criticism becomes a part of your self-image you struggle with. Especially if the critic is someone you respect (Chapter 34), the criticism—be it, "Math isn't your strong point, is it?" or "You're an impractical dreamer, aren't you?"—soaks right in and becomes something you fixate on. (Beth, from Chapter 12, is another example, perpetually worrying about her work being clichéd after the harsh writer told her it was.) Please note that a criticism doesn't have to be valid to trigger a fixation.

As with many of the problems I discuss, it's often the most caring and dedicated students who fall prey to fixations, because their caring makes them vulnerable.

Of course, our society and media are themselves fixated on certain things, including wealth, looks, and popularity (including social media popularity), so it's easy to get fixated on those even if no one directs a criticism specifically at you.

Notice how all the perfectionist behaviors can reinforce each other, so that, for instance, labeling and comparisons can cause a fixation, which, in turn, can cause hoarding—which you might then try to cover up, or compensate for, via boasting. Notice, also, how all the perfectionist characteristics I've been discussing both in Chapter 13 and this chapter are prevalent in academic settings. And notice, finally, how exhausting it all is. Constantly struggling against perfectionism will wear you out until you have no energy or enthusiasm left for your work or anything else.

Exercise 5

Go ahead and expand Exercise 3's Obstacle List using the perfectionist characteristics we've been discussing in Chapters 13 and 14. If you've been overfocusing on outcomes, narrowly defining success, overidentifying with the work, etc., describe the effect that that behavior is having on your productivity, health, and happiness.

Exercise 6

List all the perfectionist attitudes and behaviors you see in Beth's story (Chapter 12) and discuss how each might be blocking her ability to do her work.[27]

---

[27] Some answers (you may find more): narrow definition of success (wants to create, "as true and nuanced...a portrait...as she could"); an overfocus on others' responses (fear that she would be accused of betraying her family); grandiosity (expectation of easy success and an initial reluctance to ask for help); impatience (both with the writing process and in her desire for a quick career success); yet more grandiosity (anticipating a "home run" career, especially without a viable plan for achieving it); comparisons (with Alice Munro, a Nobel laureate!), labeling ("serious writer"), fixations (worries about being clichéd), rigidity (rewriting the same story over and over); and overidentification (wanting the project to validate her choices). Whew!

15. Where We Learn Perfectionism

The perfectionist attitudes and behaviors discussed in the previous chapters all have one thing in common: they go against accepted best practices for productivity, learning, and growth. So where do we get the idea they're useful? From the media, to start with. Perfectionist narratives are simple and compelling, and so the media loves them. That's why you see so many:

- Stories of "spectacular," "easy," "overnight," "solo," and "against-all-odds" success in education, business, sports, romance, etc.

- Stories that gloss over the process a person used to succeed, focusing instead on the glorious outcome.

- Stories that glamorize or exalt poverty, deprivation, and suffering. (For instance, depictions of "starving artists" who don't mind their poverty.)

- Stories that exalt punishment, suffering, or "tough love."

- Stories where the characters live in what I call "magical affluence"— e.g., the barista or freelance writer who somehow manages to afford a fabulous New York City apartment. These households also magically clean and stock themselves, which is also perfectionist.

- Stories where the person supposedly has the high-paying job needed to support the fancy lifestyle but you never actually see them doing that job. (In the real world, high-paying jobs dominate your life.)

- Stories that trivialize the realities of human existence and relationships. If you've read Atlas Shrugged, for instance, you may recall how, at the end of the book, Ayn Rand's capitalist heroes all manage to live together in effortless peace and harmony despite their many economic and romantic conflicts. Come on! Have you ever seen that happen in real life? (For the record, Rand's own personal relationships were, to put it mildly, a mess.28)

A lot of advertising is also perfectionist. Many ads overfocus on product at the expense of process ("Just do it!"), grandiosely trivialize human suffering ("No pain, no gain!"), depict narrow and unrealistic outcomes ("Use this mascara and you'll look like a supermodel!"), use flawed comparisons ("before and after"), promise quick solutions to difficult problems ("Lose ten pounds in two weeks!"), and trivialize human relationships ("Drink this booze and you'll be sexy and popular.").

The Parents' Trap

Perfectionism is so pervasive that even many parents, teachers, coaches, and other mentors have internalized it. See if you can identify the perfectionist characteristics in these common parental statements:

- "How come you only got a B?"
- "It's easy!" (When you're struggling with something.)
- "Why can't you do as well as your brother?"
- "Get over it!" (When you're hurting from a painful rejection.)
- "Sam is great at science and Amanda is great at art."[29]

Make no mistake: just as it's often the most dedicated and caring students who fall prey to perfectionism, it's also often the most dedicated and caring parents who do. But it can still hurt, as this real-life episode illustrates:

A friend once got a call that her twelve-year-old daughter had broken her wrist during soccer practice and was on her way to the emergency room with her father, who had been coaching. My friend hurried to meet them there and when she arrived was surprised to find a daughter who wasn't just injured, but irate. Apparently, at some point during the drive, Dad had told Daughter, in

---

28 See Barbara Brandon's biography, *The Passion of Ayn Rand.*

29 Some answers (you may find more): (1) narrow definition of success; (2) overfocus on product/trivializing of process; (3) comparison; (4) grandiosity (you shouldn't feel pain); (5) comparison and dichotomizing.

response to her crying, to "stop being a wimp." Talk about adding insult to injury! Small wonder, then, that Daughter's first words to her mom weren't, "My wrist hurts!" but an outraged, "He called me a wimp!" The emotional and moral pain of being perfectionistically labeled had trumped her actual physical pain.

Dad, meanwhile, just stood there looking guilty and confused. He hadn't meant to cause his daughter additional pain, of course. But he, too, had grown up surrounded by perfectionism and had internalized many of its messages.

Sometimes someone pushes back on the don't-pressure-or-punish-your-kids idea, saying something like, "My parents pressured [or punished] me and I turned out okay." Of course, we have no idea what kinds of pressure took place, or how the person's life might have differed had they not been pressured. Perhaps the pressure was mild and occurred in a context of authoritative parenting (lots of rules but also lots of affection), as opposed to authoritarian parenting (lots of rules but little affection). (See Chapter 2 for more on how our parenting influences us.) Or perhaps the person had a nonparental role model whose kindness helped to neutralize the perfectionist harshness.

Or perhaps they were resilient for another reason.

No matter. As discussed in Chapter 13, it doesn't matter whether punishment "works," or seems to. It's an inhumane practice that you should take an ethical stand against, both for yourself and others.

Situational Perfectionism

People often ask me whether someone can be "born perfectionist." It's a good question. Every parent knows that kids are born with different temperaments, and that some have a tendency to be critical or judgmental. Such kids, if they're lucky enough to receive compassionate parenting, can avoid the trap of perfectionism. Unfortunately, what many of us get, in a perfectionist society, is perfectionist parenting, and so, even if we weren't born with a critical temperament, we may still wind up falling into the trap. (And, obviously, those who were born with a critical temperament are at risk for having that tendency reinforced.)

Many events can also trigger what I call situational perfectionism, which is when an event or circumstance causes your perfectionism to spike. These include:

- A transition, like those discussed in Chapter 2.
- A failure or rejection (Chapter 22 and Part IV).
- A success (Chapter 23), especially if it causes you to feel more visible and scrutinized. An example would be the many writers, like Ralph Ellison and Harper Lee, who, after having had a notable success with their first book, either failed to produce a second or took decades to do so.
- An opportunity you're afraid of squandering. For instance: "Now that I've got this scholarship [or new computer, or paid tutoring, or some other advantage], I'd better get all A's!" Or, during winter break: "I've got a whole month off so I'd better make it count!" (Either in the sense of having fun or studying for the next semester.)
- A need to justify others' efforts on your behalf. Even students from affluent backgrounds can feel pressure to justify their parents' tuition payments, but those from working-class or poor backgrounds can obviously feel that pressure more. As a student once told me, "My mom cleans rich people's houses so I can be here [at college], so I'd better do well."

Being a first-generation student, or one from an under-represented group, especially if your situation causes you to feel extra-scrutinized or that your success or failure reflects on your group. Speaking of which...

Members of so-called **model minorities** face an additional challenge. That stereotype—of an ethnic or other group whose members excel academically and professionally—is problematic on several levels. It's a trigger for situational perfectionism, with everyone, including maybe you yourself, putting more pressure on you because of your heritage. (The cliché that "a B is an Asian F" is as perfectionist as it gets.) It also creates competition, resentment, and other barriers between you and others, both within and outside your group.[30] And it can lead some to trivialize your achievements by either crediting them to your culture or making the assumption that you didn't face any barriers.

---

[30] See, for instance: www.npr.org/sections/codeswitch/2017/04/19/524571669/model-minority-myth-again-used-as-a-racial-wedge-between-asians-and-blacks.

If you're a member of a supposed model minority, or subject to any form of situational perfectionism, that's one more hurdle you'll need to overcome in your quest for joyful productivity. Remember: there's nothing wrong with wanting to do great work. The problem is when you cross the line into perfectionism and your work becomes painful, pressured, or stressed.

Exercise 7

Reread Beth's case study (Chapter 12) and list the factors that might be creating some situational perfectionism for her.[31]

Exercise 8

Revisit the situation you examined for Exercise 3 and see if you can find some situational causes that caused your perfectionism to spike.

We've finished our discussion of the nature and origins of perfectionism. Time to move on to the solutions!

---

[31] Some answers (you may find more): senior project (a special project, and also a longer and more difficult one than she had ever done), "lifelong dream," and challenging (highly personal and emotionally fraught) subject matter. Also, earlier successes setting up an expectation of success, while at the same time—and, yes, paradoxically—last year's harsh critique set her up for a simultaneous terror of failure. Also, framing the project as the vindication of her major, culmination of her college experience, and foundation for her post-college career. Finally, the fears of being criticized by family and community, and of betraying them by doing a bad job.

16. Nonperfectionist Attitudes and Behaviors

Nonperfectionists hold the opposite of the attitudes, and do the opposite of the behaviors, described in the previous chapters. Specifically, they:

Focus on the *process* of doing their work. Meaning their actual math, English, political science, etc.—as opposed to the grade or other desired outcome. A process focus not only takes a lot of the pressure off, it helps connect you with the work's intrinsic pleasures (which helps you stay motivated) and yields better outcomes.

As the novelist Gustave Flaubert put it, "Success is a consequence and must not be a goal."

Define success broadly and holistically. Yes, nonperfectionists want those great grades and other great outcomes. But they mostly measure success based on whether or not they've done their best—meaning, whether they've worked steadily and with good focus. After that, it's whether they've accomplished some good learning, with "learning" interpreted broadly. (Sometimes, as per Chapter 28's discussion of trial and error, the valuable lesson is a greater understanding of what *doesn't* work.) Other important accomplishments might be: staying cool under pressure, treating others well under difficult circumstances, overcoming (even partially) a personal or institutional barrier, and connecting with a new mentor or collaborator.

Another example of a broadly defined success is when someone joins a sports team, or a musical or other group, not primarily to compete, but for the health, recreational, teamwork, camaraderie, coaching, and other benefits.

Stay grounded. Nonperfectionists know grandiosity is delusional. (It's a gambler's mentality and linked to low self-esteem.[32]) So, they try to err on the side of humility and do *extra* planning, get *extra* help, etc. They also choose their projects out of a sincere interest rather than a desire to impress. And they take their time management (Part V) seriously: never, for instance, trying to cram ten hours of work into an eight-hour workday.

Maintain a healthy emotional distance from their work. Nonperfectionists know that even their "important" work is merely something they do and not a justification for their existence or a source of legitimacy. They also know that obstacles are a normal part of any project and not a reflection on them personally, and so, when they encounter one, they don't pathologize. And they also know that everyone is better at some things than others, so they don't expect themselves to be exceptional in every area. (Or, necessarily, in any area: as discussed in Chapter 13, you should avoid having expectations.)

Take the long/broad/high view. Nonperfectionists understand that there's a point in pretty much every big project—and sometimes more than one—where you feel stuck and hopeless. (See Chapter 31's discussions of the Anti-Honeymoon and Vast Middle.) Also, that many problems that seem serious at the time turn out not to be (Chapter 22). And that all projects, including the biggest and most important-seeming, are mere "station stops" along the journey of their life and career.

These and other long-range perspectives help them stay grounded and motivated, even in the face of obstacles and setbacks.

Are patient. Nonperfectionists understand that it takes time to do quality work—and often way more time than we anticipate. (More on this in Chapter 26.) They also understand that most successful careers are built over time. And they also understand that, when they rush their work or other activities, they not only compromise their chances of success, but cheat themselves out of potential joy and fulfillment. (More on the evils of rushing in Chapter 42.) So they strive to remain patient even when the pressure's on.

---

[32] www.pubmed.ncbi.nlm.nih.gov/29455443/

Are positive. Nonperfectionists work to stay objective—or, even better, a bit positive. Positivity (a.k.a., optimism) is often disparaged as naive, but it is a fantastic basis not just for joyful productivity, but a happy life.[33] Sure, it's a form of expectation, so you don't want to overdo it. But a little too much positivity is way better than negativity and way, way better than cynicism (which is when you expect the worst from everyone and everything around you). Not only are negativity and cynicism disempowering, they also repel others and thus can damage your professional and personal relationships.

Nonperfectionists also have an (8) **"abundance mentality"** that encourages them to not only fully utilize all available resources, but to persevere in finding new ones. (Resourcefulness is, in my view, an underappreciated quality.) This doesn't mean you have every single resource you want or could use, but enough to get you mostly where you want to go. (I'm not denying that many people don't actually have enough money, time, or other resources, due to either their personal circumstances, societal inequalities, or both. The problem I'm addressing here are the many people who do have enough but don't think they do.)

Are comfortable owning their successes. If anything, they take a bit of extra pride and satisfaction from them. (Since it never hurts to err a bit on the side of nonperfectionism.)

Nonperfectionists also don't waste time questioning whether they are challenging themselves enough. If they're in any doubt, they ask their professor—who, let's not forget, happens to be an expert in evaluating student potential.

Nonperfectionists also know it's okay—and a wise strategy—to take on the occasional easy project and benefit from the occasional lucky break.

Reject impostor syndrome. Nonperfectionists recognize that impostor syndrome is a narrative that has the power to harm us. They therefore do their best to reject it.

---

[33] Also, a healthier and longer one: www.nytimes.com/2020/01/27/well/mind/optimism-health-longevity.html.

Are flexible. If a solution isn't working, nonperfectionists quickly seek out another one. They also always have a Plan B in case their primary plan doesn't work out.

Never punish themselves. Unfortunately, even after you intellectually and ethically reject punishment, it can still be a hard habit to break. (Chapter 20 offers suggestions.)

Resist labeling and hyperbole. Nonperfectionists use precise and nuanced descriptions, such as: "I've got ten pages to read tonight" or, "I've got a sixty-minute workout." This precision may sound boring in comparison to perfectionist labeling and hyperbole, but at least you aren't disempowering yourself via your language.

Avoid comparisons. Nonperfectionists are comfortable evaluating their achievements on their own merits without constant comparisons. While they may look to more successful people as role models and inspirations, they avoid strong or over-direct comparisons, especially if they don't know the whole story behind the other person's success. Especially, they are careful not to get sucked into comparisons on social media.

Nonperfectionists also avoid envy, which accomplishes nothing except for making the envious person miserable. Nor do they dwell on their former successes except to: (a) appreciate them and (b) figure out, and try to replicate, the conditions that made them possible.

Avoid excessive competitiveness. When nonperfectionists compete, their goal is not to triumph over others, but to do the best they can while, as much as possible, enjoying and otherwise benefiting from the experience. (If they win, that's the icing on the cake.)

Ultimately, nonperfectionists understand that creative and intellectual endeavors are individual journeys of discovery, as is life itself. (More on this in Chapter 25.) While it is possible, and essential, to learn from others, in the end, we each need to chart our own course. As the novelist Bernard Malamud put it, "Eventually everyone learns his or her own best way. The real mystery to crack is you."

Don't boast or indulge in misplaced pride. If they feel the need to do so, they take that as a sign that something's wrong and do some journaling or other work for insight and healing.

Share their work early and often. Nonperfectionists know that, in contrast to the "walls" hoarding builds between you and others (Chapter 14), sharing creates "bridges." They also understand that the more you share, the more bridges you create, and the easier it is to keep sharing. So they share early and often. Early on in a project, for instance, a nonperfectionist might share their idea and plan with their professor and get feedback. Then, as they proceed with their work, they'll share pieces of it with their professor, teaching assistants, tutors, advisors, classmates, and friends. Sometimes they'll do this in the context of asking a question. ("Here's what I've done so far; what do you think?" Or, "I'm not so sure about my conclusion, is it okay?") And sometimes they'll share just for the heck of it, because they know sharing is empowering. ("Hey, I love this thing I wrote, just wanted to show it to you, no reply needed.") Obviously, the more casual forms of sharing are best done among friends.

Hand their work in on time. Nonperfectionists don't give themselves permission to miss deadlines. A great technique for achieving this, by the way, is to give yourself an early deadline. Tell yourself often enough that your problem set is due on Wednesday, for instance, and you'll eventually start to believe it—and then it will come as a pleasant surprise when you remember it's actually due on Friday and so you have a couple of extra days. (Of course, sometimes we miss a deadline due to an extenuating circumstance like an illness or family crisis. That's not what I'm discussing here.)

Keep moving. After they've handed in their work, nonperfectionists don't sit around waiting for the grade or other outcome, but move right on to the next project. This not only helps them get more done; it also helps them to not overreact when the grade or other outcome, be it "positive" or "negative," does arrive. Yes, you want to pay serious attention to the feedback you get on your work: that's a crucial part of learning. But it's possible, and advisable, to do that without getting emotionally caught up.

Work to overcome their fixations and avoid developing new ones.
Nonperfectionists use journaling and, if necessary, counseling to help over-come their fixations. They might even take a media literacy class to help them better understand media manipulations and machinations. And they are also careful to filter their media and other inputs to limit their exposure to unhelpful and sabotaging messages.

Nonperfectionists also understand that, while some fields—like, say, theoretical physics and professional athletics—do have extreme require-ments of one kind or another, most of the time we do have sufficient intel-ligence, creativity, talent, originality, and other personal qualities to achieve our goals. (And even in the "extreme" fields, hard work and a willingness to ask for help will often take you further than you might think.) Nonperfec-tionists also understand that we mostly use labels like "talent" and "original-ity" retroactively after a creative work or career turns out well, and so it's best not to get too worked up about them. As novelist Stephen King puts it: "Talent is cheaper than table salt. What separates the talented individual from the successful one is a lot of hard work."

Ditto for money, time, help, and other resources. As discussed above, many people who think that they don't have enough of these actually do, especially if they're willing to ask for help.

So that's our list of nonperfectionist attitudes and behaviors. Do nonper-fectionists do all of these things 100% of the time? Of course not: they have their slip-ups like everyone else. (And that "100%?" Perfectionist!) The im-portant thing is that, when they do make a mistake, they skip the self-re-proach and focus on learning from the experience—and especially on making a plan to do better in the future.

I'll share the techniques nonperfectionists use to overcome their per-fectionism starting in Chapter 18. But first, we need to discuss the three most important things every nonperfectionist knows.

Exercise 9

Is there an activity you love but aren't perfectionist about? Maybe you love to cook, even if your meals aren't gourmet quality. Or knit, just for fun. Or swim, even if you're not on a team. Maybe you've even had a "disaster"—like a meal where everything went wrong or a scarf where you dropped a whole bunch of stitches—and been able to laugh it off. That's some excellent nonperfectionism right there! See if you can bring that same playful and process-focused approach to your schoolwork and other "serious" endeavors.

17. The Three Most Important Things Nonperfectionists Know

The most important things nonperfectionists know are:

All Perfectionist Narratives Are Lies

Poke any perfectionist statement and all kinds of inconvenient truths come flying out: the "overnight success" turns out to have worked for years prior to their breakthrough; the "young" or "solo" success was helped by family money and connections; the "natural beauty" required days of preparation before the photo shoot, plus photo-editing afterwards; and the "glamorously" broke artist or activist didn't actually enjoy being broke (and their work suffered).

Perfectionism *never* Helps and *always* Makes Things Worse

And not just with your work, but your life. Remember, from Chapter 14, the perfectionist student who responded to the Quora.com query about what it was like to be a top student? Here's more of her reply:

> I spend hours and hours doing my work to make sure that I can get a 100 to keep my grades, and I am worn out and exhausted. I never feel the joy of receiving a good grade anymore because I expect myself to do that well. On the flip side, I am completely

devastated every time I make anything less than a 95.

That's no way to live—and even if you want to argue that success (however you define it) is worth the sacrifice, it's an unsustainable path for most people.

As mentioned earlier, we should ethically reject perfectionism's punishments regardless of whether or not they work. But really, they don't work—and we succeed despite our perfectionism, not because of it. One of the very worst perfectionist lies is that you need to suffer to succeed. (More on this in Chapter 20.)

So, yes: work hard. Work a lot. Make your commitments, investments, and sacrifices. But don't work past the point of health, happiness, and a balanced life.

All of which brings us to the most important thing nonperfectionists know:

Never Go There

Never succumb to the urge to do the things I discussed in Chapters 13 and 14. That's easy enough to do when your work is going well. But we all have times when we're underproductive or otherwise think we've failed, and when that happens, the temptation to revert to pressure and punishments can be strong. But you need to be stronger. **The key is understanding, not just intellectually but deep in your bones, that perfectionism *never* helps and *always* makes things worse.**

This may all sound philosophical but it is deeply practical. By refusing to give in to the temptation to be perfectionist, nonperfectionists not only keep themselves healthy and safe, but ensure that they get back on track as soon as possible.

"Never go there" is a very strong instruction, but strength is what's needed. Procrastination and perfectionism are strong and sneaky habits that are fed, often, by denial and self-deceit: you won't get far trying to counter them with weak, wishy-washy measures. You need to confront them with strength and certitude.

Relatedly, nonperfectionists also understand that **there is no cheating in antiperfectionism work**. I don't mean you shouldn't cheat: I mean you literally can't. Overfocus on product, overidentify with your work, try to motivate yourself through punishment, or otherwise indulge in perfectionism even a little and you're back in the realm of perfectionism.

No one ever achieves zero perfectionism—and the idea of "zero perfectionism" is, you guessed it, perfectionist—but don't be fooled that, "a little perfectionism is okay."

18. The Nonperfectionist Mindset: Introducing Your Inner Compassionate Adult

Nonperfectionism is a collection of attitudes and behaviors that support your ability to do your work. Unfortunately, just as there are myths around perfectionism, there are also myths around nonperfectionism. Many people confuse it with "having low standards," "being self-indulgent," or "not being accountable for my mistakes." Not so! It's about doing your best and holding yourself accountable, but not crossing the line into inhumane and counterproductive punishments.

Remember the three personae from Chapter 11's Disempowerment Cascade: the Fragile Creator, Terrified/Terrorizing Perfectionist, and Rebellious Procrastinator? Someone's missing, and that's the Compassionate Adult. That's the persona who not only understands and respects your ambitions, but knows how to do the work, and is an expert at recognizing and overcoming obstacles.

The core work of overcoming perfectionism is developing your Inner Compassionate Adult persona/voice. Below are two techniques for doing that. They sound simple, but don't let that fool you: they are transformational.

Reframing to Compassion

The first is a reframing technique: you catch yourself thinking perfectionistically—often after some kind of mistake or "failure"—and *gently* interrupt that train of thought and reroute to nonperfectionism.

Instead of thinking: "I did badly on the test. I'm stupid."

You think: "Well, I'm disappointed in my grade. But it was a hard test in a difficult subject. Still, I know I should have studied more. I won't waste time feeling bad or calling myself names. Instead, I'll make a plan to do better next time."

Instead of thinking: "I can't believe I didn't get the internship. I'm such a failure."

You think: "I knew I should have practiced more for the interview. I'm pretty disappointed, but will try to get past that. I'll apply for some other internships this week. Also, I hear that the career center can record you doing a practice interview and give you suggestions for improvement. So I'll sign up for that."

Instead of thinking: "I can't believe I dropped my phone and broke the screen. I'm such a klutz!"

You think: "That sucks, especially since I don't have the money to fix it right now. But getting upset won't 'unbreak' it—and besides, everyone drops stuff. But yeah: in the future, I'll be more careful when taking my phone out of my bag."

Notice how the nonperfectionist statements are longer than the perfectionist ones. That's because, in contrast to reductive perfectionism, nonperfectionism aims for a more nuanced and accurate view. Also notice how, even though the nonperfectionist statements skip the guilt, shame, blame, and other punishments, they still maintain accountability. Nonperfectionism isn't about giving yourself a pass (a perfectionist's worst fear). Rather, nonperfectionists know you don't have to punish yourself to learn and grow.

A good way to locate your nonperfectionist voice is to ask yourself, "What would I tell someone else in this situation?" This works because we're often more compassionate with others than with ourselves. Treating ourselves worse than we treat others is a common mistake, but it's as misguided as every other perfectionist behavior. We need to be at least as compassionate with ourselves as we are with others.

Some have described the nonperfectionist voice as that of the "good grandparent" or "wise teacher." These adult designations are no accident:

nonperfectionism is an empowered mature viewpoint. Your Inner Creator, Inner Perfectionist, and Inner Procrastinator are all fearful and thus psychologically regressed—because fear causes us to lose our capacities—which is why they keep coming up with the same ineffective solutions. But once you introduce an Inner Compassionate Adult into the mix and let them lead, your Inner Perfectionist will start to relax, as frightened children do when a competent adult steps up. Then your Inner Procrastinator will see that they are no longer needed and exit the scene.

Leaving your Inner Creator free to do their job!

If the idea of reframing your thinking (or doing your inner monologue, see below) sounds silly or shallow, remember that perfectionism itself is a learned behavior that harms you every day. So why not work to replace it with something better? When you do, you should see a boost in both your productivity and your mood. In fact, the more reluctant you are to do this reframing, the more you need to do it.

Developing a Nonperfectionist Inner Monologue

It's great to interrupt a perfectionist self-criticism and replace it with something more self-affirming. But it's even better not to have that self-criticism to start with. Replacing your perfectionist inner monologue with a nonperfectionist one will strengthen your nonperfectionism and make it less likely you'll succumb to perfectionism in the first place.

Perfectionists, as discussed earlier, live with a more-or-less constant sense of failure, which is fed by a more-or-less continuous self-critical inner monologue: "What's wrong with you? Why you so lazy?" etc. You need to replace that monologue with a nonperfectionist, self-affirming one like this:

> "Okay, let's get started...Good work starting on time...Okay, that sentence has got a few problems, but I can fix those later...And hey! That's a great point I just made! Let's have some fun expanding it.… Okay, that part doesn't work, but let's leave it in for now. Plenty of time to fix it later.… This is a really interesting topic. I'm glad I chose it..."

This kind of monologue helps to build your confidence and enthusiasm—and again, please note that you are not abandoning your critical judgment and accountability. You still see the problems with your work and are committed to fixing them: you're just not panicking or shaming yourself over them.

Pay particular attention to your monologue at the beginnings of work sessions because that's when your fears are at their highest. If your monologue, at that fragile moment, is all about how, "My homework is a chore...How tedious...I'd rather be partying...Why me?...This sucks...etc.," of course you're going to have trouble starting your work. Instead, monologue in an affirming way. When I sit down to work, I greet my project like an old buddy: "Hello! How're we doing, today? It looks like we're going to be working on the section on developing your nonperfectionist inner voice. How cool is that?" Weird as that may sound, it helps defuse any initial fear and also provides a graceful entry into "our"—meaning, my project's and my—creative conversation. (More on the creative conversation in Chapter 25.)

The above techniques will help you develop a nonperfectionist mindset that will make it easier for you to do your work. One word of caution, though: try not to rush or put pressure on yourself while learning to use them, because that's perfectionist. Yup, I'm telling you **not to be perfectionist in your quest for nonperfectionism**. (It happens.) You'll know you're doing your nonperfectionism right when you're able to sit down and do your work as planned. Also, because you're not self-censoring, you'll be getting more ideas for your work, even when away from your desk. Nonperfectionists know there are lots of good ideas out there. You just gotta: (a) be nonperfectionist and (b) take notes.

But what about when perfectionism strikes during a work session and you're tempted to procrastinate? The next chapter tells you how to deal with that.

Exercise 10

Pick one of the perfectionist characteristics from Chapters 14 and 15, and start *gently* (always gently) reframing it to nonperfectionism. When you've mostly eliminated it, start working on another.

Remember to be patient, and to give yourself lots of affirmation for your successes; also to ignore any mistakes or "failures," except to learn from them.

Exercise 11

Here's a sweet little exercise that packs a nonperfectionist punch. All you have to do is send out some emails or texts with intentional errors in them. The errors could be anything from aN typo, to a mispeling, to some wEiRd formatting, to any kind of random STR*&^qq(ANGENESS.

That's it! "What's the catch?" I hear you ask. The "catch" is this: perfectionists hate making errors, and the idea of making one intentionally is inconceivable (as Vizzini would say). But what's the harm? (So long as you're sending them out to friends and not, say, the chair of the scholarship committee.) This exercise is useful in both helping you to see just how perfectionist you are, and in helping you to loosen up a bit and build your nonperfectionism.

I've seen people try to cheat at this exercise by sending "artful" errors, "clever" errors, "subtle" errors, and "faux," "ironic," and "meta" errors. Don't do any of that! I want full-on silly, stupid, and goofy errors. (Remember: there's no cheating in antiperfectionism work.) It's okay, however, to let your friends know what you're doing, and why—and if you encourage them to respond similarly, you'll be helping them to develop their own nonperfectionism.

19. Interrupting the Disempowerment Cascade

Perfectionism doesn't just show up and announce itself. ("Hello! My Name is Perfectionism.") Mostly what happens is you start feeling guilty, stressed, scared, stuck, or otherwise bad about your work—a feeling that's followed, pretty quickly, by an urge to do something else. Instead of letting yourself get derailed, however, try writing out a dialogue between your Inner Perfectionist and Inner Compassionate Adult. Here's an example:

Inner Perfectionist (panicked): What's wrong with you? Why are you so lazy? This stuff isn't hard! Anyone could do it! Anna's already finished! Why can't you be disciplined like her? C'mon! If you don't get to work, you're gonna fail and everyone will know you're a loser…and did I mention that the stuff you've already done sucks?

Inner Compassionate Adult (keeping cool): Okay, I hear you. And I want to address the problem. But no name-calling, okay?

IP: But it's hopeless! We've got to stop being lazy!

ICA (kindly but firmly): We can talk about everything you want to talk about, but you have to be respectful. And factual too, okay? No more hyperbole like, "It's hopeless!"

IP: Okay, I guess.

ICA: Great. Can you rephrase your concerns?

IP: Our paper's in bad shape and it's due on Friday.

ICA: Okay, I hear you. Do you have any suggestions?

IP: We could stay up all night working on it.

ICA: That's one option. But is it really a good idea?

IP: I guess not. We probably wouldn't get much done and it would wreck tomorrow.

ICA: Anything else?

IP: Not really. What are your ideas?

ICA: Maybe we should delete that third section. It's got a lot of problems and I don't think we need it. What do you think?

IP: If we do that, the paper won't be as good, so that's kind of disappointing. But I guess this is an emergency and we should delete it.

ICA: Great. The paper just got way easier, didn't it?

IP: I guess so.

ICA: How about if we go to the writing center for some help with the organization and grammar?

IP *(glumly):* You know I hate asking people for help.

ICA: Oh, I know…but is that a good thing?

IP: I guess not.

ICA: We should also find someone to take Thursday's shift at work.

IP *(a bit shocked at this "radical" suggestion):* Really?

ICA: Sure. We need all the time we can get.

IP: But I don't know who to ask.

ICA: We took Jasmine's shift last month when she had a test, so let's see if she can take ours. If she can't, maybe Michael can. We also took one of his shifts a couple of months back.

IP: Okay.

ICA: So now we've got a lot less work to do, and a lot more time to do it in. It all seems more doable now, doesn't it?

IP: Yeah, I think so.

The more you use this dialoguing technique, the more you'll internalize the Compassionate Adult's voice and problem-solving wisdom—until, eventually, you skip the perfectionism entirely and go right to the wisdom.

It's especially useful to do this dialoguing at times you think you've "failed." At such times, the perfectionist voice tends to be ascendant, and so you need to do everything you can to neutralize it.

Incidentally, the above example is short compared with many real-life dialogues. As with all the exercises in this book, be sure not to rush it.

How to Stop Fighting Your Inner Perfectionist

Did you notice how, when the Inner Compassionate Adult refused to let the Inner Perfectionist bully and insult them, it set the stage for a productive conversation? That's no accident: "limits are love," as the parenting manuals say. When the Adult set some limits, it helped the Perfectionist manage their fears.

Also, did you notice how the Inner Compassionate Adult refused to accept the Inner Perfectionist's fake solution of pulling an all-nighter? Many Inner Perfectionists have:

1. good general goals (do excellent work, meet deadlines, etc.)
2. terrible specific goals ("Get an A or die trying."), and
3. ridiculous solutions ("stay up all night," "take no breaks," "never ask for help," etc.).

That's a confusing mix, but it's the Compassionate Adult's job to respect and act on (1) without indulging in (2) and (3). Use the above dialoguing technique and your Inner Perfectionist will eventually realize that your Inner Compassionate Adult is not only serious about achieving your goals, but has some good strategies for doing that. Then they'll relax and retire from the scene, taking your now-unneeded Procrastinator with them.

20. Overcoming a Punishment Habit

Many people are afraid that, if they stop punishing themselves, they'll lose whatever shreds of willpower they have. As already noted, however, many of us have been punishing ourselves, or been punished by others, for years or decades: if punishment worked, we'd all be superachievers by now. The truth is, **we're productive in spite of the punishments we've endured, not because of them**. As the psychologist B.F. Skinner said, "A person who has been punished is not less inclined to behave in a given way; at best, he learns how to avoid punishment."

You'll pass through three stages as you work to overcome your perfectionism/punishment habit:

1. **Mostly Perfectionist.** You're still mostly perfectionist but catch yourself at it and self-correct to nonperfectionism.
2. **Mostly Nonperfectionist.** You're now mostly nonperfectionist, although you occasionally lapse into perfectionism during stressful times, or when you've made a mistake, or are in the midst of a challenging project.
3. **Nonperfectionist.** You remain resolutely nonperfectionist even at times you're tempted to "cheat" with a little harsh self-talk or deprivation. (Again, there's no cheating in antiperfectionism work.)

It's the bone-deep knowledge that perfectionism never helps, and always harms, that will help you move as quickly as possible through the stages.

Like any behavioral change, the shift to nonperfectionism can feel weird at first. And giving up punishments (e.g., harsh self-talk and deprivation) can feel especially weird, because:

We're so used to our punishments they feel normal.

Society keeps telling us our punishments are useful.

We often use punishments performatively to reassure ourselves (and others) we're taking our work seriously.

We often use our punishments as a form of penance or atonement for perceived underachievement. (Another type of performance.)

If you're having trouble kicking your punishment habit, ask yourself which of the above purposes it might be serving. (Journal about it.) That knowledge, combined with your obstacle resolution process (Chapter 9) and other tools, plus your foundational ethic of non-punishment, should help you liberate yourself from the habit.

Once you stop punishing yourself, however, you'll probably encounter yet another barrier to progress and productivity. Both procrastination and perfectionism are dramatic and noisy habits. (All that monologuing, justifying, rationalizing, denial, distraction, shame, blame, guilt, regret, remorse, etc.) When you start to give them up—meaning, when you start to be able to sit down and do your work with a minimum of fuss—the simplicity, ease, and quiet can be unnerving. Plus, because you're no longer procrastinating, you now have lots more time on your hands. Not coincidentally—because procrastination often is, or resembles, a kind of addiction, as discussed in Chapter 2—this is all pretty similar to what many addicts experience during the early stages of recovery.

You'll need to learn to tolerate all this weirdness, at least for a while. You'll especially need to make sure it doesn't send you back into perfectionism and procrastination. Persevere gently—always gently—and the weird feelings, which are kind of like "perfectionism's last stand," should dissipate. Meanwhile, time management (Part V) will help you to deal with the "problem" (not really) of "too much time."

Hopefully you'll decide, at some not-so-distant point, that, "Dammit, I am *not* going to treat myself badly anymore, no matter how badly I think I've screwed up. It's not worth it, it feels terrible, and it doesn't help anything." That's when you'll know you've turned the corner away from perfectionism and towards a brighter, happier, kinder, more abundant, and more productive future.

Exercise 12

Think back on times you've punished yourself and answer the below questions. (Journaling works well for this exercise, and you may also wish to discuss your answers with a friend or counselor.)

1. Were there unspoken motives underlying the punishments? Did you, for instance, punish yourself because you thought you were "supposed" to do that? Or because you didn't know what else to do in the face of a "failure"? Were you using the punishments performatively to show yourself or others that, despite what happened, you were serious about the work?

2. How did the punishments affect you and your work?

3. What might have been healthier and more productive ways to respond to the situations in question?

21. How to Distinguish Between High Standards and Perfectionism

High standards are great and so are ambitious goals. But how do you know when you've crossed the line into unrealistic standards, otherwise known as perfectionism? This is yet another confusing area, but here are some guidelines:

Unrealistic standards are often realistic ones taken a bit too far. Right now, for instance, you might be capable of reading ten pages of your textbook in an evening, but not eleven. Or of doing math problems for two-and-a-half hours, but not three. Or of getting a B+ or A- in a course, but not an A.

We all have limited time and energy. In addition, we all find some tasks harder than others. Productivity work is all about getting real, especially about our all-too-human limitations. Sure: you can, and should, aim for improvement—and that's kind of the point of education. But bashing yourself for not being where you'd like to be, or not progressing fast enough, is perfectionist.

Unrealistic standards are often the wrong standards. Grades aren't the most important thing: doing your best is.

A high salary isn't the most important thing in a job: a healthy and humane work culture is.

Some people aim to never disappoint their parents, but a better goal is to have a healthy and loving relationship with them—which inevitably means disappointing them from time to time. (You need to be able to stick up for yourself.)

Obviously, I'm dichotomizing: you can get A's *and* learn, get a job where you're paid well *and* treated well, and please your parents *and* have a healthy relationship with them. But one goal should be paramount, and perfectionists often choose the wrong one.

Unachievable goals are grandiose and therefore perfectionist *Really?* I hear you say. *Why would anyone set an unachievable goal? That doesn't make sense.* You're right, it doesn't. But people set unrealistic goals for themselves all the time, and you've done it too, if you've ever...

- Taken on an overly ambitious project, as discussed in Chapter 13.
- Taken on more work than you could possibly accomplish.
- Expected any outcome to be 100% positive. (See Chapter 23.)
- Expected yourself to stay healthy and productive while stinting on self-care.

There are many other examples. Many working parents, for instance, berate themselves when they are working and not with their kids, and also when they are with their kids and not working. Basically, they're berating themselves for not being in two places at once, which is pretty grandiose. (And unfair.)

Finally and most confusingly:

The same goal can be perfectionist and nonperfectionist at different times. It can be more reasonable to expect a high grade in some classes than others. Or for some projects than others. Or at certain times of your life more than others. That's why **your final and most important clue as to whether you've crossed the line into perfectionism is this: perfectionism hurts**. If you're feeling stressed, pressured, or otherwise bad about your work, you've crossed the line into it. Stop what you're doing and do some journaling and obstacle resolution work (Chapter 9), so you can get back on track as soon as possible.

22. Learning the Art of Failure

The most important time to put your Inner Compassionate Adult in charge is when you've "failed," experienced a rejection, or had some other kind of setback. It's a natural temptation, during such times, to get self-critical, but nonperfectionists have better ways of coping. They know that:

Everyone fails. It's an ordinary part of life. In fact, successful people probably fail more than most because they take more risks. To be precise: they're successful both because they take the risks and because they react productively—meaning, in the ways described in this chapter—to the inevitable occasional failure.

Failure is essential. You learn things from it you never would from success, including resilience, humility, how to compromise, and how to play defense. (As well as, of course, how to avoid or correct the mistakes that caused you to fail in the first place.) As Malcolm X said, "Every defeat, every heartbreak, every loss, contains its own seed, its own lesson on how to improve your performance next time." And as adrienne maree brown says in *Emergent Strategy*: "I don't experience failure much these days; I experience growth." Which brings us to...

There's no such thing as a complete failure. Nearly all failures yield some positive outcomes, and even the worst are valuable learning opportunities.

The more serious a failure seems, the more important, and healing, it is to sit down and list those positives.

Most failures turn out to be unimportant. This includes even some that seem awful at the time. A week later, you wonder what you were so upset about, and a month later, you've forgotten the entire incident.

A surprising number of "failures" turn out to be lucky breaks. Like when you get rejected for a job you later realize wouldn't have been a good fit. Or rejected romantically by someone you later realize wouldn't have been a good partner.

A failure can also clear the way for you to start on a new and better path. As the philosopher Laozi put it, "New beginnings are often disguised as painful endings."

Only rarely is one person solely responsible for a failure. So, yeah, someone could do poorly on a test because they didn't prepare well. But if the class happened to be badly taught or the test badly designed, those would be contributing factors. And if the student were distracted by personal or family problems, or had some bad luck with their schedule (e.g., two tests in one day), that might also contribute.

It's important to acknowledge all the causes of a failure, not to negate your own responsibility, but so you don't take on an unjust burden of shame. (To be clear, you shouldn't feel ashamed even when you did do something wrong: see below.) This is even more important in the work world than in school, by the way. In school, your professors and the other institutional employees are ethically—and, in some cases, legally—obligated to look after your interests. No such obligation exists in much of the work world, however, and so many employees do wind up getting mistreated. A common scenario is when an employee is given responsibility for a project, but not the authority, resources, or support needed to succeed. Then, when they inevitably fail, they're unfairly blamed and penalized (up to and including being fired). This is not only devastating when it happens, it can lead to years or decades of shame.

Situations where you did your best but still got a suboptimal outcome aren't failures. They're life! Again: none of us ever has 100% control over our outcomes.

You have to be really, truly willing to fail. These days, many people do, in fact, understand that, "you have to be willing to fail." But ask them what they mean by that, and they'll say things like, "I wouldn't want to get less than a C," or, "I'll be disappointed if I'm not in the top ten." Even though these goals sound reasonable, they're still overfocused on outcomes. If you find yourself getting stuck, therefore, ask yourself if you're really, truly willing to fail, or just think you are.

What "being willing to fail" really means is that you are prepared to get an F, come in last, bomb, even embarrass yourself. Obviously, we all hope that this doesn't happen *this time*, but it will happen eventually if you're taking some good risks. When it does, it won't feel so bad if you're focusing on process, maintaining a proper emotional distance from the work, not being shortsighted, etc.

The most important thing nonperfectionists know about failure is that **regret, remorse, shame, blame, guilt, and other negative reactions are pointless**. So skip them! The only useful way to respond to a failure is to: (a) analyze what went wrong, (b) make amends to others if needed, (c) make a plan to do better in the future, and (d) move on.

Or, as the spiritual teacher Ram Dass put it, "It is important to expect nothing, to take every experience, including the negative ones, as merely steps on the path, and to proceed."

Exercise 13

Examine some of your "failures" from the standpoint of the information in this chapter. Did they, in the end, turn out to have some positive aspects? Has time revealed them to be less important than they initially seemed? Were you really 100% responsible or did others, or bad luck, play a role? Write out your answers and, if desired, discuss them with a friend or counselor. Hopefully, after you're done, you'll feel more at peace with these incidents.

23. Learning the Art of Success

Do we really have to learn how to succeed? Isn't success simply the party that comes after all the hard work? Not quite. Success is great, and I wish you lots of it. But it can complicate things and lead to situational perfectionism (Chapter 15). Laozi put it plainly when he said, "Success is often as dangerous as failure."

Perfectionists often gloss over their successes—or, worse, reframe them as failures (Chapter 13). But nonperfectionists are careful to acknowledge and celebrate their successes. Doing so not only helps neutralize perfectionism, it fixes your successes in your memory so you can call on them when needed for motivation. ("Okay, I'm feeling stuck—but I remember that, a few weeks ago, when I felt equally stuck, I persevered and everything turned out fine. So I guess I'll persevere now.")

Take a moment to acknowledge your successes—and not just the outcome itself, but the broader success (e.g., what you learned or what barriers you overcame) and any personal qualities (courage, kindness, perseverance, etc.) you demonstrated. And if you want to celebrate—say, by treating yourself to a dinner out, a new outfit or piece of gear, or some other splurge—go for it. It's okay to be generous with yourself.

Be Sure to Acknowledge and Celebrate Your "Small" and Partial Successes

For one thing, they're often bigger and more important than they seem. Even something as "small" as reviewing your notes for a project you've been avoiding can take real courage, so why not acknowledge and celebrate that? (Especially since doing so will empower you to take further steps.) Also, acknowledging and celebrating your small and interim successes can help you to stay positive and motivated throughout the course of a long project. In fact, **big successes, as such, don't exist: they're just accumulations of small ones**. George Eliot didn't cough up her epic novel *Middlemarch* all at once like a hairball, for instance: she created it one paragraph, page, and chapter at a time. And before she even started it, she had written many smaller works, and also succeeded at a lifetime of study and other preparation. (Your own college graduation will similarly be a "big" success that is really an accumulation of small ones.)

Of course, the minute you try to celebrate your small successes your Inner Perfectionist will likely show up to scorn you as unambitious, self-indulgent, etc. As always, treat them with compassion, but don't let them abuse you, and don't take their advice.

While understanding that acknowledgement and celebration are important, nonperfectionists also know not to take things too far. In particular, they know your successes shouldn't be a source of exaggerated pride ("I'm king of the world!"), self-justification ("That'll show 'em!"), or professional legitimacy ("After I'm published, then I'll be a real scholar."). Your successes should also not be a route to popularity, love, sex, status, or any other form of personal validation. All of these attitudes are extremely overidentified—and so, to some degree, this problem is theoretical, because people who view success in these kinds of ways tend to be too terrified of failure to do their work.

The Costs of Success

Nonperfectionists also know that:

Success Leaves You Busier. Many successes create more work: for example, when you win a fellowship and then have to do the project. Success also can be a magnet that draws new people and projects to you. Don't get me wrong: these are excellent "problems" to have! But you still have to be able to deal with them. (See Chapters 46 and 47 for solutions.)

Success Raises the Stakes. It raises questions like: "What if my next paper [or performance, etc.] isn't as good as this one?" Or, "Now that I've gotten that great job, what if I can't handle the responsibilities?" Or, "Now that the newspaper is publishing my editorial, what if I get blowback on social media?" These kinds of questions are all natural—and I'd actually be worried if you weren't asking them. But dwelling on your fears or, worse, letting them dictate your behavior, won't get you far. Instead, **always answer your rhetorical questions**. What will you do, for instance, if your next paper isn't as good? (And what does "good" mean, in this context, anyway?) Or if you can't handle your new job's responsibilities? (And which responsibilities are we talking about?) Answering these types of questions is not only empowering in and of itself, it gives you a chance to avoid, via planning and consultation with mentors, the potential problems.

Success Always Involves Compromise, Loss, or Sacrifice. Some examples:

You may decide to forgo partying for a weekend so you have a better chance of doing well on a test. (Or to forgo many parties so you have a better chance of getting into graduate school.)

Later on, you may decide to give up your dream of living in the mountains so you can pursue the big-city career you want. (Or maybe you settle for a less-ambitious career so you can live in the mountains.)

Do well at your career and you might become a public figure, losing some of your precious privacy.

Find a wonderful romantic relationship and you lose some of your independence.

You need to be aware of these kinds of losses because it's easy to get caught off guard by them; also, because fear of them—a.k.a., fear of success—is a major cause of hoarding and procrastination.

Now we see that procrastination's "purpose" isn't just to protect us from potential criticism or rejection (Chapter 2), but potential loss. That's a powerful double punch, so be sure to use your journaling, discussions with mentors, counseling, and other techniques to anticipate and minimize those losses, and cope with any that remain. Step one is to stop dichotomizing: in the above examples, you can still go to some parties, live near the mountains if not in them, retain some of your privacy, and retain some of your independence. You also want to do the work of mourning and accepting those losses you can't avoid, so you can proceed wholeheartedly, a.k.a. unambivalently, with your work. Journaling and discussions with friends (or a counselor) work well for this, or you can go deeper via a spiritual discipline like Buddhism or a secular one like Acceptance and Commitment Therapy. Russ Harris's book *The Happiness Trap* is a good starting point for the latter, and there are also counselors who specialize in it.

Despite the complex nature of success, I hope you have lots of practice coping with it!

Exercise 14

Journal about a school or other project you're procrastinating on to see if any success-related fears and potential losses are contributing to that procrastination. If so, keep journaling and, if necessary, consult a friend or counselor with the goal of defusing the fears and minimizing (and accepting and mourning) the losses.

When you're done, hopefully you'll be able to approach your work with less ambivalence and procrastination.

24. Overcoming Ambivalence

Ambivalence is when you're caught between two or more contradictory goals or motives. Ambivalence about small things—"Should I have a doughnut or a muffin, I can't decide!"—is no big deal. (Unless it becomes chronic, in which case it's Quasiproductive Procrastination. See Chapter 5.) But ambivalence about bigger things, like your schoolwork, relationships, career, or identity can be awful. You're stuck in an exceptionally uncomfortable and confusing place, often doing the one-step-forward-two-steps-back kind of behavior that is so frustrating to you and others.

Here are some examples of ambivalence:

- Your parents want you to spend winter break with them but you would rather do something else. But you are reluctant to have that conversation and so wind up procrastinating on your travel plans until all the cheap flights are gone.

- You hate your job but don't want to go through the hassle of finding another. So you stay put—only you keep getting less and less motivated and focused on your work until, eventually, your boss fires you.

- You've taken on an extracurricular project you don't have time for. So you procrastinate, hoping some time will magically open up. Only that doesn't happen, and so you wind up, finally, only doing part of it, thus disappointing everyone involved, including yourself.

As these examples show, ambivalence is a disempowered—and often passive-aggressive—response to pressure often characterized by indecision, dithering, and busy work. Yup: we're talking Quasiproductive Procrastination *big time*. Two important things to keep in mind, however, are that:

1. Although the ambivalence, like all forms of procrastination, is a disempowered reaction to pressure, it also, as discussed in Chapter 11, represents the best part of you: the part that is fighting for freedom, authenticity, and self-expression, and against bullying and coercion.

2. We're often ambivalent not just because others are pressuring us, but because we partly agree with their viewpoint—so that, for instance, while you don't really want to go home for the holidays, a part of you thinks you should.

We see both of these dynamics in Jeremy's story:

From childhood onward, Jeremy's passion had always been art. When it came time to think about college, however, he didn't see art school as an option. His family had always struggled financially, and while his parents had always been proud of his artistic ability, they had also impressed upon him and his younger sister the importance of choosing "practical" careers that offered financial security. Jeremy decided to do pre-medical studies, hoping to also be able to minor in art.

Mostly for financial reasons—the tuition was low and he could live at home—he attended a nearby state college. To his dismay, however, he found himself struggling from the very beginning of his freshman year. His biology and chemistry courses were harder than he had anticipated and he was also much busier than he had anticipated. Between his classes, laboratories, piles of homework, commute, and his part-time retail job, he was constantly rushing from one commitment to the next.

Something had to give, and it turned out to be his art class, "Introduction to Digital Methods." It was his favorite class, and he felt comfortable with his teacher and the other students in a way he didn't in his other classes. Given a choice, he would have gladly spent most of his time hanging out in the studio. Being perpetually rushed for time, however, he couldn't do that. In fact, he wasn't even able to spend enough time there to do his assignments properly. More and more, he was doing them at the last minute, which wasn't fun and yielded only mediocre grades. He did manage to pull himself together for his final project, however, and wound up getting an excellent grade. "Where have you been hiding all semester?" his professor joked.

Jeremy ended the semester with two good grades (art and a required freshman writing course) and two mediocre ones (his sciences). His advisor warned him he would need to do better in the spring if he intended to go to medical school. She also suggested he not take the second semester of the Digital Methods course so he'd have more time for his science courses. Jeremy was disappointed but had to agree, and so he signed up instead for a less time-intensive art history elective.

Spring semester, his grades picked up at first. But they soon dropped again. His science classes turned out to be even tougher than the first semester's, and he was also having a harder time concentrating. At the same time, his social life had also taken a downturn. His best friends had all been in his Digital Methods class, and now that he wasn't taking the follow-up, he wasn't seeing them very often.

Feeling ever more hopeless and discouraged, Jeremy started skipping classes.

One day, when he was at a real low point—it was late morning and he still hadn't gotten out of bed—he felt a powerful inspirational surge. He leaped out of bed and, for the first time in ages, started sketching. He soon found himself creating a series of comic strips entitled, "College: The Dream Versus the Reality," that told a fictionalized version of his freshman year experience. He worked on it for a week, devoting every spare moment he could to it. When he was done, he was prouder of it than anything else he had accomplished that year. He posted a couple of the strips on his social media and was caught by surprise when, a few minutes later, his sister Bee showed up at his bedroom door. "The strips are great!" she said. "But what's up with school? Something's obviously wrong."

Jeremy tried to evade the question but she wouldn't let him. She invited herself into his room and made herself comfortable in his reading chair, then asked again: "Seriously, what's up?"

Once Jeremy finally started to open up, he couldn't stop. He told her everything that had happened since he had started school, including all his fears, discouragements, and confusions. When he was done, she said, with true sisterly candor, "I didn't think the pre-med thing was going to work out. You need to switch majors."

"I know!" Jeremy said, relieved to hear the obvious spoken aloud. "But to what?"

"Duh—art."

"Mom and Dad will freak out if I do that. They want us to earn money, remember?"

"They're freaking out now, in case you hadn't noticed," said Bee. "Anyway, whose decision is it?"

Jeremy paused. The truth was, he didn't know. "Mom and Dad should have a say since they're paying for everything," he began. "And they're right that there aren't a lot of good jobs out there for artists."

"It's your life, not theirs," was Bee's prompt reply. "Anyhow, I do think there are jobs out there. You know Sherry, from down the street? Her best friend's sister's girlfriend majored in something like 'Applied Art,' and she got a job at a high-tech firm."

"But how do you get those jobs?"

"*I* don't know," she said, rolling her eyes. "Ask your professor—and then come back and have the conversation with Mom and Dad. You know I'll have your back."

Jeremy made an appointment to talk with his former Digital Methods professor. The professor listened sympathetically as he told him about his situation, then reassured him that there were good jobs for art graduates with lots of enthusiasm and a great portfolio. "Animation and video game design are the glamor jobs, right now, and there's a lot of competition for those," he said. "But there are also good jobs in advertising, product design, Web design, marketing, and some other fields."

The professor suggested Jeremy do a double major, saying, "That will strengthen you on the job market and it will also be good for your art. Psychology, sociology, marketing: those are all good choices." Then he handed Jeremy a couple of brochures on art careers. "Give these to your parents. Don't forget to tell them that, when you start looking for work, you can contact people in our alumni network for advice and referrals."

The professor then added, "If it would help, I'd be happy to talk to your parents myself."

Jeremy was moved by his professor's caring; and as they planned his fall courses—two art classes (including the second term of Digital Methods), a psychology class, and an English Literature class—he felt his spirits soar. It was like he was starting college fresh, only this time on the right path. Right after the meeting was over, he called Bee and told her everything that had happened. "I told you!" she said, then added, with true sisterly pride, "Of course they want you in the program. You're a genius!"

That night after dinner, Jeremy told his parents he wanted to switch majors to art and psychology. They listened as he talked about his unhappiness in pre-med and explained why switching majors would help. Then they took a few moments to look over the career pamphlets he had brought home. Although they expressed skepticism, they were less averse to the idea of his switching than he had imagined.

Jeremy suggested his parents talk with his professor, which they did, a few days later—and that conversation did the trick. "That professor is a big fan of yours," his father said afterwards, proudly. "So, I guess if you want to switch majors that would be okay." His mother agreed: "Your art has always been a big part of who you are and what makes you special. Maybe we were wrong not to encourage you to continue with it."

Jeremy could hardly believe it: he was going to be an art major! He still had to get through the rest of his current semester—but that turned out to be easier than expected. Knowing he would be free to study what he wanted was enough to lift his spirits and boost his motivation.

Jeremy wound up doing very well in his art and psychology double-major. He developed "College: The Dream Versus the Reality" into a graphic novel, his first. It became his senior project and the centerpiece of what his professors assured him was a strong portfolio.

And yes, he did get a good job after graduation.[34]

Solutions to Ambivalence

As Jeremy's situation shows, one solution to ambivalence is to **get clear on your relationship boundaries**. (More on this in Chapter 48.)

Also, **work on your perfectionism**. Dichotomization is an obvious trigger for ambivalence, since it can cause you to reduce all of your options into two extreme and unappealing opposites—so that, for instance, you think you either have to spend all of your winter break with your parents or none of it. Or, worse, that you have just one unappealing option, like poor Jeremy thought he had. **Perfectionism can also cause you to dismiss good, or even excellent, solutions that are right in front of you while you carry on a quest for a mythical perfect solution with no negative aspects.**

---

[34] As this book went to press, Pulitzer Prize-winning novelist Viet Thanh Nguyen published a great piece on issues similar to those discussed in this case study: www.nytimes.com/2021/07/08/opinion/culture/parents-expectations-writing-art.html.

Philosophers call this the "Ideal Solution Fallacy," and it's a close relative of the Nirvana Fallacy (where you compare things to an idealized version of themselves) I discussed in Chapter 14—which, no surprise, can itself also cause ambivalence.

Find a mentor. Often we're ambivalent because we don't have enough information to make a decision. The person who hates their job, for instance, may not know how to go about finding another. (Or may erroneously think they're not qualified for anything else, or that "there are no good jobs out there.") Because that lack of knowledge is often buried underneath layers of emotional turmoil and interpersonal strife, the ambivalent person may not be aware that that's the problem. Go ahead and do your obstacle-resolution process (Chapter 9); then discuss your findings with a mentor or counselor.

Please note that Jeremy had *two* mentors who helped him back on the right path: his professor and his younger sister, Bee. Be open to mentorship from any caring source. (More on mentors in Appendix A3.)

Watch out for situations where you're having both halves of a conversation in your own head. (As Jeremy was doing when he assumed he knew how his parents would react to his changing majors.)

Finally, **learn to take the long view** (Chapter 16). It's always tempting to avoid the pain of dealing with the wrong major, a difficult relationship, a bad job, or some other problem. But ask yourself whether you want to spend the next few months, years, or decades dealing with it, especially since it's only likely to get worse. Ask yourself, also, if you want to develop a habit of avoidance and denial, or one of problem-solving. Hopefully, it's the latter, because—wait for it—you don't want to be ambivalent about tackling your ambivalence.

Exercise 15

Look back at an incident where you were ambivalent about something in your school, work, or personal life. List the ways that (a) perfectionism and (b) unclear interpersonal boundaries might have played a role. Also, think about how you responded to your ambivalence and what might be a better way to respond in the future.

Okay, we're done with perfectionism. Thanks for hanging in there. In Part III, we'll discuss a nonperfectionist work process called the Joyful Dance. It's as much fun as it sounds and I can't wait to introduce you to it!

PART III

JOYFUL WORK

25. Introducing the Joyful Dance

The goal is easy, effective, and joyful productivity, which is nonperfectionist productivity. To see why, look at the way many perfectionists work. They're relentlessly linear, for one thing: always trying to do everything in what they consider to be the right order. When writing a paper, for instance, they try to do all the research before moving onto the outlining, all the outlining before starting to write, etc. And when they do finally start to write, they trudge through the manuscript from beginning to end, trying to perfect (red alert!) each sentence, paragraph, and page before moving onto the next.

Similarly, perfectionists try to do their problem sets rigidly in order, completing the first problem before moving onto the second, the second before moving onto the third, etc.

Linearity isn't just boring, it's precarious. Get stuck during a linear process and you really are stuck, because the one direction you think you can move in is blocked off.

Linearity also invites a kind of do-or-die perfectionism. ("Okay, so I finished Section 3. Now it's time to start Section 4 AND I'D BETTER GET IT RIGHT!")

The fundamental problem is that linearity undermines your creativity. **Creativity is a kind of conversation** between you (your knowledge, ideas, thoughts, beliefs, and perspectives) and your subject matter (including past and present experts), collaborators, materials, processes, and techniques. Like many conversations, these "creative conversations" go best when information flows in many directions. This includes backwards, by the way: because creativity is also an act of discovery. The things you discover later in a creative conversation can illuminate some of the things you discovered earlier, making you want to go back and change it. As poet May Sarton once observed, "Revision is not going back and fussing around, but going forward into the process of creation."

Creativity, in other words, is organic and holistic—pretty much the opposite of a linear process.

For all of these reasons, nonperfectionists work nonlinearly on whichever parts of the project they feel like working on at the moment. Also, they work on whichever stage of the project they feel like working on. Organizing, writing, editing, etc.—they combine it all into one big jazzy jumble, switching among them with ease. (This includes sharing the work: as discussed in Chapter 16, nonperfectionists share early and often.) The only stage you should leave out of your jumble is research, which, as discussed in Chapter 5, is a common vehicle for Quasiproductive Procrastination (QP). It's okay—and desirable, as I'll be discussing in the next chapter—to write, outline, etc., while doing research, but you should avoid slipping into research when you're supposed to be working on the other stages. (More on how to handle research in Chapter 32.)

I call this jazzy, jumbly, nonlinear work process the Joyful Dance, because that's what it feels like when you use it: a joyful dance through your work. And I call the perfectionist way of working the Dreary Slog, because that's what it feels like. (Yup, I'm labeling and dichotomizing to get my point across. In real life, no one is 100% Dancer or Slogger.) The Joyful Dance supports and catalyzes your creative conversation, and so, when you use it, your work goes easier and faster, and is a lot more fun. You're also far less likely to get stuck because "getting stuck," to a Dancer, simply means it's time to switch over to another part of the project. (Which Dancers do without fuss or drama.)

Remember Chapter 4's point about how empowerment means having the best possible options? The Joyful Dance is all about that. When Dancing, you get to choose, at every moment, not just which part of your project to work on, but how to work on it. In contrast, the Dreary Slog only ever offers you the same bad choice: to keep working on whatever it is you're currently working on until you get it "right." Notice how your personal preferences and situation—not to mention, the specifics of the project itself—don't even enter into it.

Is the Joyful Dance actually joyful, though? Sometimes! Other times, it's "merely" interesting, satisfying, fulfilling, or fun. Don't knock it, however: those are excellent work experiences to have. What I can promise you is that the Joyful Dance will maximize your odds of not just an easy and effective work process, but a good outcome. When you work nonlinearly, you're like a surfer on a beach with some great waves, each wave being a bit of inspiration comin' atcha. You see one, rush over to it, grab it, and ride it. Then, when it peters out, you look around and see another great wave, rush over, grab and ride it. Then another and another. You keep doing that throughout your whole work session. What fun! And look how much you're getting done!

Meanwhile, your poor Slogger friend is standing forlornly with their surfboard on the section of the beach where they think the next great wave is supposed to hit, just waiting, and waiting, and waiting, and…

Get Random

Nonlinearity can feel weird if you're not used to it. But give it a whirl and you should soon see the advantages. This randomizing technique should help:

Assign a number to every section of your project (assuming they're not already numbered, like a problem set). Then roll some dice[35] and work on whichever numbered section you rolled. If you get bored or stuck, roll again and hop on over to the new section and work on that. Or if you feel a sudden urge to work on a section—say, because the current section gave you an idea for it—hop on over there and start working on it. Hop around as much as you like until you've completed your Timed Work Interval (Chapter 6), while resisting, as always, the temptation to judge your output.

Randomization works not just because it's fun, but because it subverts perfectionism. Instead of, "Now it's time to do Section 4 and I'D BETTER GET IT RIGHT!" you're all: "Hmmm, just rolled a '4.' Not sure what I want to do with that section, but I'll just play around with it and see what happens." And what often happens is that you get a good creative conversation going.

---

[35] Even fancy dice are pretty cheap (and fun): check out places that sell gaming supplies or ask a gamer friend for a set they're no longer using. (Or grab the dice from an old board game no one's using.) And yes, I know you can download a random number-generator app for your phone, but *puhlease* no phones while working.

Randomization also works well with another technique for avoiding perfectionism, chunking. That's when you divide a big project into manageable chunks and then focus on one at a time. A chunk could be a page or a paragraph of a paper, or one math or science problem out of a set. Go ahead and assign numbers to your chunks, then roll those dice.

You won't need to keep using the dice forever, by the way. Soon you'll learn to ask yourself, when you sit down to work, "Which part of my project do I feel like working on right now?" And whatever it is, you'll start working on it.

But you should feel free to return to the dice if you ever feel yourself slipping back into linearity.

26. Speed It Up!

We all want to work faster, but make sure you're aiming for the right kind of speed: not the frantic and stressful kind that depletes you (and triggers procrastination), but the cool and steady kind you can maintain for long periods without getting bored or tired. (What marathoners call their "stride.") The kind of speed, in other words, that helps you get a lot of work done while also supporting your learning and other objectives.

Pretty much every technique in this book will speed your work, but to reach your stride you need to do what the marathoners do and organize your life and work around that goal. Below are some tips for doing that:

Do your time management. See Part V to make sure that: (a) you're getting enough sleep, exercise, and other self-care, and (b) you have lots of high-quality time for your work. ("High-quality" means time when you're alert, energetic, and free from interruptions.)

Get comfortable. Remember that, as discussed in Chapter 9, a lot of procrastination begins in the body.

Optimize your workspace. If you need quiet, find quiet. If you need a certain temperature, find that. And if you need a window, or no window, find that. Don't settle for a space that's not a great fit because that will be just one more obstacle to doing your work.

Work alongside other focused workers. Many of us work faster when we're among others who are themselves focused on their work. So find a library or café full of quiet and industrious people and enjoy the boost you get from working alongside them. (The more you overcome perfectionism, however, the easier you should find it to work alone—and if solo work becomes your preference, you shouldn't hesitate to do that.)

Do some preemptive obstacle work (Chapter 9) before starting projects so you can eliminate obstacles while they're still small—or, better yet, prevent them from occurring at all.

Plan your large or complex projects. Planning not only helps you stay on track, it helps you visualize your project as a whole, which further boosts your productivity.

Reduce your project's scope. As discussed in Chapter 28.

Give Your Work Time to "Marinate." The most efficient work method is often to do the best you can on a bit without pushing it; then take a break so you can let that bit marinate in the back of your mind before returning to it later with fresh eyes. (See, also, the discussions of trial and error in Chapter 28, the importance of not forcing/controlling the work in Chapter 29, and QuickDrafting in Chapter 30.)

Perfectionists often fear that, if they stop working, they'll never start again, but **"I don't have to solve this problem right now. It's okay to put it aside and work on something else"** is one of the most calming and empowering things you can tell yourself in the middle of a difficult project. (And if you're nonperfectionist, you will be able to start again.)

Remember that the main goal of any project is always to finish. Nonperfectionists know that the main goal for any project is to, "get this done and off my desk, so I can move onto the next interesting thing." That doesn't mean you rush through it and do a shoddy job, but rather that you don't overwork/hoard your project to try to perfect every little detail. (See Chapter 7's discussion of quantity versus quality, Chapter 16's point about how nonperfectionists don't give themselves permission to miss deadlines, and Chapter 31's discussion of the importance of finishing one's work.)

Pilot/Prototype your scientific, technical, and artistic projects. When doing a science experiment, for instance, collect and analyze a small amount of data first, just to make sure your setup is working as planned (as Aisha does in the next chapter). If you're writing a computer program, first create a "minimalist" version without any fancy bells and whistles to ensure it does the basic things it's supposed to do. And if you're doing an art or writing project, start with a storyboard, outline, beat sheet, or sketch.

Do some of your work right after you get the assignment. Your creativity and enthusiasm are often at their peak then.

Alas, many students do the exact opposite and wait till the last minute, either because they're procrastinating or not managing their time well, or both. This results in them rushing, having a miserable time, and getting a mediocre result. Waiting until the last minute is also, I'm informed, one of the student behaviors that most upsets professors, both because they know you're capable of doing better and because it creates more work for them when you miss your deadlines.

Do a bit of work on all your subjects (or projects) most days. Productivity-wise, there's nothing worse than a "cold start," where you return to a difficult project after days or weeks or months of neglecting it. And so, try to do a bit of work—even if just five or ten minutes—on all your projects, most days. This not only keeps the material fresh, it will leave you with much less work to do during your final push.

While working, **keep a light touch and a light heart**, even if the work itself is serious. You may have difficult problems to solve, and serious points to make, and intense scenarios to explore, but try to do it all while keeping some emotional distance. This can be difficult, so if you do find yourself getting caught up emotionally, try journaling about the situation or discussing it with a friend, your professor, or a counselor.

Above all, you want to **resist the perfectionist stereotype of the tortured creator or scholar**. Like many perfectionist stereotypes, it has some dramatic appeal and is therefore promoted in the media. But it is a terrible model to follow for reasons of both productivity and health.

The above techniques are all humane and effective alternatives to trying to shame yourself into working faster—which, in any case, is likely to backfire. But let's take a deeper look at the whole "speed" question.

Make Haste, Slowly

Perhaps you've heard of the global Slow Movement, which urges that, in an age of technological speedup, we all become more deliberate and mindful about our various activities. The movement has spawned several sub-movements, including Slow Food, Slow Schooling, Slow Travel, and Slow Parenting.

Let's talk about Slow Work. Over the years, I've spoken with teachers in many fields, including science, the arts, engineering, the building trades, and automobile mechanics. They all said that one of their major challenges was getting their students to slow down enough to focus on the details of their work. Students tend to rush, in part because they don't realize how long it takes to do good work. The truth is, it can take a shockingly long time, especially when you're still learning, but even when you're more experienced. (I still can't believe how long it can take me to write a "simple" blog post.) A physics professor I know gives his students time estimates for their homework (e.g., "one to two hours per problem") and also suggests that, if the work takes much longer, they check with him to make sure they're using their time well. If your professors aren't offering similar guidance, ask them for it.

Working too fast yields not just sloppy work, but a difficult and joyless process. Plus, it's an obstacle to learning. You need to slow down enough to not only get the details right, but understand why they're right. In fact, **whenever you sit down to do your work, it should be with the attitude that, "I have unlimited time to do this."** This will slow you down to your natural, relaxed, unhurried speed, the speed at which you can focus on the details. Now, I know you don't have unlimited time. But in yet another one of those happy productivity paradoxes, pretending you do can speed your work because it minimizes perfectionism and procrastination. As Carl Honoré says in his book *In Praise of Slowness*, "Performing a task in a Slow manner often yields faster results."

I can't emphasize this enough. There have been countless times, during the writing of this book, when I caught myself thinking with perfectionist impatience, "This bit of writing is taking too long! If I spend this much time on every page [or paragraph or sentence], the entire book is going to take forever!" Whenever I caught myself thinking that way I immediately adopted the opposing view: "I have unlimited time to work on this." Almost always, the stress and pressure would melt away, leaving me relaxed and eager to do my work, which then went much faster. This example also illustrates how **you must always counter perfectionism with a strong opposing stand**. Weak neutrality isn't sufficient. If I had responded to my internal pressures by saying, "I'll give myself a day to write this paragraph. That's a generous amount of time," I still would have felt pressured and constrained. (This is an experiment you can try for yourself.)

This "infinite time" trick also aligns with Anne Lamott's technique, from her book *Bird by Bird*, of viewing your work as if through a "one-inch picture frame"—meaning, you focus on just the tiny bit that's in front of you without worrying about the rest.

To recap: you want to work with focus and intentionality and commitment, but not with any sense of urgency. Obviously, there will be times when you're facing an urgent deadline and need to step on the gas. But the more you learn to, as one of my mentors put it, "make haste, slowly," the better and faster you should be able to work, and the fewer of those urgent deadlines you should encounter.

At the same time you're doing your Slow Work, **choose short and simple projects**. That's especially important when you're a student or are working to overcome your perfectionism, for five reasons:

All projects are harder than they seem. Even seemingly "simple" ones will be hard enough.

Keeping things simple will allow you to focus on the details while still completing your project on time.

Novices tend to overstuff their projects, so keeping things simple will help to counteract that.

As noted in Chapter 7, quantity (i.e., finishing lots of small/simple stuff) will help you build your quality.

"Finishing" is a vital skill, and working on smaller/simpler projects will allow you to practice it more often. (More on this in Chapter 31.)

What if you want to do longer and more complicated projects? No problem! Just build up to them gradually. Every new project can be as long and complicated as you like—until you start feeling scared, pressured, under-resourced, or otherwise perfectionist.

If, while you're keeping it small, a critical internal voice pops up saying stuff like, "Wow, you're unambitious. Step it up!" I believe you now know who that voice is and how you should handle their advice.

27. Get Fresh!

Ideas are like cookies: better when fresh. A fresh idea is rich with meanings, associations, connotations, and other "flavors." It's also soft and malleable, so you can use it in different ways. But old ideas, like old cookies, go stale, losing a lot of their flavor and becoming stiff and brittle. When a Slogger uses a linear process that involves, for instance, doing all the research and organizing first, and only then starting to write, they're doing the intellectual equivalent of eating stale cookies. (Yuck! No wonder they procrastinate.)

So use your ideas while they're fresh. You do that by doing your writing and other "output" work in parallel with your planning, research, and other preparatory steps. Let's say you're researching a paper and find a useful nugget of information. Don't write it on an index card or in a notes file with the idea of later transferring it into your manuscript. Just plunk it right down into your manuscript, in the spot you think it best fits. Then start writing and editing around it. (Obviously, always be sure to use proper citations. Plagiarism is bad.) Then, when you run out of steam with it, go back and do some more research until you find your next useful nugget.

As noted in Chapter 5, however, you shouldn't do the opposite and research when you're supposed to be writing or doing other output work, because research is a prime vehicle for Quasiproductive Procrastination.

Aisha's story demonstrates how you can use this "parallelism" technique even for scientific work that would seem to require a linear approach:

For her senior chemistry capstone project, Aisha is investigating the process of nucleation, in which the addition of a tiny amount of an impurity (e.g., clay or talc) can cause a supersaturated solution to crystallize. It's a dramatic and beautiful effect—and, by the way, without the impurity, the solution would just sit there unchanging, forever boring in its static perfection.

Her initial plan is to use nucleation to create several types of organic and inorganic crystals, measuring both the speed and thoroughness of the crystallization process. Her professor, however, says that's too ambitious for a single semester, and advises her to build her experiment around just one type of crystal, testing its growth rate and purity under conditions of varying temperature and pressure. She'll still learn a lot, but every phase of her experiment—hypothesis formation, experimental design, apparatus setup, data collection and analysis, comprehensive literature review, and writing up her results—will be simpler, and she'll have plenty of time to get it all right.

She agrees—and is relieved, actually, because she had suspected her plan was too ambitious. (Hopefully, in the future, she'll listen a bit better when her Inner Compassionately Objective Adult whispers such wisdom to her.)

Aisha is also required to produce a research paper and a 20-minute slide presentation summarizing her work. Her professor suggests she start working on those immediately so she doesn't get stuck with a lot of work near the end of the semester. She follows this advice, and because she's using the Joyful Dance techniques we've been discussing, the work goes pretty easily and is fun.

Her professor also suggests she do a small pilot project, just to make sure her experimental design is solid and her apparatus is working as intended. This advice she's not so enthusiastic about, since she's short on time and certain everything works. Still, she follows it—and it's a good thing she does, because her solution doesn't nucleate (probably because of some contamination). Once she recovers from her shock, she rebuilds everything from scratch, this time working much more slowly and carefully. Then she repeats her pilot.

This time she gets a great crystal! And so, in a confident frame of mind, she continues on.

Thanks to her parallel work process, by the time Aisha's finished her data collection and analysis, her paper and presentation are already largely done. She feels great about that, and relieved not to be facing a mound of raw data and disorganized notes, like some of the other students. Later on, she's happy to get a great grade on her project, but her gratification mostly comes from her deeper understanding of, and appreciation for, the scientific process in general, and nucleation in particular. She's looking forward to doing more experiments—and will always work slowly and carefully.

And she'll always run a pilot.

28. Wizard-Level Problem-Solving

The problem, often, is problems. We can be chugging along doing our work and then be stopped cold by one. Our tendency, at such times, is to sit there and ponder, á la Rodin's sculpture, "The Thinker." Most of us aren't great at abstract thought, however, and so our efforts don't yield much—at which point, there is a strong temptation to flee via procrastination.

To do better, you need to first understand that most of what you're doing, when you're working, is making decisions. It doesn't matter whether you call those decisions, "physics," "anthropology," "music theory," or something else: it's still just decisions. Even a "small" project can require hundreds: a few large, some small, many tiny. Some you make consciously, while others are automatic. (But weren't always: while you can now write simple sentences and do simple math automatically, those tasks would have involved some very big decisions, back in elementary school.)

In between the decisions is the time we spend "implementing," or doing what we decided to do. But decision-making is usually a much bigger part of our projects than we realize, and even when we're implementing, we're still making some decisions.

The next thing you need to understand is that what we refer to as a "problem" is just a set of decisions that requires more time and effort than most. (Again, watch the labeling.)

So, a key to working fast is to make efficient decisions—and a key to that is, again, nonperfectionism. Dichotomizing, pathologizing, rigidity, impatience, etc. are all obvious barriers to decision-making. Perfectionism can also convince you that none of your solutions are any good, thus getting you stuck on looking for "the right one."

One of the saddest things about perfectionism is how it can suck the joy out of a fun process. Think about it: many people solve problems for fun via crossword puzzles, sudoku games, mystery novels, and "brain teaser" puzzles. Why should the problems you solve for your schoolwork be any different? This may sound silly if you're used to viewing "work" and "fun" as opposites, but, as discussed at various points in this book, you absolutely do want to approach your work as play.

Here are some other ways to speed up your problem-solving:

Trial and Error

Instead of sitting there and pondering, go ahead and try out some solutions. This gets you out of the realm of abstract thought and into the far more productive (and fun) one of using your skills. (You're "thinking by doing," in other words.) Sooner or later, you'll come up with a solution that works.

The key to successful trial and error is to not censor yourself. The whole point is to give yourself the freedom to experiment and play. But if you start preemptively shooting your ideas down—say, as "unlikely to work" or "silly"—that defeats the whole purpose. (I don't need to tell you which part of you is likely to do that.) Also, "unlikely" or "silly" ideas often turn out, with tweaking, to be winners.

Trial and error is another example of Chapter 7's idea that quantity yields quality. Generally speaking, the harder your problem is to solve, the more trials it will take to solve it. But solutions can often come quickly. Or, to put it another way: **our problems often aren't as tough as our inner perfectionist would have us believe.**

Trial and error isn't just a problem-solving technique, but your main work method. It's what writers do when they Quickdraft, for instance (see Chapter 30) and what coders do when they use iterative development techniques. Architects and engineers often develop their ideas by creating multiple models, and many visual artists and performers work by adding and subtracting bits until their vision emerges. Trial and error is the main "format" of your creative conversation, in other words—and it's no coincidence that it also provides you with lots of empowering options (Chapter 4) for proceeding with your work.

Write for Help

You do this either by journaling about the problem—as always, in a non-judgmental, nonperfectionist way—or writing an email to someone summarizing it and asking for help. Doing this gives you some emotional distance from the problem, while at the same time allowing you to look at it from a fresh angle. (As discussed in Chapter 10, often you don't even need to send the email: just writing it is enough to get you unstuck.)

Cut it Out!

As noted earlier, novice scholars and creators, and even experienced ones who are perfectionist, tend to overstuff their projects. And guess what? It's often that excess that clutters up your argument and otherwise causes problems. So, try removing the problem bit. This advice applies not just to entire sections of your work, but to individual sentences, phrases, and even words. (Even a tiny bit of excess can cause problems.)

It's amazing how often this trivial-seeming action of cutting works, and how good it feels. There's something satisfying about giving a troublesome part of your project the boot. One caveat, however: don't cut out of fear. **Some of the most valuable work happens when you arrive at a mess, take a deep breath, and then dive in and try to work it out.** A general guideline for when to cut is: if there's a problem with your central thesis or theme, try working it out. But if the problem is a tangential bit, go ahead and cut. (Obviously, keep a backup in case you change your mind.)

The worry, when you cut, is that the project is going to wind up too short. This is often both a perfectionist worry—because perfectionists mistrust "easy" success—and a pragmatic one: if the assignment is for ten pages, you can't hand in eight. Sometimes you can gather the more interesting cut bits into a new paragraph or section devoted to "secondary issues" or "topics for further research." Even when you can't, however, there's probably some part of the work you can expand, which brings us to...

Expand It

Often a bit of work won't come together because we're trying to cram too much information into too few words. So another technique is to expand the troublesome bit. First, copy it into a new window so you have lots of room to experiment and play; then let your creativity take charge. Often, the piece will open up in interesting and fun directions.

Finally, for very tough problems that are resisting any solution...

Start Over

This time letting the work find its own way. Impatient and rigid perfectionists are often horror-struck when I suggest this, but productive people do it all the time. And you know what? The new version usually goes way faster. That's often because: (a) you finally do know what it is you're trying to say, and (b) you're less controlling this time around. (See the next chapter to learn why trying to control the outcome isn't helpful.) Please note, however, that there's a difference between occasionally starting a difficult project over from scratch and constantly starting all of your projects over from scratch because you're afraid to finish. The former is great while the latter is a perfectionist behavior I discussed in Chapter 13.

29. How to Get, and Stay, Inspired

Poets, philosophers, and others have been pondering the mystery of inspiration for thousands of years, but all "being inspired" means is that you're ready and motivated to do the work. And all "being uninspired" means is that you're not—yet. So what does it take to be ready? A few things, including an understanding of the process you need to follow, confidence, a detailed knowledge of how to do the next couple of steps, and abundant preparation. Let's discuss each individually.

An Understanding of the Process

This may seem like a no-brainer but many people who think they know what they're doing don't. They're operating from a mix of hunches and guesswork, perhaps with a dash of shallow media advice (e.g., "Ten Tips for Writing Your Thesis" or "How to Succeed as a Musician") mixed in. What often happens, in such cases, is that the person gets mired in Quasiproductive Procrastination—e.g., busy work, redoing the same work over and over, over-researching, etc.—that gives them the illusion they're making progress. On some level, though, they know they're stuck, and their doubts keep growing until, one day, they're tipped over the edge by a "failure," harsh criticism, or other crisis. Then they quit—and maybe not just the project, but also their class, major, school, or career.

You need to think carefully about whether you're in this situation if you're working in isolation, and especially without mentors.

Confidence

Even if you understand your process, it's easy to get discouraged if you don't feel confident. You need confidence in your skills, in the availability of help, and—most of all—that if you make a reasonable effort you have a reasonable chance of success. (As mentioned in Chapter 4, futility is the most disempowering emotion.) This is yet another reason to maintain an expansive and holistic—otherwise known as nonperfectionist—view of success. For example: "Even if I don't achieve the entirety of my primary goal, I still will have achieved something. Also, I'll have learned a lot and had a great time. So my efforts weren't wasted."

Along with understanding and confidence, you also need to know **how to do the next couple of steps in detail**. Otherwise you might get stuck on one of them, or on your current step. (Because you're aware, at least subconsciously, that you don't know how to proceed.) Good ways to test whether you know enough are to: (1) write the steps down in detail, and (2) try explaining them to someone else. Any holes in your knowledge should become apparent. (If you're working without a mentor you should assume you don't, in fact, have all the information you need to proceed.)

One of the benefits of being in school is that, in theory, you should always understand your assignments, have confidence they're doable, and have a detailed knowledge of the steps. But people make mistakes and miscommunicate. Especially when working on important or complex assignments, check in frequently with your professor.

Finally, to be inspired you need to have done **abundant preparation**. Here are the typical steps of a writing project: conceptualization (a.k.a., brainstorming or idea generation), research, organization/outlining, first draft, revisions, and sharing the work. Notice how the step most people think happens first, "first draft," happens more than halfway through. If you get stuck, therefore, try going back and spending more time on the conceptualization, organization, and research stages, and you should regain your inspiration. Similar advice applies to science, math, and engineering: if you're stuck, go back and review the fundamentals. It often turns out we don't understand them as well as we think we do.

The word "inspiration" literally means "breathing in," and that's what you're doing during the early stages of your project: "breathing in" the work of experts past and present, which you then combine with your own ideas and insights in your creative conversation. But if you rush through those early stages, as many students do because they are in a hurry to get to what they consider "the real work," you starve yourself of the inputs needed for inspiration, pretty much ensuring your work will be a grind.

Know Thyself and Thy Motivations

Even if you do have the understanding, confidence, detailed knowledge, and preparation needed to proceed, you can still find yourself stuck. In such cases, try answering these four questions:

1. **Am I being perfectionist?** I know, I know: again with the perfectionism! But it will rob you of your inspiration faster than just about anything. Ask yourself, especially, whether you're overfocusing on outcomes or being overidentified, grandiose, impatient, mistrustful of success, or rigid. If the answer is yes, then use your reframing, dialoguing, and other solutions.

2. **Am I doing this project for the right reasons?** Especially ask yourself if you're doing it to impress others. That's a sign of overidentification and other possible problems. I can usually tell when someone is in this bind because their project is overserious, overcomplicated, and overintellectualized—e.g., "My paper is about death as a metaphysical protest and ecstatic reaction, as interpreted by Tolstoy and Dostoevsky, with supplementary analytical comparisons using Gogol and Chekhov." Also, it's pretty clear, usually, that the person's heart isn't in the topic. (Also see Chapter 13's discussion of overambitious projects.)

3. **Am I ambivalent for other reasons?** Perhaps your project revisits some difficult personal or family history, or explores challenging issues such as war, domestic violence, or animal cruelty. If so, try the solutions in Chapter 24, and always remember that empowerment means creating more good options for yourself—including the option to not work on a project, if you don't feel ready to do so.

4. **Am I trying to force the work?** Imagine you're having a fun conversation with friends. Then, all of a sudden, someone starts talking over everyone else, insisting that the discussion be held in a certain way and arrive at a specific conclusion.

Not so fun or productive anymore, is it?

It works the same way with creativity: the moment you try to control it, you shut it down. Often, when we do this, it's because we're aiming for a certain quality standard like "excellence" or "comprehensiveness" or "originality." That's admirable, but repeat after me: You Can't Force the Work. (Also recall Flaubert's point that, "success is a consequence and must not be a goal.")

Therefore, a final thing to ask when you're feeling stuck or uninspired is, "Am I trying to force the work? Or, alternatively: "Am I trying to control the outcome?" or "Am I trying to dominate the creative conversation?" Any of these can stop your creativity cold.

If this turns out to be the problem, then ask your Inner Perfectionist (and ego) to step aside so your creative process can unfold. The only potential problem with doing that is that the work might start going beyond the bounds of what your professor assigned. If that happens, go ahead and talk with them. Hopefully they'll be understanding, because what you have here is an honest-to-gosh case of creativity. But if they aren't—and they may have their legitimate reasons—then you get to practice another valuable skill: working on something you don't want to be working on. (The "boredom" discussion in Chapter 32 offers tips for that.)

30. How to Write Like a Pro

Writing is a paradox. On the one hand, it's a common activity many of us feel we mastered in elementary school. On the other, it's easy to get stuck when doing it.

Clearly, there's a lot more to the "simple" act of writing than many of us think. The main problem is that, along with the intellectual and creative challenges we expect, writing presents a whole other set of challenges we don't: challenges of solitude, sedentariness, and—let's face it—monotony. (All those endless rounds of putting down words and taking them out again.) Add to all that the reality that it often takes a lot more work than expected to create a good piece of writing, and it's no wonder many people struggle.

Fortunately, there are some groups of professional writers who are taught how to deal with all that, and whom we can learn from. They include journalists—who often must make weekly or even daily deadlines—and the genre writers (science fiction, fantasy, romance, etc.), many of whom write a book (or more!) a year. Below is a suggested writing process that incorporates techniques used by these productive writers. Even if you're not a self-described "writer," but someone who is expected to write a lot for class—and, later, on the job—they should work for you.

Stay Grounded

Some people approach their writing like it's a holy mission: an overidentified and grandiose approach which, needless to say, isn't helpful. In his book *On*

Writing, Stephen King suggests you view your writing as, "just another job like laying pipe or driving long-haul trucks."

Stay Playful

Writing, like all creativity, demands freedom and a light touch—and that's true even when you're working on serious projects. That doesn't mean you should be all ha-ha jokey when writing about, say, climate change, but only that you shouldn't fall into the trap of thinking you're supposed to be actively depressed while doing so. It's always good to maintain some emotional distance from your work, especially when dealing with intense subject matter.

It can be difficult to maintain that distance, however, so if you do find yourself getting depressed or otherwise affected by what you're working on, talk to your professor, a friend, or a counselor. And as noted in the previous chapter, don't feel obligated to tackle a subject if it's too emotionally challenging.

Daydream Productively

Prolific writers invest heavily in the "conceptualization" step of the writing process. Charles Dickens, for instance, would often take, "a vigorous three-hour walk through the countryside or the streets of London…'searching for some pictures [he] wanted to build upon.'"[36] I imagine him pondering the next scene in *Oliver Twist* or *Great Expectations*, then coming upon a real-life scenario that helped put everything in focus.

Ursula K. LeGuin told an interviewer that, after waking up, she spent around forty-five minutes lying in bed and thinking, before having "lots of" breakfast and then sitting down to write for around five hours.[37] We can assume she used her early-morning thinking time to fuel her ideas for her writing, just as she used the big breakfasts to fuel her physical energy.

---

[36] From Mason Currey's book *Daily Rituals*.
[37] www.openculture.com/2019/01/ursula-k-le-guins-daily-routine-the-discipline-that-fueled-her-imagination.html

I'm guessing Dickens kept a notepad handy while he was walking so he could jot down his inspirations. And perhaps LeGuin kept one by her bedside. I similarly recommend you carry a notepad, or use your phone's voice recorder, when daydreaming away from your desk.

Create Your "Shitty First Draft"

The idea of a shitty first draft was popularized by Anne Lamott in *Bird by Bird*. She describes it as follows: "The first draft is the child's draft, where you let it all pour out and then let it romp all over the place, knowing that no one is going to see it and that you can shape it later. You just let this childlike part of you channel whatever voices and visions come through and onto the page."

Lamott also describes shitty first drafts as self-indulgent, boring, stupefying, incoherent, hideous, and "almost just typing, just making my fingers move." She also notes how perfectionism—which she calls "the voice of the oppressor"—is the main obstacle keeping you from completing your shitty first draft, because you can't tolerate the shittiness. When I ask perfectionists to describe a shitty first draft, they often say something like this: "It's rough in places but mostly organized, and the major points are there..." Perfectionists' shitty first drafts, in other words, are like nonperfectionists' near-final drafts! Make sure you're comfortable creating truly shitty, shitty first drafts.

Once you've written your shitty first draft, it's time to move onto my favorite part of the writing process...

Quickdraft

During writing productivity classes, I sometimes ask the trick question, "How many drafts should you do of a paper or other piece of writing?" The students who are creative, academic, or business writers answer something like, "three" or "five" or "ten." But the journalists always answer, correctly, "As many as it takes." But you need to know what they mean by a "draft": not a slow, linear slog through your paper (or chunk), but a kind of nimble dance through it, during which you stop to make only the easiest and most obvious edits.

The goal, in other words, is to do lots and lots of fast drafts. Now, sooner or later, while you're doing that, you'll come across a bit you feel like focusing on, and you should do that. That feeling is called "inspiration," and you shouldn't waste it. When it passes—meaning you've written or edited as much as you can, at that moment, on that bit— return to your nimble dance.

Your writing process, then, consists of alternating fast and slow work, with you shifting as desired between those two modes without hesitation, fuss, or drama. Then, when you reach the end of the paper (or chunk), you return to the beginning and start over.

Repeat all that until you finish your Timed Work Interval (Chapter 6).

I call this process Quickdrafting and it offers some terrific advantages, including that it's:

Nonlinear and fresh. You can start wherever in the piece you want and are also free to stop and focus on whichever bits you'd like.

An active, easy, interesting, and fun way to write, so you don't get bored.

Preserving of your energy, so you can work longer without getting tired.

Generative. Each time you do a Quickdraft, you gain ideas and insights that fuel the next.

Accelerative. Meaning that, the more Quickdrafts you do, the faster the remaining ones should go. (In contrast to linear work, which tends to, first, slow down, and then bog down.)

Quickdrafting is particularly useful for big projects because it helps you to comprehend your project as a whole, leading to more speed and a better, more integrated product. Quickdrafting also helps you to avoid the kinds of rabbit holes, tangents, and other time-wasters (see Chapters 31 and 32) that are easy to fall into when you overfocus on one part of a big project. Just as visual artists do preliminary sketches to make sure they've got their overall composition right before starting work on the details, your early Quickdrafts will, in effect, be "sketches" for your final written product.

How many Quickdrafts does it take to complete a paper or other piece of writing? (Not a trick question, this time.) The answer varies. It could be as high as ten, twenty, or even more—but don't panic: a nonperfectionist can do dozens of Quickdrafts faster than a perfectionist can do one "Slowdraft." (Assuming they even finish it.)

Be Extra Patient when Handling Feedback and Criticism

The moment when you get comments back on your piece, from a professor, classmate, friend, or someone else, is one of the most fraught in the entire writing process.

The first pitfall is emotional. Obviously, you want to set your perfectionist ego aside and evaluate those criticisms and suggestions without being defensive.

After you decide what changes you want to make in your work, there's another challenge, which is that it can take a surprising amount of work to integrate even small changes into an existing text. Sometimes that's because you have to do a lot of writing and editing around a change, and sometimes it's because a change triggers more changes, and then more, in a kind of domino effect. And sometimes it's because a change requires you view your text in new and unfamiliar ways. In all cases, the key is to stay nonperfectionist and not panic. Start just by recording, right in your manuscript, notes about the changes you want to make. (I often list them in bullet point format.) Then start Quickdrafting around those notes, working with even more patience than usual.

Remember the Primary Goal

As discussed in Chapter 26, it is to finish, so you can move onto the next project. (So, don't get sucked into endless perfectionist revisions.)

Remember the Rewards

It's noteworthy that, despite writing's many inconveniences, so many people are drawn to it. That's because, like all creative and intellectual pursuits, it offers numerous and profound rewards, including meaning, growth, transcendence, transformation, and joy. As Flaubert put it, "Writing is a dog's life, but the only life worth living." And in *remembered rapture*, bell hooks writes of, "that moment of grace when the words come, when I surrender to their ecstatic power," and also that, "We write because language is the way we keep a hold on life. With words we experience our deepest understandings of what it means to be intimate."

Staying mindful of the rewards of writing can help you stay motivated throughout the course of your projects. And if you use the techniques in this chapter, the writing itself should go much more easily.

Casey's story, below, shows how you can combine the above techniques with nonlinearity and parallelism, to wind up with not just a great paper that is written efficiently, but an enhanced understanding of, and appreciation for, a vivid aspect of the human experience.

For their comparative religion class, Casey is writing a paper on the Japanese concept of *wabi-sabi* (finding beauty in the imperfect and transient). They start by doing some research, then lay out their ideas in a very rough—a.k.a., "shitty"—first draft.

Then, they start Quickdrafting, gradually improving that draft.

After doing some more research, they find this exciting quote from Kakuzo Okakura's classic work, *The Book of Tea*: "Perfection is everywhere if we only choose to recognize it." They copy it, with attribution, right into the relevant section of their manuscript, then start writing and revising around it.

The Okakura quote inspires some other ideas, so Casey starts writing about those, too. Eventually, they decide that all the Okakura-related material would work best gathered into one section, and so they do some bold reorganizing. (An example of working with their creativity and letting the work take its own course.) Of course, they save their current version as a backup, just in case.

Casey keeps Quickdrafting. When they encounter a problem, they resist the urge to ponder, and instead do some trial and error; and so, all the problems get resolved quickly. Still, for what seems like a scarily long time, their paper resembles a giant mishmash, and they worry they're not making enough progress. They keep the faith, however—and, in particular, are careful to resist the temptation to try to force the work in any particular direction. Sure enough, the compelling themes soon start to emerge.

The more Casey focuses on those themes, the more their paper gels. Pretty soon—and with some judicious cutting of some sections and expanding of others—all of the paper's major problems have been resolved, and it starts to resemble a coherent whole. After that, it's mostly smooth sailing—or, more accurately, smooth QuickDrafting—until the end of the project.

When it's time to hand their paper in, Casey does so with satisfaction and the confidence they've done their best. Not surprisingly, their professor gives them a great grade, and also praises their "depth of analysis" and "ability to capture the subtleties of the concept." Casey's happy about all that, but even happier to have engaged with such a fascinating topic. They're eager to learn more about Japanese culture, and one day visit Japan.

31. Navigating the Project Life Cycle

Just as humans go through life stages—infancy, childhood, adolescence, adulthood, etc.—projects also go through life stages. In this chapter, I discuss each stage individually, so you can anticipate its characteristic challenges and prevent them from stalling your projects.

The Honeymoon

The Honeymoon is the very beginning of your project. At this stage, the project exists mainly as a glorious golden vision in your head—and what you are probably envisioning is not the product itself, but how amazed and impressed others will be when they see it. Even when you do envision the process, it's probably all smooth sailing, with few, if any, serious problems.

This golden vision is super motivational and so for a while you work like gangbusters. But then, inevitably, the vision starts to crack and tarnish as you realize that:

- The work you've done so far isn't great. In fact, it's pretty bad. (Shitty first drafts and other early attempts always are.)
- The project's got some serious problems you don't know how to solve, or even if you can solve them. And even if you can...
- The project is going to turn out very different from, and not nearly as good as, the golden vision. (Because nothing could turn out that well.) And finally,
- You still have an enormous amount of work to do.

The Anti-Honeymoon

Welcome to the Anti-Honeymoon, the stage of peak disappointment, disillusionment, and demotivation. It's the stage at which many people abandon not just projects, but classes, jobs, careers, relationships, etc. English Literature majors will recognize it as the "Slough of Despond" from John Bunyan's classic 17th century allegory, *The Pilgrim's Progress*. And college students in all majors may experience it in the form of "Sophomore Slump." (See Chapter 2.)

What's really going on is—you guessed it—perfectionism. The Honeymoon/Anti-Honeymoon cycle reeks of overemphasis on product, a narrow definition of success, overidentification, grandiosity, shortsightedness, impatience, and pathologizing. The key to coping, therefore, is to moderate your perfectionism and expectations. Optimism at the start of a project is great, but avoid grandiose fantasies that will inevitably trigger a backlash of disappointment. And when the Anti-Honeymoon does arrive, keep cool and keep working, always keeping in mind the problem isn't your work, but your perfectionist attitude toward it. (Just as, in *The Pilgrim's Progress*, the Slough consists of the Pilgrim's, "fears, and doubts, and discouraging apprehensions.")

Also, double down on your other solutions. Bunyan's protagonist, the pilgrim Christian, finally escapes from the Slough with the assistance of "a man whose name was Help," hint, hint.

The Vast Middle

Get past the Anti-Honeymoon and you'll soon enter the Vast Middle. If the Honeymoon/Anti-Honeymoon combination and Home Stretch (see below) each represent around 10% of your project, that leaves 80% for the Vast Middle. (That's vast!) The real problem, however, isn't the Vast Middle's vastness, but the fact that, much of the time when you're in it, you don't feel like you're making progress. In the midst of what can feel like endless rounds of trial and error, it's easy to get discouraged.

The solution, again, is to keep your cool and keep working—keeping in mind that the "Vast Middle" is simply another name for "doing the work." Joyful Dancers and process-focused people don't mind the Vast Middle: it's only those who are overfocused on product—or, I guess, late on their deadlines—who see it as something to be rushed through.

Hang out long enough in the Vast Middle and eventually something great happens: you see the faint outlines of your destination. (As Casey did while writing their paper.) Other ways of describing this exciting moment are: you discover what it is you're trying to say; your creative conversation zeroes in on a conclusion; your project gels; and your meaning emerges out of all the chaos. Your work will get easier at this point, and should continue to get easier, until you arrive at...

The Home Stretch

The Home Stretch, where what's left to do is formatting, proofreading, and other easy "polishing." Many people enjoy this stage: just be sure not to enjoy it too much and get stuck there, because that's a common form of Quasiproductive Procrastination. (Also see Chapter 14's discussion of Hoarding and the discussion of Fear of Finishing in the next chapter.) Avoid that trap, however, and you soon should experience...

The Finale

A mere moment in time, but a satisfying one. Take a moment to acknowledge and celebrate your achievement before moving onto...

Sharing

Sharing, a.k.a., handing the work in. After you do, don't sit around and wait for the grade or other outcome: start working on your next project. (As discussed in Chapter 15.)

What's Taking So Long?

Sooner or later, someone's going to ask you about the progress of one of your projects. If you're lucky, the inquiry will be phrased something like this: "How's your work going?" If you're not so lucky, it might be more along the lines of, "Still working on that thing?" Or, "Haven't you finished yet?" Or, "What's taking so long?"

Let's agree that, regardless of the form of the inquiry, the asker probably means well. But the last three phrasings are all perfectionist. So how to handle them?

First, be nonperfectionist. Obviously, if you yourself are impatiently overfocused on product, or are devaluing the work you've already done (an example of negativity; see Chapter 13), then having someone ask about your progress is bound to be painful. So keep your focus on your process, keeping in mind that many projects that "aren't going well" or "are going too slowly" are just in their Anti-Honeymoon or Vast Middle stage.

Next, remember that your goal, during the conversation, shouldn't be to convince the other person—you have no control over that—but to share as much of your truth as you want, in an empowering way.

Finally, instead of trying to justify or defend yourself, educate. For instance: "Actually, senior projects usually do take a few months." Often, however, before we can educate others, we have to educate ourselves—and here, once more, mentors can help. Acclaimed writer of massive biographies, Robert A. Caro, tells this story in his autobiography *Working*:

> I was bothered, too, by the length not only of the manuscript [of his book *The Power Broker*, about New York City "master builder" Robert Moses], but also of the time I had been working on it.
>
> That was the thing that made me doubt the most. When I had started, I had firmly believed that I would be done in a year, a naive but perhaps not unnatural belief for someone whose longest previous deadline had been measured in weeks. As year followed year, and I was still not nearly done, I became convinced that I had gone terribly astray. This feeling was fed by the people Ina and I did know. I was still in the first year of research when friends and acquaintances began to ask if I was "still doing that book." Later I would be asked, "How long have you been working on it now?" When I said three years, or four, or five, they would quickly disguise their look of incredulity, but not quickly enough to keep me from seeing it. I came to dread that question…

A bit later, Caro has been given desk privileges in the New York Public Library's prestigious Frederick Lewis Allen Room, where he finds himself working alongside, among others, two of the 20th century's most celebrated biographers: James Flexner (author of a multivolume biography of George Washington) and Joseph Lash (author of *Eleanor and Franklin*, a big biography of the Roosevelts). One day, Caro looks up from his work:

> The expression on [Flexner's] face was friendly, but after he had asked what I was writing about, the next question was the question

I had come to dread: "How long have you been working on it?" This time, however, when I replied, "Five years," the response was not an incredulous stare.

"Oh," Jim Flexner said, "That's not so long. I've been working on my Washington for nine years."

I could have jumped up and kissed him [...] as, the next day, I could have jumped up and kissed Joe Lash...when he asked me the same question, and, after hearing my answer, said in his quiet way, "*Eleanor and Franklin* took me seven years." In a couple of sentences, these two men—idols of mine—had wiped away five years of doubt.

This anecdote also illustrates why it's important to have mentors who have accomplished the same type of thing you are trying to accomplish. None of Caro's journalist friends could give him the information and perspective he needed. It had to be biographers—and not just any biographers, but those whose goals, in terms of scope, quality, and ambition, were similar to his own. And in case you're wondering, not even fame and acclaim will put a stop to the perfectionist inquiries. Caro reports that he is still, "constantly being asked why it takes me so long."

More Techniques for Dealing with Perfectionist Inquiries

"When will it be done?" isn't the only perfectionist inquiry you'll likely receive. You might also hear, "Got a job yet? What's taking so long?" Or (for those not majoring in business, engineering, or medicine): "Can you make any money doing that?"

The above techniques (nonperfectionism, stating your truth, and educating) will work for those as well. And here are a few others:

Argument from authority can work well, especially when talking with skeptical or condescending elders. E.g., "Actually, my advisor says I'm right on track."

Set boundaries. You don't have to answer every question put to you. So think about what you're comfortable sharing and with whom, and practice gracefully pivoting away from unwanted requests for information. Example:

Questioner: How's the job search going? Found anything yet?

> *You:* Nope, still looking. [Resists the temptation to offer further details.] How are things with you?
> *Questioner* (persisting): The job market's pretty tough, eh?
> *You:* Let's talk about something else, okay? How are the Phillies doing this year?

Boomerang the focus back on the listener. Example: "Did you ever go through a period where you had a hard time finding work? What did you do?"

Humor is a risky tactic because it's easy to screw up, and if you do screw it up, you risk sounding not just unfunny, but bitter or condescending. But give it a try, if you want. Example: "Why don't I get another job? Great idea! Maybe I'll stop by the job store on my way home and pick one up." By the way, professional comedians are able to get the jokes right because they spend a lot of time refining and practicing their routines. Which brings us to…

Plan ahead and practice. Plan your answers to difficult questions and practice saying those answers with confidence. Each time you practice, you should hear yourself improve, and knowing that you've practiced will, in itself, aid your confidence.

The ability to respond to challenging inquiries with ease and confidence is a great skill to have, and a sign of some excellent empowerment.

Exercise 16

Think back on some projects that took longer than they should have. Did you spend too much time on one or more of the project stages? More generally, is there a stage you enjoy—like research or revision—and tend to get stuck at? If the answer to either question is "yes," then recognizing the problem will hopefully help you avoid it in the future.

32. Avoiding the "Big Four" Project Derailments

Along with the project stage-related challenges I discussed in the last chapter, there are four other common project derailments you should watch out for. They are Beginning Bias (and other forms of avoidance), Reckless Research, Fear of Finishing, and Boredom. I discuss each below.

Banish Beginning Bias and Other Avoidance-Related Problems

Beginning Bias is what I call the tendency some of us have to overwork the beginnings of our projects relative to, and usually at the expense of, the middles and ends. (Quasiproductive Procrastination in action.) Years ago, a professional book reviewer told me she could always tell when an author had this problem because the beginning of their book would be much more polished than the rest, which obviously got done in a hurry after their editor told them to, "hand it in or else."

Running out of time on tests is also often partly a Beginning Bias problem. With the test-taker spending too much time on the first part of the test, thus leaving themselves too little time for the rest.

Beginning Bias is a subset of a bigger problem with the Joyful Dance, which is that, by giving yourself "permission" to nonlinearly work on any part of your project, you're also giving yourself "permission" to *not* work on any part. Especially, we avoid those parts that are difficult, tedious, scary (e.g., a presentation), or collaborative (because collaboration is hard). Even worse, the more we avoid a piece of work, the scarier it gets, and the more we want to avoid it.

Chapter 25's Randomization technique can help with mild cases of Beginning Bias and other avoidance problems. You can also use a "semi-random" technique that ensures you do some work on every part of your project. When writing this book, for instance, I made sure to devote some Timed Work Intervals to each of the five main sections every week.

For stronger cases of avoidance, I recommend a technique I call **Microintervals**. Every hour or so while you're working on the easier stuff, switch over to the scary bit and work on it for a very brief amount of time, like a minute. You might edit a sentence, research a math or science problem, or send out a quick email for a collaborative project. As always, don't judge your work. (Obviously, you shouldn't be expecting to accomplish much in a minute, anyway.)

After a few Microintervals, the scary bit won't seem so scary anymore. You'll be able to do longer Microintervals, and then even longer ones. Then, eventually, the scary bit will become just another *un*scary part of your project.

Rein in Reckless Research

Research is a common vehicle for Quasiproductive Procrastination because:

- It can be endless. You can take even "small" topics in dozens of directions. Plus, new source materials are constantly being created.
- Many people enjoy it. Rooting around in archives, or falling down an Internet "rabbit hole," is fun.
- Every project is different and so it's hard to come up with general guidelines for what, and how much, research you should do.
- You learn how to research your topic partly by researching it— which is why so many scholars, after finishing their research, wish they could start over from scratch. (And some do just that, starting over and over and over, and never finishing.)

Perfectionism, as usual, makes everything worse because, along with the usual types of fear of failure, you now have the additional, research-related fear of, "leaving something out." One solution to over-researching, therefore, is to build your nonperfectionism. Another, as discussed in Chapters 5 and 25, is to not do research during your writing and other "output" work intervals.

If you think you're slipping into Reckless Research, use your Obstacle Analysis, Timed Work Intervals, Microintervals, and other techniques to get back on track. It's also a great idea to ask your professors, at the beginning of projects, what kinds of research you should be doing, and how much. Rest assured that these are not naive questions, but pretty savvy ones that they themselves probably still occasionally ask their own colleagues or mentors.

Finish Off "Fear of Finishing"

Finishing your work is important, and not just for the obvious reasons. You gain confidence from finishing and also learn valuable lessons, like how to persevere through the Vast Middle or at other times you're feeling unmotivated. Finishing lots of projects will also help you build your skills and knowledge—Chapter 7's "quantity yielding quality," again—and gain a sense of who you are as a creator and what specialties you'd like to develop (Chapter 46).

Finishing is a skill. You learn it the same way you learn other skills: by practicing. Start by finishing small and easy projects, then work your way up to bigger and more difficult ones. All the obstacles and barriers discussed in this book can cause you to quit your projects before they're finished, but developing a commitment to finishing, and a self-image as a "finisher," will help you to persevere through them. One way to do that is to learn to recognize and celebrate your finishes as you would any success (Chapter 23).

Being a finisher doesn't mean you have to finish every single thing you start. (Even professionals experience the occasional false start.) But you should finish most of them—and also have a good reason for not finishing something. Above all else, you want to avoid becoming the poor short-sighted perfectionist (Chapter 13) who abandons projects because they can't see past ordinary obstacles and "bumps."

Give Boredom the Boot

As discussed in the last chapter, the Vast Middles of projects can seem boring and your job, when there, is to maintain perspective and keep working.

But there are two other common causes of boredom: (1) you're just not that interested in a topic (or project) and (2) the work is too simple, repetitive, or otherwise tedious.

Let's discuss those one at a time.

Lack of Interest. Since nearly all college courses examine some fundamental aspect of the human experience, in theory, at least, no college course should be boring. As the playwright Terence said, "I consider nothing human alien to me." Strive, therefore, to have as wide a range of interests as possible, and also to reframe any "boring" classes so they become more interesting.

Sometimes the boredom is a reflection of another problem, such as:

perfectionism (it destroys all fun).

bad teaching (Chapter 35).

bad study habits (see Chapters 8 and 36) or poor time management (Part V).

lack of commitment (e.g., the only reason you're taking the class is to fulfill a requirement).

personal problems. (If you're feeling bored, tired, or unmotivated a lot, that could be a sign of depression, so please see a counselor.)

Resolve these and other obstacles, to the extent you're able, and you should find yourself getting more interested.

Some other techniques for alleviating boredom:

Select classes based on the quality of the professor. As discussed in Chapter 8. An excellent teacher can make even "boring" material exciting, while a not-so-great teacher—like the "droners" who read from their notes or the textbook—can turn even the most fascinating topic into a snooze.[38]

See the big picture. Students sometimes overfocus on details but you often have to connect the dots to have a subject come alive.

Don't make snap judgments. If the first session of a class isn't to your liking, hang in there for another session or two. Sometimes professors have

---

[38] Apparently J.R.R. Tolkien was the ultimate droner. A professor of medieval philology at Oxford University, he not only spent the entire class lecturing, but did so with his back to the students while writing on the blackboard. I guess he saved all the excitement for his novels.

to convey a lot of information at the very beginning of the course, but after that, things get more interesting and interactive.

Connect the subject to your own experience. Admittedly, this is easier with some classes, such as history and psychology, than others, such as math and physics. But be open-minded, recalling that many of our most enjoyable activities, including music, cooking, gardening, and sports, have a fascinating science or math component.

Go Slow. As discussed in Chapter 26. When we encounter boring stuff, our tendency is to try to blitz through it and finish as quickly as possible. Unfortunately, this pretty much guarantees a miserable work experience and an inferior result. Instead, try slowing down and savoring the details. You'll have more fun and get a better result—and maybe even finish sooner, since blitzing often leads to procrastination.

Now for the second type of boredom: **when the work is too simple, repetitive, or otherwise tedious**. Please note that there are two types of this repetitive work:

1. The practice work you do to build your skills, like when a musician practices scales or an athlete does drills. This work is important and if you do it mindfully and with proper support it shouldn't be too boring. (If it is, try slowing down.)
2. Any task, chore, or other work you're either not learning anything from or that is outside your mission. Sometimes the boring task could be one you once found interesting but have outgrown. (You see this a lot in people stuck in a job rut.) Or it could be something you're doing because it's "normal" or other people expect it. (You see this a lot in people caught in a rut of perfectionist housekeeping or overgiving; for solutions to the latter see Chapter 48.) In both cases, your boredom is a kind of rebellion against using your time unrewardingly, and is thus a good thing. The first rule of coping with this kind of boring work, therefore, is to do as little of it as possible. (Section V will help.) **Always strive to follow your passions, and to live and work among others who are following theirs.**

Even if you're terrific at the above techniques, you'll never entirely eliminate the boring stuff. When you find yourself stuck working on something you'd rather not be working on, try working alongside a Study Buddy or two. Working in community can be fun, even when the project you're working on isn't.

Exercise 17

The next time you're stuck on a project, use journaling to answer these questions:

- Which part of the project life cycle (from Chapter 31) is your project at? Does your answer add any clarity to the situation or suggest any solutions?
- Are any of the derailments listed in this chapter present? If so, hopefully the solutions offered will help you get back on track.

33. How to Take Excellent Breaks

Breaks are essential from both a health standpoint (especially if you're doing a lot of sitting and screen work) and also from the standpoint of avoiding fatigue and other triggers for procrastination.

They're also great for problem-solving. Many people have had the experience of struggling with a tough problem, only to have the answer magically pop into their head while taking a coffee break or walking the dog.

Your Inner Perfectionist disagrees. For them, breaks are just so much wasted time. "If you must take one, at least make it productive," they insist. You know: by doing some other schoolwork, or learning a musical instrument, or aerobically running up and down five flights of stairs. (All real-life examples people have shared with me.) Important reminder: as per Chapter 19, you should empathize with your Inner Perfectionist, but never take their advice.

Your breaks should be easy and enjoyable. Sure, pick out a few guitar chords if you want. Or do a few dishes or fetch the mail. Even do a few push-ups or pull-ups. But no strenuousness, unpleasantness, intensity, depletion, deprivation, coercion, etc. Also avoid the use of screens during your breaks, since using one neutralizes many of the health benefits and can also lead to your getting sucked into an app.

The best breaks are enjoyable, active, low-stress, and not intensely interactive or otherwise distracting. A walk, some stretches, a romp with an animal companion, or meditating are all great choices. As always, do what works for you.

As for the interesting question of how long your breaks should be, I recommend tracking your **"Break Percentage"**: the percentage of time, out of your entire work interval, that you devote to breaks. While you're still working on overcoming your perfectionism, your Break Percentage might be 50% (equal time spent working and on break) or higher (more time breaking than working). That's probably not a number you're happy with, but keep the faith: as you get more nonperfectionist, your work should flow more easily and your Break Percentage should drop. A good goal to aim for is around 20% (twelve minutes of break time out of each work hour, perhaps divided into two or three chunks). But again: do what works for you.

Finally, **learn to distinguish a true break from procrastination.** Many people, when they encounter a problem with their work, zip through the entire Disempowerment Cascade in an instant and then "decide" to take a break. They're not breaking, they're derailed! Instead, stay calm and either use your obstacle-resolution (Chapters 9 and 10) and problem-solving (Chapters 28 through 32) techniques to resolve the problem, or switch—as always, without drama or fuss—to an easier bit of work. (While letting the problem "marinate" for a while.)

So that's the Joyful Dance. Use it and you'll create, finish, and share more work than ever before—perhaps more than you ever thought possible. And you'll also enjoy your work more than you ever thought possible. But there are even bigger yields than that because, once we learn how to easily work on the things that are truly important to us, we become more free to develop into our truest self, and help others do the same.

The Joyful Dance is a tool not just for productivity, but liberation and love.

Finish and share more of your work and you'll start getting more feedback, some of it critical. Part IV tells you how to handle that.

PART IV

RESILIENCE

34. The Many Forms of Criticism and Rejection

Criticism and rejection can take many forms. There's "classic" criticism: when someone has something negative to say about you or your work. And "classic" rejection; i.e., denial of a request or opportunity.

Then there's all of these: bias, callousness, carelessness, contempt, deprecation, devaluation, dismissal, disparagement, labeling, marginalization, mockery, neglect, ostracism, ridicule, sarcasm, snark, shaming, and tokenism.

And these: passive-aggressive withholding of information, time, or other support, and non-accommodation of reasonable requests.

(Throughout the rest of Part IV, except where indicated, I use the words "criticism" and "rejection" interchangeably to refer to all of the above.)

Constructive criticism—meaning criticism that's useful, appropriate, proportionate, and sensitively delivered—is essential to learning and growth. Painful as it can be, it's a sign that others are taking you seriously.

But harsh, arbitrary, or otherwise unconstructive criticism can be destructive. You know how an oyster responds to an irritant, like a grain of sand, by coating it with layers of nacre, creating a smooth and non-irritating pearl? We often do something similar with harsh criticism: "coat it" with denial and procrastination to protect ourselves from present and future hurt. (Denial is when you bury the hurt and pretend it's not there. Procrastination, as discussed in Chapters 2 and 14, "protects" you by making you and your work invisible.) This process continues until you have, not a pearl, but a block—and I know this happens a lot because frequently, in classes, after I mention a type of harsh criticism or rejection, a student will get one of those

Whoa! looks and say, "I just realized that that happened to me and afterwards I never wrote another short story."

Or, "...I dropped the class and switched majors."

Or, "...I stopped applying for internships."

It can also work the same way in our personal lives: after someone rejects us cruelly, we may stop approaching others for friendship or love.

I call any criticism or rejection that leaves you feeling ashamed, unfit, fearful, or hopeless, "traumatic." I'll discuss how to handle the different types of traumatic rejections throughout the rest of Part IV. First, however, let's discuss a common piece of advice given to those hurting from a rejection: the suggestion that they "toughen up" or "grow a thicker skin." It's lousy advice for three reasons:

First, it's vague. How, exactly, do you do that?

Second, it implies you're being weak and is therefore shaming. In fact, it literally adds insult to injury. (Recall Chapter 15's story about the soccer dad who wounded his daughter with a similar comment.) And third...

We—meaning society—don't need any more thick-skinned people. Thick-skinned people go around stomping on others' feelings and causing trouble. And it's not true that they don't feel the hurt of a criticism or rejection. They might be in denial about it but the pain is there, causing them to suffer and, often, mistreat others.

The goal, in other words, isn't toughness, but resilience. You want to be open, caring, and sensitive, but also capable of coping with the inevitable hurts and disappointments. To achieve that resilience, it's helpful to understand why criticisms hurt, and why some hurt more than others.

Why It Hurts

If your adored but somewhat-out-of-touch parents tell you they dislike your new hairstyle, you probably won't get too upset and might even take it as a good sign. But if your fashion-forward friend says the same thing, it can really hurt. The same criticism (or rejection) will hurt more or less, in other words, depending on who's delivering it.

It will also hurt more or less depending on a few other factors, including:

- How much you care about the thing being criticized.
- How hard you worked on it.

- Whether the criticism occurs publicly (for instance, in front of a class or on social media).
- If you're criticized at a time when you're also coping with other difficulties.

The content of a criticism will also (obviously) determine its hurtfulness. **The most hurtful criticisms are harsh, cruel, or shaming.** And the worst are personal attacks, such as, "Do you really believe those things you wrote in your essay?" or "What makes you think you can be a [fill in the blank]?" People sometimes say these kinds of harsh things in a caring or reasonable tone of voice, which can be confusing. But the pain is real.

Bigoted or biased criticisms and rejections are also hurtful—not to mention, violations of basic principles of social justice. (And also, if they cross the line into discrimination or harassment, illegal.) Bias can also lead to internalized oppression, which is when you believe the bigoted view, thus limiting your sense of yourself and your potential.

Callousness is another common offense. It's when someone criticizes or rejects you without making a reasonable effort to minimize the hurt. Along with the pain of the criticism itself, it sends the additional painful message that you don't merit ordinary consideration and respect. Form letter rejections, especially for opportunities you were personally encouraged to apply for or had to do a lot of work to apply for, are a common type of callousness.

Don't be fooled if a harsh or callous criticism comes labeled as "tough love" or "fun ribbing." It's still hurtful and irresponsible, especially if coming from either someone who says they care about you, or from a professor or other educational professional with a responsibility for your welfare.

Finally, we have **blindsiding**, which happens when we either don't expect a criticism or don't expect it to be as harsh as it is. Because your defenses are down, blindsiding can be very painful, and take a long time to heal. A common form of blindsiding is when someone whom you would expect to be on your side—like a parent, professor, lover, or friend—attacks or betrays you. But you can also blindside yourself by expecting a success that doesn't happen. (Recall Chapter 13's discussion about how expectations are always risky.) Even when all indications are that a project will succeed, always be prepared for the unexpected possibility.

As Luke Skywalker warned the evil Emperor Palpatine in *Return of the Jedi*, "Your overconfidence is your weakness."

How to Be One of the Good Ones

I hope this discussion will help you better understand and cope with any criticisms and rejections you may have received or might receive in the future. I also hope it inspires you to be a kind and competent critic. You achieve that by doing the opposite of everything I've been discussing—i.e., delivering your criticisms (and rejections) as kindly, fairly, privately, etc., as possible—and by not criticizing too much. Criticism is a very strong spice and in most cases just a pinch or two is fine—and only after getting the person's permission for such feedback. Also:

1. **Always follow through** when you offer to critique someone's work, and do so in a timely way. If you don't, it can be not just inconveniencing, but hurtful, to the person who trusted you. A corollary to this is: think carefully before agreeing to critique someone's work, especially if it is outside your specialty. I've gotten stuck a few times by agreeing to critique, only to realize later on that I didn't know enough to do so. The ensuing conversations were, to say the least, awkward. (An exception would be if they want your opinion as a non-specialist in their field.)

2. **Always find something good to say.** If you don't like the work itself, then find something to praise in the person's process (as discussed in Chapter 14) or approach.

3. **Be specific.** As Joni B. Cole writes in *Toxic Feedback*, "Writers...can handle specifics. It's the generalities that bring them to their knees. 'Your story didn't work for me.' 'I don't get it.' 'This isn't my thing.' Those...only serve to leave writers feeling more at a loss than usual."

4. **Be generous.** You don't have to write (or speak) pages, but going into detail about two or three points will be helpful, and also show you care.

5. **Ask the person what specific types of feedback they'd like.** Along with helping ensure your critique is useful, this also narrows the task so it's easier and quicker for you.

6. **Sandwich a criticism between two compliments.** It's kind of obvious, but still helps.

7. **Critique the project on its own terms** instead of comparing it to the project you would have done. This can be difficult—and if you

sense it's going to be too difficult, then you should decline the request to critique.

8. If your opinion is mostly negative, do your best to deliver it **either in person or via phone or videocall**. Email and text don't allow for much emotion and nuance.

Everyone should learn how to deliver compassionate and constructive criticism, especially if they desire to mentor or teach others. And it also goes without saying that you should be an effective receiver of constructive criticism. Don't get defensive or angry when someone is trying to help, especially if you asked for the help.

Exercise 18

1. Journal about some criticisms and rejections you've experienced, both in and out of school. See if you can link them to any procrastination, perfectionism, or blocks you might have experienced or may still be experiencing.

2. For each incident, list any elements of context (e.g., the critic's identity or the time or place of the incident) or content (e.g., harshness or callousness) that increased the hurtfulness. Hopefully, identifying these amplifying factors will help you to further process the event and defuse any lingering pain. If it's still painful, however, you might want to talk to a counselor.

Exercise 19

Can you think of any times when you criticized or rejected someone in a hurtful way? What could you have done differently and what will you do differently in the future? (It may not be too late to apologize and make amends.)

35. When Professors Screw Up

I think professors[39] are the bomb. (Okay, I'm a bit biased, being the partner of one.) Many are fascinating people who do interesting and important work, and also work hard to support their students. But it's also true that some professors aren't great at their job, just as some people in every field aren't great. Bad professors waste students' precious time and money, worse professors can kill your love for a subject, and the very worst can derail careers and even lives.

Professors are human and are thus capable of screwing up in all the ways listed in the last chapter. And they can also screw up by being...

- **Unprofessional**: unskilled, unknowledgeable, arbitrary, or unprepared.
- **Uncaring**: negligent, neglectful, unsupportive, or unresponsive.
- **Biased** against you and/or your ideas. We all have biases, but a professional educator has a special responsibility to not let theirs interfere with their job. This is not to say that all ideas are worth defending or discussing, however. A biology professor has a professional responsibility to refuse to discuss ignorant creationism or evil "race science" in their classes, except perhaps as cautionary tales.

---

[39] As per the Vocabulary Note, when I use the word "professor," in this chapter and elsewhere, I am referring to all teaching professionals.

- **Negative, fatalistic, or cynical**. A professor should be candid about their field's drawbacks, such as a lack of jobs, but shouldn't exaggerate them.
- **Arrogant, aggressive, condescending, or patronizing.**
- You should also watch out for professors who:
- **Prioritize their own needs** (e.g., for friendship or a fan) over their professional relationship with, and obligations to, you.
- **Play favorites.** (Bad for the favorite *and* the rest of the class.)
- **Exploit you** as free professional or personal labor. If you must take on an unpaid research assistantship or similar gig, make sure you're getting "paid" in quality mentoring.
- **Target you** sexually or otherwise.

If a professor is mistreating you, don't blame yourself. Instead, talk with your advisor (or a department head, counselor, or provost) immediately. This can be a difficult step, but as Leslie's story, below, shows, it can help you to reclaim your power. (Content warning: sexual harassment.)

Leslie, an ambitious and confident biochemistry major, was thrilled when she was offered a part-time laboratory assistant job with Dr. Patrician, a world-famous biochemist at her university. It was a great opportunity that would also look terrific on her graduate school applications. Her enthusiasm was somewhat diminished, however, when she told her news to a graduate teaching assistant for one of her classes. His reaction was, at best, mixed. "Congratulations," he said. "They don't take just anyone. But be careful. Some people have had problems working in that laboratory." When Leslie pressed him for specifics, he said, "I've heard they can be a little sexist." Then he added, about Dr. Patrician himself: "He's a genius, but not the easiest guy to work for."

The conversation was a downer, but Leslie never considered not taking the job. It was too great an opportunity—and besides, she saw herself as a strong person, capable of handling anything.

Her first few weeks on the job went great. Everyone was friendly and welcoming, and she quickly got up to speed on the procedures for washing and sterilizing glassware, organizing and restocking the supplies closet, preparing batches of simple reagents, and her other duties. People seemed appreciative of her efforts—and that included even the hard-to-please Dr.

Patrician. He always greeted her when they passed each other in the laboratory or hallway, and once even complimented her on her reliability and attention to detail. Leslie felt proud, but also relieved, because by then it was evident that the teaching assistant had been right: Dr. Patrician wasn't easy to work for. He was impatient and often harsh, and didn't refrain from criticizing people publicly. People tiptoed around him.

As for sexism, Leslie couldn't help but notice that nearly all of the laboratory's senior positions were filled by men, and that even the senior women were doing support work for those men, as opposed to running their own experiments. They were also doing a lot of emotional labor, including comforting people after Dr. Patrician yelled at them.

It all made for a weird and unpleasant work situation, but Leslie persevered. Soon, however, one of the senior researchers, Bill, started behaving in ways that made her uncomfortable. He would stand a bit too close to her during conversations, and sometimes touch her on the shoulder or arm. If she moved away—sending a clear signal she didn't want the physical contact, she thought—he would just move closer and continue with the touching. She spent a lot of time wondering whether this behavior was deliberate, but when he escalated to touching her on the back or waist whenever he walked past her in the laboratory, she no longer had any doubts. He always murmured an apology, as if the space between the benches was too narrow and he had no choice. But no one else needed to touch her like that.

And that wasn't all: at times, Leslie would look up from her work and see him creepily staring at her from across the laboratory. He always held her eye for a couple of moments, a slight smile on his face, before turning away.

Soon she was going out of her way to avoid Bill, and was also constantly on the alert lest he approach her. Not surprisingly, her work began to suffer. Once, distracted, she dropped a whole tray of glassware: the crash echoed throughout the entire laboratory, bringing all activity to a halt. It was mortifying. Another time, she screwed up ordering some chemicals—in part because she had been reluctant to check the order over with Bill—costing the laboratory money and delaying some research.

After these incidents, Dr. Patrician's attitude toward her changed. Now, when they passed each other in the laboratory or hallways, he just stared at her coldly.

Leslie started to wonder whether she was on the verge of being fired. That would be humiliating—not to mention, a blot on her record—so she resolved to "suck it up" and be more focused at work. Then Bill started asking invasive questions about her personal life, such as what she did on the weekends and what her relationship was to the woman who sometimes picked her up after work. Leslie jokingly told him to mind his own business, but he persisted.

She knew she had to talk to someone, and chose Rosemary, a senior scientist who had often presented herself as a mentor to Leslie and the other young women in the laboratory. Rosemary's reaction, when Leslie told her what was happening, was less than helpful, however. "Bill? Really?" she asked, in obvious disbelief. "I know he can be a bit touchy-feely, but he doesn't mean anything by it." And about the staring: "I don't understand...it's a problem that he's looking at you?" And the invasive questions: "People talk about their weekends and social lives all the time."

Rosemary obviously saw Leslie, and not Bill, as the problem. Frustrated, Leslie just stood there and stared at her. After a few awkward moments, Rosemary said she'd talk to Bill.

That night, Leslie called her parents and told them what was happening. They were outraged and told her to quit immediately. But Leslie balked at the idea of quitting without notice, which she felt would be unprofessional. She decided to give the standard two weeks' notice.

It was a decision she would soon regret.

When she returned to the laboratory the next afternoon, it was clear that Rosemary had spoken to Bill, who was now keeping his distance from her. That was great, but the laboratory itself now felt full of bad associations. She hated every moment of being there—and was it her imagination or were others besides Bill also now avoiding her?

She gritted her teeth and focused on getting through the next two weeks.

Then, late on the Friday afternoon after she had spoken with Rosemary, Dr. Patrician called her into his office and berated her for, "making accusations against my people." Clearly, Rosemary had told him about their supposedly confidential conversation. He then went on to attack what he called her, "bad attitude," "poor attention to detail," "lack of teamwork," and other deficiencies. Caught off guard, Leslie didn't even try to defend herself, but just stood there, apologizing.

Dr. Patrician ended the conversation with an abrupt, "Your services are no longer needed." In a daze—and conscious of everyone's eyes on her—

Leslie returned to her bench to pick up her coat and backpack. Then she left, never to return.

Over the next week, she was assailed by doubts. Had she somehow misconstrued Bill's actions? Or overreacted to minor offenses? Should she have handled the conversation with Rosemary differently? She debated these and other questions endlessly with herself, to the point where she couldn't concentrate on her schoolwork or anything else. She also suffered from headaches and insomnia, and spent her days in an exhausted and demoralized fog.

Her parents, girlfriend, and friends all assured her that, not only had she not screwed up, she had done as well as anyone could have hoped to, given the toxic environment. They also urged her to talk to her advisor or a school counselor, but she resisted doing so, partly because she was afraid that that would trigger a mandatory sexual harassment (Title IX) investigation she wasn't sure she'd be able to handle.

A couple of weeks later, however, she knew she had to talk to someone. She was still distracted and unhappy, and her schoolwork was continuing to suffer. She realized that, if she didn't do something, she was in danger of compromising everything she had worked so hard for. And so, she made an appointment with her advisor.

Sitting in his office, a few days later, Leslie felt a turmoil of shame and anger and confusion as she told her story. But her advisor didn't seem confused at all. As he listened to her, his easy-going expression turned serious. "I'm really sorry that that happened to you," he said, after she had finished. "It was completely unacceptable." Hearing those unambiguous words of support from an official college representative, Leslie felt a huge relief. He believed her! She wasn't overreacting! They discussed the incident some more and then her advisor reminded her that he was mandated to report the harassment to the school's Title IX Coordinator, who was in charge of setting and enforcing campus policies against harassment and discrimination. "She'll call you to set up a meeting to discuss your options," he said, adding: "Whatever you decide, I'll support you."

That night, Leslie felt better than she had in weeks, and was also able to better focus on her schoolwork. Seeing these positive changes, her girlfriend noted, "You're taking your power back."

During their meeting, later that week, the Title IX Coordinator told Leslie that she would assist her in submitting a "complaint," meaning a document outlining the events in question. After that, the school would start a formal grievance process that would include an investigation into what had happened, followed by a statement of the investigator's findings. That statement would then be submitted to an Adjudication Committee, which would make the final determination on whether a Title IX violation had occurred and also decide which penalties, if any, to impose.[40]

Leslie welcomed the grievance process, but had two worries. The first was that Bill, Rosemary, and Patrician would likely defend themselves by attacking her work and character, which wouldn't be pleasant. The Title IX Coordinator assured her that, while their statements were likely to be critical of her, the experience typically wasn't as bad as people anticipated, and the investigator would also be sure to disregard any inappropriate statements they might make.

Leslie's other big worry was the possibility of getting a reputation as a troublemaker that could hurt her chances of getting into graduate school. (The Title IX Coordinator told her she would be identified only as "complainant" on the public documents, but she knew that, sooner or later, her identity would get out.) Her advisor assured her, however, that such repercussions were unlikely. "People outside the campus probably won't know it's you," he said. "Besides, your academic record is strong and you'll have great references from me and others, and those are what really count."

The whole process took several months, and yes: Bill, Rosemary, and Patrician did attempt to defend themselves by attacking Leslie. At times it was hard, but Leslie, with the full support of her loved ones and advisor, hung in there. When the Adjudication Committee announced its decisions that (a) Bill had violated her Title IX rights, (b) Rosemary and Patrician had violated school policy by not reporting the possible violation, and (c) Patrician had engaged in illegal "retaliatory behavior" when he fired Leslie, it was a moment of triumph. Perhaps because of Dr. Patrician's institutional status and power, however, the announced penalties were disappointingly small. Bill was put on probation for five years, with a warning that any additional episodes of harassment could lead to his firing. (That "could," especially, rankled Leslie.) Rosemary and Dr. Patrician were given no penalties at all, just warnings. And the entire laboratory was mandated to take Title IX training.

The Title IX statute mandates general procedures for dealing with sexual harassment and related complaints, but the specific processes, penalties, etc., can (within the bounds of the law) differ from school to school. Had an actual crime, like sexual assault, been committed, Leslie would have had the option of filing a criminal charge with the police.

The investigation was written up in the local press and even in the science press, which pleased Leslie. As she had predicted, even though her name hadn't appeared in those accounts, some people in the biochemistry department guessed that she was the student involved. Several approached her and expressed their support and appreciation for her having taken action, a positive response she hadn't anticipated. Even better, a student from another department wrote to her saying that, because of her brave example, she herself was filing a Title IX complaint against one of her own professors.

These were all good outcomes. But for the rest of her time at college, Leslie avoided going into the building that housed Dr. Patrician's laboratory. This meant she missed some seminars and other events that could have been useful to her. And the few times she happened to see Bill, Rosemary, or Dr. Patrician out on campus, it was scary. At the Title IX Coordinator's suggestion, she got some counseling, which helped.

Happily, however, Leslie's advisor had been right: the grievance process did not prevent her from getting into a good graduate school. As her career progressed, she made two strong pledges to herself: (1) to never again work in a known toxic work environment, or with a known toxic person, no matter how great the opportunity seemed; and (2) to always do her best to believe and support anyone who came to her for help with harassment or other workplace problems.

Leslie's story reminds us of the importance of always seeking out those who hold themselves to a high standard not just in terms of their work, but how they treat others. Make the same decision she did—to never work for cruel people, harassers, or exploiters—and you'll not only save yourself lots of pain, but find more pleasure, ease, and success in both your work and personal life.

Exercise 20

Think of some difficult interactions you've had with professors. Did they behave in any of the ways described in this chapter? If so, did you recognize the problem at the time? Did you blame yourself, or feel guilty, for problems you didn't cause or weren't responsible for? If the answer to any of these questions is "yes," then journal about the situation to understand it better and hopefully neutralize any remaining guilt or shame. If necessary, discuss what happened with a friend or counselor.

36. When Students Screw Up

While some professors go around saying stuff like, "some people can't do math," or "creative writing can't be taught: you've either got talent or you haven't," I strongly believe that, if a student is really trying, then any learning failures are the professor's or institution's responsibility. First, because those kinds of sentiments are flat-out wrong. (It's well known that U.S. K-12 mathematics education is dismal[41] and students shouldn't be blamed for that; also, as I discussed in Chapter 16, abstractions like "talent" are meaningless.) But also because helping students identify and overcome their barriers to learning happens to be one of the core responsibilities of professors and other university staff. Even in the relatively uncommon cases where a student is not up to doing the work, it's those professionals' job to identify the problem early and help the student to find an alternative course or major that's a better fit.

Note, however, that, "if a student is really trying." Students also have responsibilities, including:

- Doing your work.
- Using effective study habits (see Chapter 8).
- Working to overcome, as much as possible, internal barriers including procrastination, perfectionism, and poor time management.
- Asking for help early and often, as discussed in Chapter 10.

---

[41] As documented in Amanda Ripley's book, *The Smartest Kids in the World: And How They Got That Way*.

- Showing up early for meetings. (The paradox of time management is that you can either be early or late, but never exactly on time. So be early.)
- If you must cancel a meeting, not doing so at the last minute.
- Responding promptly to professors' communications.
- Reaching out when there's a problem. Unfortunately, that's the opposite of what many students do, which is to hide. That's an understandable reaction, but again: isolation and invisibility aren't your friends.
- Not being perfectionist! For instance, not harping on the one thing your professor isn't great at, while ignoring all the other things they do well.

It's a short list and very reasonable, yet many students don't do one or more of those things. Students can also be pretty callous: for instance, by not paying attention during lectures or acting bored or sullen during office meetings.

I get that college is a busy and stressful time. But try not to take your frustrations out on others, especially if they are trying to help.

Exercise 21

Think back on incidents where you might have mistreated a professor. What happened and why? What might have been a better way to behave and what steps can you take in the future to ensure you do better? (If this exercise is making you feel bad—don't! As discussed in Chapter 22, regret is useless. Learn from the experience, apologize and make amends if appropriate, then move on.)

37. How to Cope

The goal, as stated in Chapter 34, is resilience—and you already know much of what you need to achieve that because 90% of resilience is nonperfectionism. Perfectionists are like burn victims: sensitive to the slightest "touch." That's partly because they're already suffering under a barrage of constant self-criticism, which the external criticism only reinforces, and partly because their overidentification, pathologizing, distrust of success, and other perfectionist characteristics make them vulnerable.

So, to be more resilient, work on overcoming your perfectionism.

Here are some other tips:

Share with care. While you want input from many sources, there is zero benefit to getting it from someone informationally, temperamentally, or otherwise unqualified to give it. So, share your work, thoughts, feelings, ideas, personal struggles, etc., only with those capable of offering a wise and compassionate response. This also applies to your family, by the way: they don't get a free pass to criticize you harshly, neglect you, marginalize you, etc. (More on coping with family in the next two chapters.)

Take the long view. Just as most failures turn out to be unimportant (Chapter 22), so, too, do most criticisms and rejections. Therefore, remind yourself when you're hurting that "this too shall pass."

Work to positively reframe your rejections. Here's a fun example from writer Chris Offutt:

The notion of submitting anything to a magazine filled me with terror. A stranger would read my precious words, judge them deficient, and reject them, which meant I was worthless. My goal, however, was not publication, which was still too scary a thought. My goal was a hundred rejections in a year.

I mailed my stories in multiple submissions and waited eagerly for their return, which they promptly did. Each rejection brought me that much closer to my goal—a cause for celebration, rather than depression. Eventually disaster struck. *The Coe Review* published my first story in spring 1990.[42]

Notice how empowering the positive reframing is, especially when combined with Offutt's playful approach. (Also, notice the overfocus on outcomes, overidentification, and other perfectionist characteristics that probably contributed to his being so scared of rejection to start with.)

Prioritize healing/cope lavishly. When you do experience a painful criticism or rejection, resist the temptation to minimize it or ignore your hurt. (In other words, ignore those who tell you to, "Get over it.") If you need to have a crying jag or a sulk—or a few—do that. At the same time, however...

Don't isolate yourself. Sure, hide out for a while if you want. But after that, discuss the situation with a trusted friend, advisor, or counselor.

Speak truth to power, judiciously. Speaking truth to power can be a healing and empowering act that can also lead to changes that prevent others from being harmed the way you were. There's always a risk, however, that the person you're speaking to will respond negatively. So think carefully before doing it, perhaps asking yourself whether the offender is a good person who made a mistake or someone who is often harsh or callous. The former may be worth having a discussion with, while the latter may not be. (This is yet another area where it's best to err on the side of caution.) All of which brings us to the most important coping strategy of all...

Minimize the stuff you need to cope with. You do this by avoiding classes, projects, personal relationships, and other prolonged interactions with known harsh people, exploiters, and other problematic types. (Personally, I

---

[42] Chris Offutt, "The Eleventh Draft." In Frank Conroy (ed.), *The Eleventh Draft.*

do my best to avoid even brief interactions with these kinds of people, as some can do an amazing amount of harm in a short time.) This rule is usually easy to follow, until it isn't. Sooner or later, you'll probably be tempted by, for instance:

- A research gig with a famous professor with great connections, but also a reputation for harshness.
- A job at a prestigious company known for burning out its employees.
- A romantic relationship with someone who is sexy and glamorous, but also mean and self-centered. Or,
- Some other opportunity that sets off your warning bells.

Just. Say. No. Relationships with toxic people and organizations rarely work out the way we hope, and frequently leave us worse off.

38. About Your Family I. Empathy is Empowering

Note: This chapter and the next are about how to handle situations where your values or choices conflict with those of your parents or other family members. They're not about how to handle racism, homophobia, transphobia, or other bigotry directed at you personally. Although there can be some overlap between the two types of problems, the latter is a much more serious one that is beyond this book's scope. If you are subject to bias from your family or anyone else, I urge you to get support from friends, a counselor, and/or organizations that specialize in helping your community.

For many years, I taught productivity and entrepreneurship classes at non-profit organizations around Boston, a town that's filled with cool and caring people, including many artists, activists, academics, and organizers. After a while, I couldn't help noticing a pattern: many of my cool friends and students would visit their families for the holidays, then return depressed and exhausted. When I asked what was wrong, the inevitable reply was that there had been lots of political and other conflicts between them and their more-conventional family members.

No doubt about it: it can be tough even for like-minded family members to get along. Add some social, ethical, political, or class differences to the mix, however, and things can get way more complicated and intense.

Unfortunately, the advantage, in these types of conflicts, tends to be with the more conventional family members, both because theirs is the majority opinion and also because they have the power of the status quo behind them—so that, for instance, the morning headlines are more likely to support their views.

There can also be conflict when you return home with different vocabularies, values, ideas, and friends from those you grew up with. "Oh, so now you think you're better than us?" and "Oh, so now you think you know everything?" are questions many students in this situation hear from their parents or others. (I heard them too.) Anthony Abraham Jack, whom I quoted in Chapter 10 on the importance of interacting with faculty and administrators, says first-generation students often have to do "a lot of translational work" for their families, and also that, "Sometimes you have to forgive family for maybe feeling a little resentment that you are doing the exact thing that they are most proud of and wanted you to do in the first place."[43]

No wonder so many of my friends and students came back from their trips home exhausted or worse.

And things have only worsened in recent years. The world's on fire, both literally and figuratively, and many of our relatives have fallen into the abyss of authoritarianism.[44] Even many families that weren't previously in conflict now are—and the conflicts seem more ingrained and intractable than ever. Below and in the next chapter, I offer some ways of coping; first, however, let's look at some of the intolerant things our relatives and others can say or do. **Mockery** is prevalent, for instance:

- "Here he goes again..." or an eye-roll, when you point out an injustice.

- "We can't all be a saint like you," when you suggest a behavioral change. A tricky type of comment in which an insincere compliment ("saint") is used passive-aggressively to dismiss your valid concerns.

- "She always takes things so seriously." This was said mockingly about *me* a few years back, after I mentioned, during an event that was held on Columbus Day but wasn't about Columbus, that he had

---

[43] www.gse.harvard.edu/news/uk/19/04/real-advice-first-gens
[44] Like Jen Senko's father: www.thebrainwashingofmydad.com.

committed genocide and shouldn't be honored. (I think my relative was embarrassed that I had brought up the topic.)

Later on, in your creative or helping or social justice career, you can be subject to these kinds of put-downs:

- "When are you going to settle down and get a real job?"
- "Aren't you embarrassed to be driving around in that old car?"
- "I don't know why you'd want to do something so depressing." (This was said to a friend of mine by one of her siblings, about her work helping refugees. And by the way, her work was amazing.)

In college and beyond, **condescension**—e.g., "You'll grow out of it."—is prevalent, since conservatives have always sought to reframe progressives' caring and concern as naive and childish. Ditto for accusations of oversensitivity, as in: "Snowflake!" "Bleeding heart!" "Tree-hugger!" etc. Don't fall for any of it! Your caring and concern are wonderful qualities.

Accusations of hypocrisy are another common "gotcha," since none of us can lead a 100% ethical life. Matt Bors skewered this one in his famous "Mr. Gotcha" cartoon.[45]

Marginalization can likewise be a problem. It's when your values, concerns, or achievements are trivialized, dismissed, treated as an afterthought, or ignored. It's often done passive-aggressively—meaning, your relatives wound you by *not* acting or speaking—which makes it even harder to identify and deal with. Some examples are when your family:

- Doesn't take your needs or values into account. For instance, when an atheist's family tries to pressure them into attending a religious ceremony or a vegan's family tries to pressure them into eating non-vegan food.
- Refuses to consider easy alternatives to objectionable practices. For instance, when your family insists on shopping at a store, or dining at a restaurant, with bad labor practices or political affiliations.

---

[45] www.thenib.com/mister-gotcha/

- Says nothing/asks nothing/does nothing about an important project you're working on or about a recent success or failure you experienced.

Make no mistake: the above behaviors can hurt, especially when coming from people you love, and especially if they happen repeatedly.[46] In situations like these, you're often caught between either sticking up for yourself and your values (and being seen as an irritant or source of conflict) or staying quiet and not advocating for yourself. The phrase "caught between" indicates your disempowerment and lack of good options.

Meanwhile, if you do speak up, you're at risk for getting DARVO'd. DARVO is a useful acronym coined by psychologist Jennifer J. Freyd to describe a common response to accusations of abuse: the abuser Denies, Attacks, and Reverses Victim and Offender.[47] An example would be when you get upset because a family member is being hurtful and they turn it around and say you're the unreasonable one.

I experienced many of the above situations—and occasionally still do. They're hard to deal with! But I offer one solution below and others in Chapter 39.

To Be Understood, First Seek to Understand

I never reached any kind of resolution with my parents, who are now both deceased. But I'm happy to say that my sisters and I stuck with it, worked it out, and now get along pretty well. My first piece of advice if you're struggling with your family, therefore, is to keep trying. People can, and frequently do, surprise us. (And we sometimes surprise ourselves.) This assumes that: (a) your relatives aren't toxic, and (b) both you and they are committed to the sometimes-difficult work of listening, sharing, and self-examination.

Even if everyone is on board and well-meaning, however, these types of situations can be complicated. It can be hard when those around us seem to not care about others' suffering or catastrophes like environmental collapse. Or when they say they care about those things but aren't willing to

---

[46] Research by psychologist Naomi I. Eisenberg and colleagues found that rejection and other forms of "social pain" activate the same brain areas as physical pain. See: https://ncbi.nlm.nih.gov/pmc/articles/PMC3273616/.

[47] www.dynamic.uoregon.edu/jjf/defineDARVO.html

take even small steps to mitigate harm. You may even be right that their failure to act constitutes a moral failing. But don't be so quick to judge. We all have our strengths and weaknesses, including morally.

Never forget that capitalism excels at distracting people, lulling them,[48] exhausting them (e.g., by forcing them to work long hours at difficult jobs for little pay), frightening them (e.g., with scarcity or an invented external threat), and limiting their view of themselves and their options (so that, for instance, they see their civic responsibilities as limited to voting).[49] Also, don't forget that the oligarchical capitalism we're all suffering under right now tends to extol and promote the worst behaviors, including greed, selfishness, technocratic paternalism, and coming up with fake solutions to serious problems (like privatization or the self-interested "philanthropy" many oligarchs engage in).[50]

Beyond all that, your relatives might not like talking about politics. Or, they might feel guilt or regret about some of their choices and have a sense that the topics you raise are going to make them feel worse. When people sense that their actions don't match their beliefs, they often experience cognitive dissonance, an uncomfortable feeling that can cause them to lash out.

Always strive for empathy and understanding. A wise friend reminded me, while I was writing this chapter, that people's worst behaviors often develop, "as the residue of strategies that empowered their survival," and also that, "not everyone has the luxury of interrogating their own experience." This is not to excuse someone's bad behavior. But it can be a survival strategy for *you* to understand where that behavior is coming from. With that in mind, I did an Empathy Exercise in which I wrote a narrative about my parents, with whom I had many conflicts, trying to see them through the lens of their own experience. Here's what I came up with:

> Despite all our fighting, my parents and I had a lot in common. They were both pro-union, my father was very creative, and my mother loved animals and the environment. In different circumstances, he could have been an artist, she an environmental or animal activist. But they both grew up the children of struggling and

---

[48] Like K.C. Green's famous "This is Fine" cartoon dog: see knowyourmeme.com/memes/this-is-fine.

[49] Edward Herman and Noam Chomsky called the media's role in promoting an unjust status quo, "manufacturing consent." Here's a great explanation of the concept: https://youtu.be/34LGPIXvU5M.

[50] See Anand Giridharadas's book, *Winners Take All.*

not-entirely-acculturated immigrant parents during the 1930s Great Depression—a situation that would have constrained anyone's opportunities and sense of self. Both started working right out of high school, with no opportunity to attend college. And they kept working for decades, often at jobs they didn't like.

My parents also lived through decades of war and lost extended family in the Holocaust. [My family is Jewish.] They endured vicious anti-Semitism in the United States, much more pernicious sexism than we have now, and some nasty 1950s-era reactionary politics. (When my father wanted to take classes at New York City's The New School, where many leftists taught, his Post Office colleagues warned him that doing so could jeopardize his career.) They also suffered many personal and familial losses and traumas, including the death from cancer of my father's younger brother, Harry, when he was just sixteen.

Given everything they lived through, it's perhaps not surprising that both of my parents struggled with anger, addiction, low self-esteem, and other problems. Throughout most of their lives, solutions such as therapy, trauma work, addiction recovery, and self-care were far more limited and rudimentary than they are now. (Not that they were likely to have encountered them or think of them as something they could use.)

After doing this exercise, I felt more understanding of, and empathy for, my late parents. You can do it, too—hopefully for loved ones who are still around, and with whom you have a chance of relationship repair (see Exercise 22). Empathy is very empowering, giving both you and the person you're empathizing with additional options and potential outcomes.

The Empathy Exercise can help you deal with loved ones who are politically, culturally, or otherwise more conservative than you are. You can even use it to try to better understand and relate to those who have fallen into terrible white supremacist or other antisocial views. As Ian Danskin discusses in his animated film, *The Alt-Right Playbook: How to Radicalize a Normie*,[51] many white supremacists start out as lonely, depressed, traumatized, or alienated men (and some women) who get sucked into racist groups through social media algorithms that send someone searching for "cures for depression," for example, to an alt-right gateway video or site. From there,

---

[51] http://www.youtube.com/watch?v=4xGawJIseNY

it's only a few short steps to joining a racist group where they get psychologically groomed, primed, pressured, bullied, and otherwise coerced into staying.

So, there's plenty to feel compassion for. You may even wish to go farther and do the work of trying to persuade your relative to give up their hateful views. That's admirable, but proceed with caution, because while their racism may have begun as the "residue of strategies that empowered their survival," after years of consuming racist media and hanging out with other racists, it may be entrenched. "Deprogramming" a racist is often a big job akin to cult deprogramming.[52] Danskin advises:

> I want to state plainly that Gabe [his film's fictional main character, who becomes a white supremacist] went off the deep end because he found a community willing to tell him that, because he is a cishet white man, the world revolves around him. Do not treat him like this is true. If a fraction of the energy spent having debates with America's Gabes were spent instead on voter re-enfranchisement, prisoners' rights, protection for immigrants, statehood for DC, and redistricting, Gabe's opinions, in the societal sense, wouldn't matter.
>
> If you think you can get through to him, it is worthwhile to try. But [anti-fascism] is a fight with many fronts, and deradicalization is only one of them. It sends an awful message when we spend more time trying to get bigots back on our side than we do on the people they are bigoted against.

Even if you decide you don't want to take on such a "deprogramming" project, doing the Empathy Exercise will help you in your attempts to deal with the Gabes in your life. And in the happy event that they one day start to rethink their choices, your increased empathy will have left the door open for discussion.

Exercise 22

Interview your parents (or other family members) about their lives, paying special attention to the time and place they grew up, the challenges they faced, and the choices and opportunities they had or didn't have. Do this as

---

[52] www.lifeafterhate.org may be able to help.

if you were a journalist or biographer without a personal stake in the information, and be as impartial and nonjudgmental as you can. Proceed chronologically, starting with their childhoods—or even earlier, with their parents' lives—and when you're done, write a narrative similar to the one I wrote about my own parents.

Some notes on the exercise:

1. Many people love the opportunity to tell their stories to an empathetic listener. But some don't. This could be for many reasons, including trauma. Never pressure someone to talk about life experiences they don't want to talk about. If your loved one doesn't want to talk at all, you can piece together your narrative from what you already know—as I did with my parents—and still achieve your goal of increasing your understanding and empathy.

2. It sometimes works better to ask your questions over a period of time, instead of trying to do a formal sit-down interview.

3. In your narrative, and at other times, don't compare the person to others who lived through similar or worse circumstances and made what you consider better choices. Such comparisons are perfectionist and judgmental.

4. I suggest you keep your narrative private because sharing it will put pressure on you and possibly influence the way you write it. If you want to write a separate document for others, that's fine.

39. About Your Family II: Time is on Your Side

Here are some additional techniques you can use to repair and improve relationships with loved ones:

Look at How Your Own Behavior Might be Contributing to any Conflicts

You do this not just because it's the responsible thing to do, and not as a way of excusing the other person's bad behavior, but because, in the end, our own behavior is the only thing we have any control over. Besides, it's true that when we change ourselves, others sometimes change in response.

Anger is a tricky subject. There are some who feel it's never productive, but it can be difficult to set it aside when you or others are being oppressed. C. Daniel Batson and colleagues have written about how, "moral outrage—anger at the violation of a moral standard—should be distinguished from personal anger at being harmed and empathetic anger at seeing another for whom one cares harmed."[53] And David Pilgrim, curator of the Jim Crow Museum, advises:

> There will, undoubtedly, be times when you are justly angered. How can anyone look at the infant mortality rates of poor people in the United States and not get angry? That is justified, righteous

---

[53] www.Onlinelibrary.wiley.com/doi/pdf/10.1002/ejsp.434

anger—and so is the anger directed against the patterns of sexual assault in this country. Direct your anger against systems and patterns of injustice, not against individuals. That is hard, I know. Whenever possible, try to replace anger with focused passion and a zeal to address the injustice. And, finally, as much as is possible within you, avoid the anger that simmers, paralyzes, and morphs into hatred.[54]

The reference to paralysis in the last sentence reminds us that anger can be disempowering. Anger that you don't take positive action on can fester, which doesn't do you or your cause any good. Look, for instance, at the many people whose "activism" consists of ineffectual raging on social media. No, I'm not saying that social media is a waste of time. But the ultimate test of whether your activism is working is whether you're influencing people to change their attitudes and behaviors. Many social media ragers aren't.

Keep in mind that your reactions can feed the behavior you're objecting to. Psychologists tell us that any response to an unwanted behavior, including a negative one, can reinforce that behavior. But a total lack of response can cause the behavior to fade away, a phenomenon called behavioral extinction. The trick is that you can't respond at all, not even with the teeniest eye-roll or annoyed sigh. Try that, and even if the behavior doesn't fade away, you'll still be training yourself to be less reactive.

Choose Your Battles

This is a good place to address the complaints that some of my older manuscript readers had about this chapter and some other parts of this book: complaints that can be best summed up as, "But young people today are so fragile and coddled! They grew up getting participation trophies, so if they don't get constant rewards, they feel mistreated! And all your talk of compassion, self-acceptance, etc., just encourages all that!"

Whew! Leaving aside the points that: (a) bashing the young is history's oldest and most boring hobby, (b) elders should be understanding of youth and its occasional foibles, and (c) today's elders should be especially understanding, given the mess they're leaving behind—yes, of course, members of your generation can be entitled or over-reactive. (Just as members of your critics' generations can be.) So choose your battles. Maybe Great Aunt

---

[54] www.ferris.edu/htmls/news/jimcrow/question/2009/june.htm

Grumpypants's ignorant political jabs aren't worth getting steamed up about. (Although if you interview her for Exercise 22, she might be thrilled, the result will likely be revelatory, and it could transform your relationship.)

Plan Ahead/Set Boundaries

If your family is likely to fight about politics, suggest that some topics be off-limits during the holiday dinner. (Or your whole visit.) If your family isn't going to accommodate your veganism, then bring your own food. (They'll probably object to that, too—but hey, they had their chance.)

If you know that a racist or otherwise problematic relative is going to ruin an upcoming holiday meal, then maybe you could skip that meal, or sit at the other end of the table, or just show up for dessert. Or, maybe you and some other family members could have a discussion with the racist person ahead of time and get them to agree to keep their noxious opinions to themselves. Or, if they won't do that, maybe you can convince your family to not invite them to this or future events. Note how you're creating better options for yourself, as per Chapter 4, and also how, even though the options aren't "perfect," they're still better than procrastinating.

Make Sure You're Comfortable with Your Own Values and Choices

Remember Chapter 24's point about how we're often ambivalent because we share the other person's view? Work to gain clarity on your own values and choices, and the skeptics shouldn't bother you so much.

Create Your Own "Family"

In school and later on, create your own "family" of loving people who share your values and can provide the kinds of support your family of origin can't. You can find these people online but it's best to also have a supportive community in real life.

If Persuasion Is a Goal, Then Learn How to Do It

Persuasion is a skill: you can't wing it. (Hint: it's not about nagging, hassling, harassing, judging, shaming, nitpicking, or name-calling.) Chapter A2 lists useful books for those wanting to do activism or community organizing, although those are just a starting point, as it's best to learn these skills hands-on from experienced organizers. And if your college offers a course in negotiation or sales, consider taking it. You'll most likely find it in the business or communications department and, regardless of your major or future plans, it could well wind up being one of the more valuable courses you take.

Keep in mind, however, that, regardless of your skills, your family may not be the best target for such work. In my book *The Lifelong Activist*, I wrote about how often, "your ideas are held in lower regard by the people who watched you grow up, and who in some cases diapered you, than by the general population." Save your efforts at persuasion, in other words, for those most likely to be convinced, whether or not they happen to be related to you.

Also remember that how we say something is at least as important as what we say, and that happiness and pride in your choices can be more persuasive than logical appeals. (And I have two words for you vegans out there: fabulous desserts.) And finally...

Await Your Eventual Vindication

Some of the difficulties you're experiencing are intrinsic to being a caring person and a visionary, both of which are great things to be. Later on, hopefully, you'll experience the pleasure of having the mainstream catch up with you. (I'm happy to report that, less than a decade after my Columbus Day episode, that holiday is well on its way to being replaced by Indigenous Peoples' Day.) Time, in other words, is on your side.

If your relatives are gracious, you may even experience the pleasure of them admitting that you were right all along. You might even wind up being some young person's "cool" parent, aunt, uncle, friend, mentor, teacher, or boss, which is one of the best gigs around.

Exercise 23

Before your next call or visit home, journal about any anticipated problems or conflicts, then make a plan for minimizing them. Your plan could include using Cooperative Problem Solving (Chapter 10) to set some ground rules, scheduling more "alone time" and self-care, and/or shortening your visit.

40. How to Stay Safe and Healthy on Social Media

Although the various social media platforms are amazing, game-changing, society-evolving technologies, they are also cauldrons of abuse and dysfunction where you'll find every perfectionist characteristic discussed in Part II, and every form of criticism and rejection discussed in this section, in abundance. Perfectionism may, in fact, be a big reason why psychologists have linked social media use to depression, anxiety, and sometimes suicide in teenagers and young adults.[55]

Of course, you'll also find rampant sexism, racism, religious bias, homophobia, transphobia, ableism, classism, and nativism online.

Then there's the whole set of other problems intrinsic to social media, including reductiveness (from the often terse communications); a lack of

---

[55] See, for example: www.nytimes.com/2017/10/11/magazine/why-are-more-american-teenagers-than-ever-suffering-from-severe-anxiety.html, www.ny-times.com/2019/02/20/health/teenage-depression-statistics.html, www.cbsnews.com/news/a-lost-girls-diary-alexandra-valoras/, and www.theatlantic.com/magazine/archive/2015/12/THE-SILICON-VALLEY-SUICIDES/413140. If you're in the U.S. and are having suicidal thoughts, please call or text 988. And here are two lists of global anti-suicide resources: www.befrienders.org/find-support-now/the-sa-maritans-of-new-york-city-2/page/2, www.lifeline-international.com/our-network/, and www.blog.opencounseling.com/suicide-hotlines/. And here is a long list of resources for mental health issues: www.reddit.com/r/CasualConversation/wiki/resources/#wiki_cri-sis_hotlines_by_country

body language, vocal tone, and other cues; a lack of privacy; a lack of boundaries (so that your family and boss can read stuff you'd normally just show your friends); and the pressure to post frequently. Plus, all the usual writing and editorial quandaries. As renowned blogger Jason Kottke put it:

> Doing https://kottke.org/ is this constant battle with myself: staying in my comfort zone vs. finding opportunities for growth, posting what I like or find interesting vs. attempting to suss out what "the reader" might want, celebrating the popular vs. highlighting the obscure, balancing the desire to define what it is I do here vs. appreciating that no one really knows (myself included), posting clickable things vs. important things I know will be unpopular, protecting myself against criticism vs. accepting it as a gift, deciding when to provoke & challenge vs. when to comfort & entertain, feeling like this is frivolous vs. knowing this site is important to me & others, being right vs. accepting I'll make mistakes, and saying something vs. letting the content and its creators speak for themselves.[56]

Kottke has been blogging for more than twenty years: if he still finds it challenging, I guess we can all be forgiven for feeling the same way. In any case, you probably do want and need to be on social media, to some degree. As discussed in Chapter A1, proficiency on at least one platform is a requirement for many jobs. Also, we—meaning society—need you to be on social media, to the extent you're comfortable being there. We need as many voices as possible and yours is especially important if you're a member of a marginalized or otherwise oppressed group. With all that in mind, here are some steps you can take to stay safe and healthy on social media, and even have some fun:

Use It Judiciously and Critically

Limit your use of social media (it helps to develop some offline interests) and get savvy about how advertising and celebrity culture use it to sell images of bogus perfection. (Maybe take a media studies course.)

---

[56] www.kottke.org/20/07/a-moment-of-reflection-on-the-paradox-of-individual-creative-work

Prioritize safety. Don't pressure yourself to participate more than you'd like or in ways you don't like, and don't let anyone else pressure you either.

Work on your nonperfectionism. Remember: it's the foundation of resilience (Chapter 37).

Be strategic. Figure out your goals for participation and tailor your online presence accordingly. If your primary goal is to communicate with family and friends, for instance, tighten up your privacy settings. If it's to advance your career, keep things professional. If it's to promote a political viewpoint, you might want to engage more broadly—but still, not with everyone.

Consider having two accounts. A private one just for close friends and a public one for everyone else.

Find role models whose online success you'd like to emulate. Look for those who are relatable—i.e., non-celebrities—and two to ten years further along the path than you.

Block the troublemakers. If someone is causing you stress or pain, block them, even if they happen to be related to you. Do it sooner rather than later.

Don't feed the trolls. If someone is playing devil's advocate, sealioning, being a "reply guy," or otherwise posting in bad faith, don't feel obligated to respond.[57] You don't owe them your time and attention. (Politician Alexandria Ocasio-Cortez compared one right-winger's incessant demands that she debate him to street harassment.[58]) Ignore them and they'll probably get bored and go away.

Trust your gut. If you're not mostly enjoying your time on social media, something's wrong.

---

[57] Citations for this sentence: www.reddit.com/r/Feminism/comments/dry3dn/let_me_play_devils_advocate/ (devil's advocate), https://en.wikipedia.org/wiki/Sealioning (sealioning), mashable.com/article/twitter-reply-guys (reply guy),.https://meta.wikimedia.org/wiki/What_is_a_troll bad faith).

[58] www.twitter.com/aoc/status/1027729430137827328

If you're being harassed, stalked, or threatened get help immediately. Keep records of all incidents, including not just a timeline, but printouts of messages, texts, posts, etc. Useful resources include: www.cyberbullying.org/resources/, www.1800victims.org/crime-type/cybercrimes/, and www.gameshotline.org (for harassment on gaming platforms or in gaming communities). Also, consult your college's campus safety department, department of student life, and Title IX Office.

For Those Posting Political Content

A few more steps for those posting political or otherwise controversial content:

Know what you're doing. Persuasion, as noted in the previous chapter, is a skill.

Expect pushback. Remember that your goal is to (choose one or all): shake up the status quo, speak truth to power (or take that power down), "Comfort the afflicted and afflict the comfortable," in the words of journalist Finley Peter Dunne, and "Go where you are least wanted, because that is where you are most needed," as per abolitionist Abigail Kelley Foster. You can't do those things without making some people mad, so be prepared for pushback and learn to see it as a sign you're having an impact.

Remember your "silent audience." Even if some people respond obnoxiously to your posts, there are probably others who quietly appreciate them. Speaking of which...

Support others. If you see someone being picked on online, support them with a public comment or private message.

Educate yourself on your online rights and use technologies appropriate to your values and situation. These sites will help: www.eff.org/pages/tools/, www.fsf.org, and www.aclu.org/issues/privacy-technology#current.

One of the major problems with social media is that it can eat up so much of our time. If only there were a tool that could help us keep everything in balance…oh wait—there is! It's called "time management," and I discuss it in the next section. See you there!

PART V

ABUNDANCE

41. An Awesome Liberation

The big reason to practice time management is that there's no such thing as unmanaged time. **If you're not managing your time, someone else is managing it for you.** That could be your family, friends, professors, classmates, employer, and/or coworkers. Or it could be corporations trying to sell you a particular product or lifestyle. Bad enough to let those who care about you rule your time—but corporations?

The capitalist/consumerist lifestyle common in the U.S. and some other countries emphasizes long workdays (often with additional long commutes), with much of the rest of your time spent on chores. "Free time," after all these obligations, is often limited to television, Web surfing, gaming, and other passive or isolating activities, both because those are the major options available and because you're too tired to do anything else. Meanwhile, relationships, socializing, self-care, caregiving, civic work, and activism—all the major contributors to a happy and healthy life and society, in other words—are given short shrift.[59] Is it any wonder that so many people are stressed, unhealthy, and unhappy? That so many relationships are troubled? And so many communities unraveling?

---

[59] Notice how many of the countries that provide workers with the most paid time off (https://en.wikipedia.org/wiki/List_of_minimum_annual_leave_by_country) also top the World Happiness Report's list of happiest countries (https://en.wikipedia.org/wiki/World_Happiness_Report#2019_report). Also note that many of those same countries also provide strong health, housing, and educational benefits, thus further improving individuals' lives while freeing their time by easing their caregiving and other obligations.

Our time use is also gendered, with women almost always on the losing end of the equation. Globally, we women continue to do the bulk of caregiving and chores. At the same time, far less of our labor is paid than men's.[60] Furthermore, women are still encouraged to subjugate their needs to those of others and so overgiving (Chapter 48) is a problem.

I teach, and will be discussing, what I call Values-Based Time Management (VBTM). Unlike some other time-management systems that focus narrowly on maximizing your work output, VBTM's goal is more holistic: to help you align, as much as possible, your actions with your values. VBTM also concerns itself with both your professional (in this case, school) and personal lives. That's not just because it doesn't make sense to only manage half your time, but because your personal life is important.

Like many time-management systems, VBTM involves budgeting, scheduling, and tracking your time, all of which I'll be discussing. But the core is the underlying ethos that you should organize your time as much as possible around the activities that are important to you.

VBTM, in other words, maximizes the chances that you'll live a happy, healthy, and productive life. And here are some other reasons to do it:

I've already discussed (Chapter 23) how success makes you busier. Developing a time-management practice today will help you to cope with the flood of opportunities we're all hoping you'll be deluged with tomorrow. This also applies to your personal life, by the way. Many people aspire to not just a great career, but a great family life, a comfortable home, and to do good work in their community. Despite perfectionist media that implies that such a life is easily attainable, it's a lot to handle. But VBTM can help.

Society promotes unhealthy ideas of time use. Many people still believe, for instance, that the busier you are, the more successful or important you must be. Or that multitasking is a good idea. (Chapter 5 debunked that one.) Or that they work best under pressure. Speaking of which…

No one works best under pressure. Sure, pressure may terrify you into overcoming your procrastination and focusing on your work. But there's no way that that work will ever equal the quantity or quality of work done under conditions of abundant time and attention, such as VBTM can provide.

---

[60] See, for example: www.bls.gov/news.release/atus.nr0.htm. (Scroll down to the discussion of childcare.) And www.unstats.un.org/unsd/gender/chapter4/chapter4.html.

Last but not least...

Your professors will love you. Believe me, they can tell when you've waited till the last minute and they hate that! (Partly because they know you're capable of doing better and partly because the missed deadlines create more work for them.)

Here's the good news: for all its liberating potential, VBTM often comes down to making just a few simple changes in your life and habits. Chapters 42 through 48 will continue to discuss the fundamental ideas underlying VBTM. Then, Chapters 49 and 50 will tell you how to use those ideas to create the values-driven time budget and schedule that work best for you.

42. Good vs. Poor vs. Wannabe Time Managers

Good Time Managers (GTMs) are **optimizers**. They're always asking themselves questions like, "Did I do this task as efficiently as I could have?" and "Was this event a good use of my time?" And modifying their future behavior based on the answers. **Please note that this inner Q&A is always supportive and encouraging, and never perfectionistically harsh. Always be your own best coach!**

Professionally and personally, GTMs are busy but not frantic. They meet their deadlines and do quality work. They show up on time, or a bit early, and prepared. They also prioritize sleep, nutrition, exercise, and other self-care. All of this means they're as productive, healthy, and happy as possible, given their circumstances, and that they're not just great team members, but natural leaders and mentors. And so, interesting people and opportunities are drawn their way.

Are GTMs like this 100% of the time? Of course not: they have their "off" days like everyone else, and sometimes their "off" days, weeks, or months. (And that "100% of the time" is perfectionist.) But even during difficult times, a GTM will function better than they would have without their time management skills, and those skills will also help them get back on track as quickly as possible.

Unfortunately, judging by the frequent news stories about workaholism, "time poverty," and similar problems, there aren't a lot of GTMs out there. Most people, in fact, are probably Poor Time Managers (PTMs) who frequently overcommit themselves. As a result, they're frequently late, frequently missing deadlines, and frequently handing in poor-quality work.

Also, most PTMs aren't a picture of health and happiness. Mostly, they're walking around stressed, ill, fatigued, and depleted.

Needless to say, a PTM isn't anyone's idea of a good team member, much less leader. Professionally and personally, GTMs avoid relationships with PTMs, whose chronic unreliability not only creates a huge strain but lessens the chance of a successful outcome.

Unsurprisingly, there's a perfectionist angle to all this. Both overscheduling and expecting yourself to function without adequate self-care are classic grandiose behaviors.

PTMs aren't the worst-off people, however: those would be the Wannabe Time Managers (WTMs). They're dabblers, trying a little time management here and there, but they won't commit. As a result, they often wind up experiencing all the inconveniences of the practice while getting few or none of the benefits. They also tend to be deluded about how much time management they're doing. Many think they are "almost a GTM" or "halfway between a GTM and PTM." In reality, however, most are far closer to PTMs than GTMs. (From now on, whenever I mention PTMs, you can assume I also mean WTMs.)

Slow Down, You Move Too Fast

The signature behavior of PTMs is rushing around. People in time-dysfunctional cultures often see rushing as a sign of ambition or importance. ("Sorry! Gotta run! Three meetings this afternoon!") But rushing is horrible. We've already seen, in Chapter 26, how it impairs our ability to learn, but that's just one of the problems it causes. Rushing also impairs us physically and emotionally (all those stress hormones), intellectually (see Chapter 45's discussion of cognitive capacity), and even relationally (we treat both loved ones and strangers worse when we're in a rush).

Rushing even impairs our ethical functioning. This was demonstrated in a classic social psychology experiment by John M. Darley and C. Daniel Batson,[61] in which forty Princeton seminarians were asked to write, and then later record, a sermon. Each was assigned one of two topics to write about: either, (1) the ethically instructive parable of the Good Samaritan, in which,

---

[61] John M. Darley and C. Daniel Batson, "'From Jerusalem to Jericho': A study of situational and dispositional variables in helping behavior." In Elliot Aronson (ed.), *Readings About the Social Animal*, 7th Ed. (This is the same C. Daniel Batson whom I quoted in Chapter 39 on the subject of anger.)

as you may recall, a king and a priest pass by a wounded man without stopping to help, but a "humble Samaritan" does the right thing and stops; or (2) the more ethically neutral topic of career paths for seminarians. After each seminarian had written his (they were all male) sermon, he was then told that either:

- He had plenty of time to get over to the recording studio (which was located in another building).
- He was on time, but shouldn't dawdle. Or,
- He was late! The recording staff was waiting for him and he had to get to the studio *right now*!

Here's the twist: each seminarian, while en route to the studio, encountered a man lying in the street, seemingly ill and in distress. (He was actually an actor hired by the experimenters.) In other words, the seminarian was presented with the Good Samaritan scenario in real life!

What would he do? (What would *you* do?)

Not to leave you in suspense: the experimenters found that the seminarians in the third group, who were rushing to get to the studio, were far less likely to stop and help than the others—and this was true even for those who had just written an entire sermon on the Good Samaritan. All that thought and analysis, not to mention the basic helping orientation of most seminarians, flew right out the window, just because they were rushed.

Darley and Batson concluded that, "Ethics becomes a luxury as the speed of our daily lives increases." They also urged us not to judge the "non-helpers," who, they said, were caught in a conflict between their obligation to help the needy person and their obligation to the experimenters.

The bottom line is that when you're rushing, you're not the person you're capable of being: not physically, intellectually, emotionally, relationally, or ethically. Moment by moment, you're only living up to a part of your potential.

The opposite of rushing could be defined as presence, mindfulness, or the ability to "be here now," as Ram Dass put it. Also, the ability to devote abundant—or, as abundant as possible—time, energy, and attention to the people and things that are important to you. Values-Based Time Management will help you locate and focus on all those priorities, so that you can live a life filled not just with accomplishment but interest, meaning, love, and joy.

Exercise 24

Journal about how much rushing you do every day, how that rushing affects your schoolwork and life, and how things might improve if you slowed down.

43. Investing Your Time

Our time is valuable and we should always strive to use it as well as we can. We should also value small amounts of it, both for their own sake and because they add up. Reclaim just fifteen minutes of underutilized time a day and you'll gain more than ninety hours—the equivalent of more than two work weeks—a year.

Now, many people think they already understand this. They go around saying stuff like, "Time is money." Watch as they go about their day, however, and you'll see them squander their precious time in ways they never would their cash. Also, they're wrong, because time happens to be far more valuable than money. That's not just because it's finite, with even the richest person being limited to 24 hours a day; it's also because time can create outcomes that money can't, and those happen to be the most valuable outcomes.

Consider two students. One attends an expensive college and buys the best computer, textbooks, etc., but rarely studies. The other attends a cheaper school and makes do with cheaper supplies, but studies a few hours a day. Who will get educated?

Or, think of two people trying to get fit. One spends thousands on a gym membership and fancy workout clothes, but never uses them. The other spends $100 on a decent pair of running shoes and some used weights, then runs or works out most days. Who will get fit?

Finally, think of two parents. One is always buying expensive gifts for their kids but rarely spends any time with them. The other doesn't have a lot of money to spend but tries their best to be present. Who will have the better relationship?

You get the idea—and it's not a new one. Around 2,000 years ago, the Stoic philosopher Seneca, in his essay "On the Shortness of Life," said of those who misuse their time: "They are trifling with life's most precious commodity, being deceived because it is an intangible thing, not open to inspection and therefore reckoned very cheap."

I'm not saying that money is unimportant. Of course it is. But research has shown that after our basic material needs are met, the yields of time, including good health, good relationships, and a sense of personal fulfillment, become primary.[62] Also, people who value time over money tend to be happier.[63]

Time does have something important in common with money, however: you can invest it. You're probably familiar with financial investments, like stocks or real estate, that increase in value over time, thus earning you a "return." Buy $100 worth of stocks today, and if you've chosen well you can sell them later for more. Personal financial experts tell us that anything that's not an investment is an expense, including not just your latest impulse purchase, but essentials like food, transportation, and clothing. All expenses, including the essential ones, lose value over time. (You can't resell that bag of groceries you just bought, or last month's train pass.) Experts therefore advise us to minimize even our essential expenses so we can put as much money as possible into investments.

Time investments work pretty much the same way—except that, as discussed, a time investment can yield not just money, but health, happiness, love, and even more time. So, as important as investing your money is, it's even more important to invest your time. **The major categories of time investments are:**

Self-care, including good nutrition, exercise, sleep, grooming, health care, and, for some, a meditation or spiritual practice. Poor Time Managers (PTMs) often stint on this and wind up going through their days exhausted and depleted. Good Time Managers (GTMs), in contrast, aim for abundant

---

[62] www.pewsocialtrends.org/2008/04/30/who-wants-to-be-rich/. Notice how, in the study, the most valued priority across all demographics, by a wide margin, is, "to have enough free time."

[63] www.nytimes.com/2016/09/11/opinion/sunday/what-should-you-choose-time-or-money.html

self-care and they also understand that **the more ambitious your goals, or the tougher the barriers you face, the more self-care you need**.

Some activists and others believe self-care is an indulgence in a world beset with urgent problems. But skimping on it makes you less effective and is likely to lead to burnout. As the poet/activist Audre Lorde said, "Caring for myself is not self-indulgence, it is self-preservation, and that is an act of political warfare."

Relationships. You know: that thing that, at the end of their life, many people wish they had devoted more time to?

Values-driven work, meaning work you do for love and not just a paycheck. (I also sometimes refer to this category as your "vocation" or "mission.") Since college is a time-intensive activity akin to having a job, I would include your college work in this category. Some caregiving, creative, spiritual, and other practices would also fit, if you devote serious hours and attention to them.

Education, by which I mean the lifelong education that you participate in after your college years. Some people continue to accrue degrees and certifications throughout their lives, while others take whatever online or offline courses happen to strike their fancy, while still others do a lot of independent reading and study. It's all good. The important thing is that you never stop learning and growing.

Replenishing recreation. Activities that are fun and relaxing, and that also leave you healthier and happier (a.k.a., "replenished"). They are active and engaging, and also connect you with others and/or nature and/or certain aspects of yourself, like your creativity, intellect, athleticism, or senses. Examples include socializing, sports, creative activities, outdoor activities, and travel.

Activism/Community Organizing. This is perhaps the highest yielding of all the investment categories. Don't believe me? Consider the fact that you're able to attend college at all. A century ago, it might not have been possible unless you happened to have been rich, white, non-disabled, and male. Generations of activists and community organizers fighting for social justice on all fronts, including labor, education, race, gender, and disability, have granted you this precious opportunity—which, let's not forget, is still beyond the reach of many. So, pay it forward by investing a few hours a month on whichever social justice cause speaks most to your heart. Along with the good you'll be doing, you'll also find that activism yields some terrific personal benefits, including the opportunity to do meaningful (and resume-building) work alongside some of the best people you'll ever meet.

For more information, see Chapter A2—and please note that I'm talking about activism/organizing and not volunteer work. Volunteering is good, but activism is better because it seeks to correct the conditions, such as poverty, that make the volunteering necessary to start with.

The final category of time investment is one many forget, but it's the most important one because it underpins the success of all the rest:

Planning and Management. Success doesn't just happen: you have to plan for it and manage the process as it unfolds. You should, in fact, plan and manage all of the above investment categories, including those we don't think of as requiring planning and management, such as relationships. (Many people wing it in this crucial area and wind up with a failed marriage or alienated kids.) You should also plan and manage your resources, including your information, money, property, and (hello) time. All this planning and management may sound like a lot of work, but it isn't, since a little goes a long way. Planning for a successful romantic relationship, for instance, might involve reading a few books on relationships, working with a counselor to overcome any relevant barriers, and then developing a set of principles (e.g., mutual support and open communication) and habits (e.g., weekly date nights and prompt conflict resolution) that you and your partner agree to moving forward. Career planning might involve more initial work but the effort still remains small compared with the potential yield of a satisfying decades-long career. (See Chapters A1, A2, and A3 for career planning tips.)

Assuming you're not in the midst of planning your career or some other major life goal, two hours per week should be fine for all your planning and management activities.

You want to devote time to each of your investment categories every week. Obviously, some weeks are busier than others and you might want to skip, say, your activism and some recreation during midterms and finals weeks. But the goal is to maintain a balanced and healthy lifestyle where you address all of your priorities on a consistent basis.

So those are the time investments. All other activities are time expenses, including:

Chores, including housekeeping, errands, etc.

A **"day job"** you're doing just, or mostly, for money.

Your **commute**, an often time-consuming activity that is also often stressful. The average U.S. commute (round-trip) is 52 minutes/day.[64] However, a PTM's commute is likely to be longer than average.

Escapist recreation. In contrast to replenishing recreation, escapist activities are sedentary, isolating, and disconnecting. Television is the obvious example, but social media and gaming can also qualify.

Procrastination is also a time expense. It may seem funny to think of it that way since none of us wants to procrastinate. But when you think about it, that's true of all the other expenses, too. (Except, perhaps, for the escapism.)

The final category of time expense is: **any activity you're doing just to kill time**—and what a horrible expression that is—or **out of habit, convention**, or **a reluctance to say no** (see Chapters 47 and 48).

The line between time investments and expenses isn't hard and fast: an activity could be either, depending on who's doing it and why. If you enjoy something and feel it enhances your life—like, say, cooking—then it's an investment. But if someone else finds it a tedious chore, then it's an expense for them.

It's also possible to overdo an investment, in which case it becomes an expense. We already know what that's called: Quasiproductive Procrastination (Chapter 5).

---

[64] www.census.gov/library/visualizations/interactive/travel-time.html

44. Shifting from Expenses to Investments

Similar to money management, a major goal of time management is to shift as much of your time as you can out of expenses and into investments. An investment-centered life offers some outstanding yields, including not just increased productivity and achievement, but more health, happiness, fulfillment, and joy. You do the shift from expenses to investments via budgeting, which I discuss in Chapter 49. But why not get started now? Here are a few easy suggestions:

- Quit (responsibly—don't leave anyone in a lurch) any optional activities you aren't enjoying or, if goal-oriented, aren't accomplishing much.

- Quit (but not callously) any relationships that aren't working for you (for example, people you're seeing out of habit or obligation).

- Work double shifts at your job to lower your commuting and preparation time.

- Set a time limit for household chores—say, half an hour of cleaning per room per week. (Without a limit, they have a way of expanding to fill all your available time.)

- If you live with others, make sure everyone in the household is doing their fair share.

- Buddy up with a roommate or friend for chores, so that, for instance, you do all the laundry and grocery shopping one week and they do it all the next.

- Invest in great tools that make chores easier and quicker (e.g., great housecleaning supplies).
- Say "no" and delegate wherever possible. (See Chapter 47.)

Many of these steps involve eliminating, or at least cutting down on, stuff you don't want to be doing anyway. In theory, this should be a no-brainer, but perfectionism, guilt, peer pressure, and an overgiving habit can all get in the way. Be compassionate and patient with yourself while working to overcome these barriers, but do work to overcome them.

As you eliminate expenses, start filling the liberated time with investments. Your choices will be based on your own particular values and goals, but **a good rule of thumb is to put two-thirds of your liberated time into your mission and one-third into self-care and replenishing recreation**. Doing that should lead to a quick improvement in both your productivity and your quality of life.

Reining in Your Escapist Activities

The hardest expenses for many people to cut or trim are the escapist ones, such as social media, gaming, video watching, and television. These are so much fun and so stress-relieving! (And can be essential for some, including those who are disabled.) But they're also sedentary and, often, isolating. They also often promote terrible values: see, for instance, social media's ubiquitous perfectionism and some gaming communities' misogyny. Even when one of these activities has a social component, it's often shallow or what psychologists call parasocial, which means it is one-sided and unreciprocated. Psychologists have expressed many concerns about parasocial relationships, including that they reinforce unrealistic relationship models, erode people's ability to socialize in real life, and can render people vulnerable to advertising and other influences.[65]

In Chapter 49's sample budget I allocate 1.5 hours a day for escapist activities. That's a huge chunk of your precious time—around ten percent of your waking hours—but it isn't so huge that it's likely to sabotage your success. Still, if you can do less that's terrific. (Psychologist Melissa G. Hunt, whose research on social media harms I cited earlier, recommends no more than thirty minutes a day.)

---

[65] www.pbs.org/wgbh/nova/article/parasocial-relationships

For those interested in reducing the amount of escapism they do, here are some suggestions:

- **Disconnect part-time**, as discussed in Chapter 6.

- **Use Clocks.** Remember, from Chapter 6, how removing clocks from your workspace can help you work longer? The opposite is also true: if you display a clock while gaming or watching television, that can encourage you to limit that activity. It's best if the clock is either analog or, if digital, a separate device from your phone or PC.

- **Use Timers**, as Gregory Ferenstein (Chapter 6) did. These can help to interrupt the trancelike ludic loop so you can get back to whatever it is you are supposed to be doing. Again, it's better to use either an analog timer or a standalone digital one (like the kitchen timer you're using for your Timed Work Intervals).

- **Have some low-stress and easy forms of replenishing recreation available**. It could be some light, fun reading, or a fun hobby like sketching, knitting, baking, beading, or gardening.

- **Be mindful of the opportunity costs**, meaning the more rewarding activities you could be doing if you weren't putting so much time into escapism. (Try not to be one of those people who complains online about all the cool stuff they could be doing if they weren't online so much.)

- **Slow down/stop rushing.** As noted in Chapter 41, rushing is stressful and the stress often increases our need for escapism.

- **Be mindful of apps' negative aspects.** I find social media engrossing, entertaining, and informative—but also, often, tedious, repetitive, shallow, stressful, and banal. Staying alert to, and mindful of, these kinds of downsides can make it easier for you to resist the temptation to overindulge.

- **Be mindful of apps' political and social context.** Fun as apps, games, videos, television shows, and other distractions are, they were created by corporations to hijack and monetize your time and personal data. Many of the platforms have obvious and well-publicized problems, including privacy violations and an unwillingness to deal with bigoted and otherwise harmful content. Staying mindful of these kinds of political and social concerns, along with those pertaining to your own personal welfare, can help you resist the temptation to overindulge.

So far, I've mostly been talking about small changes. But there's one major change you can make that, all by itself, can help you shift a lot of your time into investments. It's called frugality and I discuss it below.

Getting Frugal

Everything we purchase winds up costing us twice, time-wise: once in the time it takes to earn the money to purchase it and forever after in the time it takes to maintain it. "The things we own, own us," as the saying goes. And so, frugality is one of your strongest time management strategies. **Frugality isn't deprivation, it's intentionality.** Whether you think of your frugality as "living simply," "minimalism," or "living below my means," it comes down to buying only what you truly need or want: for example, the excellent wardrobe, cookware, and/or vacations that enhance your life, but not the fancy car, furniture, and electronics that don't. Again, these are just examples: you would make your choices based on your own values and goals—although a new car is *the* textbook financial expense, with most losing about 25% of their resale value the moment you drive them off the dealer's lot.

Frugality is often necessary during tough economic times when wages are depressed, but it's a wise choice even in better times. And while many people are frugal out of necessity in their twenties because of low starter salaries, I'm also talking about being frugal later in life, when you do have some discretionary funds. This kind of "optional frugality" can be powerfully liberating, freeing you to be able to, for instance:

- Work at a job or career you truly want, even if doesn't happen to pay as well as some others.
- Work part time while also pursuing a cherished but low-paid or unpaid arts, activist, travel, caregiving, or other mission.
- Live in the community you really want to live in (because it's safer, more fun, or less of a commute) instead of having to live where it's cheapest.

Frugality can also, obviously, help you save money; and that, in turn, can help you achieve costly goals such as home ownership, parenthood, business ownership, and a comfortable retirement.

So let's get frugal. It's good to pinch pennies where you can, but a Good Time Manager (GTM) will take this liberating step to the max using two techniques. The first is **living in a small space**, thus reducing your rent, utility, furniture, cleaning, and other expenses. (Alternatively, you could share your big space with others, achieving similar benefits.) This can seem like a bold move if everyone around you equates success with moving into larger and fancier spaces. But it can pay off in terms of freeing your time, money, and attention for the things you love.

Thrifting is the other great frugality technique. Find a good thrift store, resale shop, or consignment shop—meaning one in or near an affluent neighborhood, and that's also spacious, well-lit, and well-organized—and make a point of stopping by once or twice a month. Make a note of which days they put out new merchandise, and befriend the staff, who will sometimes let you know when a good shipment, or an item you need, has come in. Over time, you can acquire a great wardrobe, or great kitchenware, sports gear, furniture, decorative pieces, etc., for pennies on the dollar.

Obviously, you can thrift online, too—and many do that, with gusto. But it can be hard for even honest vendors to describe a used item accurately and the shipping costs can also be prohibitive. So try to find a local store.

Although there are plenty of online resources devoted to frugality, you want some local mentors who can point you towards discount shops, housing opportunities, thrift stores, and other resources. You'll often find them in arts, activist, and cohousing communities. Chances are, in fact, that you already know someone who's rocking their frugality, so figure out who that is and ask them for advice.

45. The Only Thing More Precious Than Your Time

The only thing more precious than your time is your cognitive capacity, roughly defined as the amount of information you're able to work with at any given moment. We all have only a limited amount and everything we do, think about, and deal with uses up some. The goal is to maximize the amount you can devote to your important projects, including your schoolwork. (Also, your important personal "projects," such as your health and relationships.)

Happily, whenever you remove a time expense or other low-value activity from your schedule, you reclaim not just the time but the cognitive capacity you would have otherwise devoted to it. Free your time, in other words, and you also free your mind.

You also reclaim cognitive capacity when you overcome procrastination and perfectionism, not just because they are ongoing sources of stress and worry, but because they can cause you to overcomplicate your projects and work with inadequate resources.

Excellent self-care, including good nutrition and abundant sleep and exercise, will also help you maximize your available cognitive capacity, and so will planning and routines. (For instance, going to the gym at the same time each day.) When Flaubert said, "Be regular and orderly in your life like a bourgeois so that you may be violent and original in your work," he meant that you should preserve your precious time, energy, and cognitive capacity for your important projects.

Recovering, even partially, from a physical or mental illness can help you reclaim some of your cognitive capacity, and so can coping (again, even partially) with a disability, learning difference, or constraining force such as poverty or bias.

Happily, the more cognitive capacity you reclaim, the more you're often able to reclaim. Every time you solve a problem, for instance, you reclaim the cognitive capacity (and time, money, energy, and other resources) you had been using to cope with it, which you can then apply to other problems or projects. This is even better news than it sounds because **some of our most difficult problems are difficult mainly because we're not setting aside enough time and cognitive capacity to deal with them.** Many who struggle with health and fitness-related goals, for instance, underestimate how much work it takes to change your habits and maintain a healthy lifestyle. Changing your diet, for instance, might require that you read up on nutrition (or consult a nutritionist), figure out a meal plan, research shopping options, and become a more careful shopper and meal preparer. It could also involve seeing a therapist and changing your routines and relationships so that you're hanging out with people who encourage healthy eating.

The first thing to do, therefore, if you have a seemingly intractable problem, is to set aside some time to think, research, and plan. Don't, in other words, make the common mistake of thinking you should already have a plan before setting the time aside.

Another excellent way to conserve cognitive capacity is to specialize, a technique I discuss in the next chapter.

Exercise 25

Is there a school, personal, or other problem you've been trying to solve but haven't made much progress on? If so, consider whether you've invested sufficient time in solving it. ("Solving" means things like research, planning, discussions with mentors, trying solutions, etc., and not worrying or feeling bad about it.) If you haven't, do so now.

Sometimes, when people do this exercise, they realize they haven't been procrastinating, but prioritizing. If that's what you've been doing, that's great. Just don't beat yourself up perfectionistically over it. (Or anything else, for that matter.)

46. Specialize!

Everyone ought to have a specialty in every investment category.

In school, it might be history—and more specifically the history of China. (And even more specifically: 19th-century Chinese history.)

Recreationally, it could be painting—and more specifically watercolor landscapes.

In self-care, it could be yoga, meditation, or knowing how to dress well on a small budget. (Less spiritual than the first two, perhaps, but still pretty fun and useful.)

Your specialties don't just enhance your life and bring you joy, they're an important part of what defines you. When you specialize in something, you love it, look for reasons to do it, enjoy reading, listening, and talking about it, and seek out—or build—communities devoted to it. One of the best things about specialization is hanging out with others who share your interest.

Productivity-wise, specialization is the bomb. It makes your work easier; saves you loads of time, energy, and cognitive capacity; helps you to develop your expertise; maximizes your enjoyment of your work; and makes you a desirable team member and a natural leader. (Because all that expertise and joy attracts others.) In other words, it's a key to both professional and personal success. Remember, from the Introduction, the advice I got from the multimillionaire to, "focus relentlessly on your unique value-add"? He was talking about developing a specialty.

Having a specialty doesn't mean you can't do other things. Our historian is free to delve into Brazilian history, our painter to try ceramics, and our discount fashion maven to meditate. And they'll all benefit from the diversity of experience. Specialization means you make an activity the main focus—but not necessarily the only focus—of your professional or personal efforts. You're also free to change your specialties at any time.

When we specialize, we're usually leveraging our strengths, which is always a good idea. And we're also usually having fun. (Because we tend to enjoy what we're good at, and *vice versa*.) The Germans have yet another great word for the special kind of pleasure you get from doing something you're good at: *funktionslust*. Specialize and you'll enjoy lots of it.

Sometimes others are better at spotting our specialties than we are. A wise student changed his entire research focus after a mentor heard him speaking about a different topic and pointed out, "You light up when you [talk about] that."[66] (And, obviously, this is terrific feedback to give someone else.)

If you're having trouble choosing a specialty, you might be self-censoring. We sometimes do that when we're afraid of failing at our specialty or think others will oppose it. Self-censorship is a form of ambivalence, so see Chapter 24 for solutions. Or you might be one of those enthusiastic types with many interests, in which case you'll need to make some tough choices and mourn the consequent losses, as discussed in Chapter 23. (Although the choice might be easier than expected: "I can live, for now, without doing A, B, and C, but I really don't want to give up D, so I guess D's my specialty.")

Perhaps you're attached to the idea that you can "do it all." Science fiction writer Robert Heinlein went for the perfectionist gold with this passage from his novel *Time Enough for Love*:

> A human being should be able to change a diaper, plan an invasion, butcher a hog, conn a ship, design a building, write a sonnet, balance accounts, build a wall, set a bone, comfort the dying, take orders, give orders, cooperate, act alone, solve equations, analyze a new problem, pitch manure, program a computer, cook a tasty meal, fight efficiently, die gallantly. Specialization is for insects.

Like most perfectionist harangues, it has a certain superficial appeal but on closer examination makes no sense. Not only does almost no one need to know most of the things on Heinlein's list—plan an invasion? Really?—

---

we want our bones set by, buildings designed by, and computers programmed by specialists. To add to the ridiculousness, Heinlein gave that speech to his character Lazarus Long, a mutant human who lives thousands of years and therefore has millennia to learn whatever useful and useless things he wants.

But we don't have those millennia—and so, I much prefer Jane Austen's sensible take in *Pride and Prejudice*, when her protagonist, Lizzie Bennet, after hearing the snobbish Mr. Darcy and Miss Bingley rattle off a voluminous list of things a woman must know to be "truly accomplished"—including "a thorough knowledge of music, singing, drawing, dancing, and the modern languages"—tells Darcy, "I'm no longer surprised at your knowing only six accomplished women. I rather wonder now at your knowing any."

You can also, and should, specialize in your personal life. **For a life of vividness, intensity, joy, and true camaraderie, organize your free time around the (replenishing) recreational activities you love most, while at the same time investing in the best equipment, classes, excursions, etc. you can afford.** If hiking is your passion, for instance, don't just settle for "okay" local hikes. Do your best to take wonderful hikes in amazing places, with excellent equipment, and in the company of other devoted hikers.

Also, specialize when it comes to helping out friends and relatives. If a friend asks you to help them move, for instance, figure out which part of that process you're best at and help with that. (It could be the packing, the heavy lifting, or the unpacking and organizing of their new home. Or you could be the one who takes care of their dog or cat while it's all going on.) When assisting an ailing or homebound friend or relative, figure out how you can best use your time to support them. Don't trudge to the grocery store or pharmacy, for instance, if you can order online and have everything delivered. And don't mow their lawn or shovel their driveway if you can get a kid to do it cheap.[67] Instead, offer higher-value support, like escorting your loved one to a medical appointment or helping them with their paperwork. Even a fun afternoon of lunch and Rummikub is a better use of your time and energy than running around doing a lot of chores someone else could have easily handled.

---

[67] Some nonprofits offer grocery delivery and other services to homebound people—check with local offices for the aged and disabled, religious organizations, and senior centers.

Specialization's Fantastic Yields

Specializing can create many fantastic yields, as Ben's story illustrates:

Ben's dorm is holding an antiracism event. He's eager to participate, but knows the importance of specializing, and so he declines suggestions that he help set up the event, publicize it, or bring food. Instead, since he's a statistics major, he volunteers to create a display illustrating the health, economic, and other impacts of racism.[68]

Since the project is in his area of specialty, it goes pretty well and he also has a great time doing it. (Or, as great a time as possible given the depressing subject matter.) He's also very willing to ask for help and so winds up collaborating with four very cool people: a sociology-major friend who helps him with his research, a statistics professor who helps him improve his analysis, an artist friend who helps him design and create some great displays, and an actor friend who helps him improve his verbal presentation. All this specialization and collaboration pay off, with Ben's display and presentation turning out to be among the event's highlights. Several people tell him he's enhanced their understanding of racism and the school newspaper features his work in its article about the event.

Beyond all this, Ben has also enhanced his skills in statistics, sociology, graphics, public speaking, and project management.

Afterwards, Ben is careful to follow up with, and thank, his collaborators. They're all happy to have helped and express a willingness to work with him again on other projects. That's great, because Ben now realizes that this project could be expanded into an excellent senior project. (So he now has a head start on that!) Plus, his collaborators have themselves gained some new knowledge and experience.

So many great outcomes just from specializing! Imagine if, instead, Ben had agreed to do setup, publicity, or food. He would have achieved much less.

---

[68] It's okay, and an act of solidarity, to occasionally take on a non-specialist task, like setting up for, or cleaning up after, an event. But you shouldn't be doing that routinely. Needless to say, this problem, like many time-management problems, is gendered, with women disproportionately being asked to take on "support tasks" like food preparation, childcare, note-taking, and cleanup. Organizations with a sincere social justice mission will make sure such tasks are distributed equitably along gender and other lines.

Crucial to Ben's success were his abilities to decline unwanted tasks and delegate tasks to specialists. I discuss both of those crucial time-reclamation skills in the next chapter.

47. The Joys of Declining and Delegating

You want to say no to ("decline") any tasks, projects, and other opportunities that aren't your specialty. Even within your specialty, you'll want to decline most of them, keeping only the best—meaning, the most interesting, important, impactful, fun, and strategic—for yourself. That way, your work itself will keep getting more interesting, important, impactful, fun, and strategic.

Unfortunately, many people have trouble saying no, either because they're afraid of disappointing others or grandiosely think they should be able to "do it all." If you're one of them, now's the time to break the habit, because **saying "no" isn't just a productivity skill, it's a profound form of self-care and one of life's great pleasures**. (One of my favorite memes is the one with the woman snug in bed with her cat, both of them propped up on many pillows in television-watching position. Meanwhile, she's saying to someone on the phone, "Yeah, can't come out tonight. Super busy.")[69]

A reluctance to say no can also lead to overgiving, a self-sabotaging behavior I discuss in the next chapter.

So practice saying "no." Do it with easy requests at first, and then tougher ones, until you're comfortable saying it even to people who pressure you. Also work on getting past needing a "good reason" to say no (like a deadline or test). You want to get comfortable saying it for the simple reason that, "it's not a good fit for me."

---

[69] www.ifunny.co/picture/sorry-can-t-come-out-tonight-super-busy-XhrUnKBr8

Delegation, or getting someone else to do part of a task, is the other great time-reclamation skill. It's often thought of as something bosses do "to" their subordinates, but you can do it more equitably by: (1) delegating tasks to those for whom they are a specialty (as Ben did) and (2) providing lots of support and mentoring.

You can also pay someone to help you. I'm a big fan of this if you can afford it. As discussed in Chapter 43, time is more valuable than money, and so it makes sense to use your money to "buy time." (It's also good to help a good person earn their living.) Also, since the person you're paying is hopefully an expert, paying is often the quickest and easiest way to get some great support. **Paying someone to tutor you on a difficult subject for a few hours each week, versus struggling for many more hours on your own, is a great investment.** Ditto for paying someone to fix your computer, versus spending days or weeks trying to fix it yourself. (Or worse, trying to live with the malfunction.)

This is all contingent on you having enough money. I know many students don't, but I also know that some—and even more employed people— do have the ability to pay but are reluctant to do so. Don't make that mistake.

Issues of payment aside, people often have lots of reasons why they "can't" delegate a particular task—or any task—including:

- "It's such a little thing I might as well do it myself." (Nope! Your time is precious.)

- "I can do it better myself." (Even if that's true—and often it's not— it's better, from an overall efficiency standpoint, to delegate.)

- "I don't have anyone to delegate to." (Help is abundant. You may have to search a bit to find the right person, but that person is out there.)

Regardless of how compelling the justification sounds, you'll often find, at the root of a reluctance to delegate, a plain old reluctance to ask for help, as discussed in Chapter 10.

Another reason to embrace both declining and delegating is that, as noted in Chapter 41, success makes you busier. Each of your professional and personal accomplishments is likely to result in yet more invitations, ideas, projects, potential partnerships, and other opportunities arriving at your door. Don't get me wrong: this ongoing flood of opportunities is a great problem to have. But it's still a problem. Say "yes" to even just a few too many and you'll run aground. So yeah: you want to get comfortable declining and delegating all but the very best that's offered to you.

A good delegator must also be a good manager. Bad managers throw a task at someone and don't want to hear from them again until it's completed. Good managers, in contrast, take as much time as needed to explain things at the beginning of the project; then check in with their helper while the work is underway.

Good delegators are also kind and patient and otherwise nonperfectionist.

So work to become a frequent decliner and delegator. Of course, if you do, then sooner or later you'll either decline a task you should have taken on or delegate a task to the wrong person. These are inevitable mistakes and not a reason to stop declining and delegating, but rather to work on improving your process. (And also your ability to tolerate "failure," see Chapter 22.)

48. The Perils of Overgiving

Overgiving is when you take on tasks, projects, relationships, and other commitments you should decline. At the very least, it's a pernicious form of Quasiproductive Procrastination. But often it's even worse than that. Here's what can happen when you overgive at your job, or to a group you belong to, or to a person:

- You're so busy doing their stuff that you don't have time to do your own.
- You're stressed, exhausted, and resentful.
- You're possibly also broke—because many overgivers are also too free with their money.
- Dangerously, you attract the wrong people: those looking, consciously or subconsciously, for someone to exploit.

While many overgivers are motivated by a sincere desire to help, the problem is also often rooted in perfectionism ("I should be able to do it all.") and an inability to say no. Some may also get an ego boost from being a "problem solver," "go-to person," or even—although they'd never say this word aloud—"savior." (Grandiose much?) Many fall into the trap of workaholism, which psychologists characterize as an addictive/escapist behavior linked to stress, depression, ill health, and impaired personal relationships. Workaholics may work long hours, but their accomplishments often fall short, both because their underlying motivation is escape (versus effectiveness or efficiency) and because their lack of life balance is sabotaging.

Sadly, many organizations encourage and exploit people's tendency to overgive. Many health, educational, and community organizations are understaffed, thus forcing their employees to constantly choose between maintaining their own healthy boundaries and meeting the needs of their patients, students, or clients. And many social justice organizations shamelessly exploit activists' guilt over taking any time off from fixing society's urgent problems.

The solutions to overgiving are to work on your perfectionism, make sure you're doing things for the right motives, learn to say "no" and delegate, and consult a counselor if the problem persists. Also, find great mentors and learn from them. Many experienced health care workers, teachers, caregivers, and other helpers have learned how to best serve their clienteles while also maintaining healthy boundaries; and many experienced activists, as noted in Chapter 43, see self-care and life balance as foundational. Finally, time budgeting (Chapter 49) and scheduling (Chapter 50) can also help. Similar to chores, overgiving often expands to fill any available time, but a budget and schedule can help prevent that.

Operating Principles

Operating Principles are also useful. They're short, easily-remembered mantras or "rules to live by" that you use to make better decisions, especially under pressure. Here are three school-related examples:

- "Except for when someone is having a true emergency, classes and schoolwork always come first."
- "On weeknights I'm in bed by 1:00 a.m.—no exceptions."
- "I always shut off my phone while working."

And three more general ones:
- "Perfectionism is always a dead end so I never go there."
- "With very limited exceptions, I only volunteer to help people when I can do so using my specialties."
- "When I'm in conflict with someone, I always respond with kindness."

The intensifiers—"always," "no exceptions," "never," "very," and "only"—are there to remind you to adhere to the principle even when you're tempted not to. It's not that you can never ignore an operating principle, it's just that you need a good reason for doing so. (You can also always revise or eliminate an operating principle if it's not working for you.)

You come up with your operating principles by researching your field's best practices, and also by observing your mentors and having discussions with them. You can also figure them out as you go along. Many Good Time Managers (GTMs), for instance, adopt the operating principle, "If someone I'm working with is unreliable or otherwise difficult, I end my work with them as soon as possible and never work with them again," after having gotten mired in a bad collaboration. And many performers adopt an operating principle similar to, "I never work for free, no matter how worthy or prominent the event is," after having been burned once too often by promises of "payment" in exposure or publicity that didn't pan out. (They might make an exception for one charity or cause they especially care about.)

Overcoming Messaging Software Overload and Social Media Overload

Email, messaging and collaborative software are tricky, from a productivity standpoint, for four reasons:

- They combine the spontaneity of verbal communication with the permanence of written communication.
- The lack of nonverbal content, like vocal tone and body language, can cause confusion and misinterpretation.
- We message all kinds of people for all kinds of reasons, so it's hard to come up with a set of general principles.
- We get so many messages that if we overwork each one even a bit, it can add up to a lot of misused time.

Messaging software overload can also be partly an overgiving problem, because many people spend too much time on their messages for fear of looking bad or disappointing others. (Ditto for social media.) Ask yourself, therefore, whether you're giving too much of your precious time, energy, and cognitive capacity to online people, conversations, topics, groups, and platforms that aren't giving you much back.

The solutions are the same as for overgiving—reduce your perfectionism, understand your motives, and develop some Operating Principles. In addition:

Reply tersely. Not every decision requires an explanation, and it's often when we're explaining, or trying to, that things get out of hand. Explanations can turn into essays, and feeling like you have to write an essay—especially when you didn't mean to, don't need to, and don't want to—can lead to frustration and procrastination. And even if we do manage to get the essay out, our long explanation can induce the other person to respond with an essay of their own, which adds still more work.

Instead of writing long explanations, therefore, try sending emails like this: "OK – thanks," and "Yes – please let me know if you have questions." And, as per the last chapter, "Thanks for asking, but it's not a good fit for me." (In cases where you feel an explanation is required, it's often quicker to communicate verbally.)

Abstain from replying. Not every email requires a response.

Learn from mentors. Many successful professionals have techniques for keeping their messaging under control. They might, for instance, set a strict time limit on their daily messaging software use, which encourages them to be efficient. Or, they might affix a signature line to their outgoing messages letting correspondents know that not all messages will be answered. Speaking of which...

Use your tech. Autoresponders can be set up to reply to routine queries. (This also helps ensure accuracy and consistency.) Filters can be set up to separate urgent from nonurgent messages—and maybe you only check the "nonurgent" folder once or twice a week. Customizing your apps to boost your efficiency is an excellent time investment that can yield an incredible return over the years, so take as much time as you need to do it.

About Boundaries

There are four things you need to know about interpersonal boundaries, from a time-management perspective:

(1) **The important "boundary" isn't between you and the other person, but within you.** It's how you define your relationship with that person, and your obligations and responsibilities to them.

(2) **You should make conscious choices about your boundaries.** Do this even in relationships with a lot of personal and societal expectations, such as those with family members. Don't, in other words, buy into clichés or traditions about how you're supposed to behave.

(3) **It's your responsibility to state your needs.** Often, others don't even know there's a problem until we tell them—and when we do, they often surprise us with their supportiveness. ("Oh, so you need to skip some of the holiday events so you can finish your paper? No problem!") Sooner or later, however, you'll encounter someone who isn't so supportive, which brings us to...

(4) **Distance yourself from unsupportive people.** And give serious thought as to whether you even want them in your life.

These kinds of decisions—and the ensuing conversations—can be among the most difficult and unpleasant aspects of time management. But defending your boundaries isn't just an essential life skill, it's a profound form of self-care and self-preservation. Remember that, in a world filled with Poor Time Managers (PTMs), disappointing people is a sign you're doing your time management right.

Also remember that GTMs are problem-solvers and optimizers who don't settle for partial solutions. They are also clear on the long-term consequences of their actions—or, perhaps more to the point, inactions. So, while a PTM might be reluctant to disappoint someone by declining an offer, "impose" on them by delegating, or "upset" them by defending their boundaries, a GTM sees the consequences of being reticent and this motivates them to act.

Exercise 26

You've already sent out some fun Intentionally Erroneous Emails (Exercise 11) to help with your perfectionism. Now, send out some Intentionally Terse Emails to help with your overgiving, as per the discussion in this chapter.

Exercise 27

Start creating your lists of professional and personal operating principles. Write down a few you're already living by and store the list somewhere convenient so you can review and edit it frequently. Especially when something doesn't go as planned, think of what you might have done differently and see if you can turn that insight into an operating principle.

Okay, we're done discussing the ideas underlying time management! On to the process itself.

49. Budgeting Your Time

As already noted, you need to budget, schedule, and, at least for a while, track your time. We discuss budgeting in this chapter, and scheduling and tracking in the next.

Budgeting is the act of defining your priorities and determining how much time, each week, you'll devote to each. Sounds simple but, as you will see, it can involve some deep thought and tough choices. Here's how you do it:

Monitor your sleep. Start by acknowledging that sleep deprivation isn't a valid time-management strategy.[70] Then, **admit to how much sleep you need each night and commit to getting it.** (For most of us, that will be around seven or eight hours.) Then, subtract your week's total sleep from 168, the total number of hours in a week. If you need seven hours of sleep a night, for instance, that's 49 hours of sleep a week, leaving 119 hours of "awake" time. This may sound like a lot, but just wait...

Create your ideal weekly time budget. That's the budget you would use if you had unlimited time each week. We start with your ideal budget so you can look at your time with fresh eyes, thus ensuring that your final budget reflects your true priorities. Go wild! If you dream of taking five classes, participating in three extracurricular activities, and going to the gym every

---

[70] www.theguardian.com/lifeandstyle/2019/feb/09/best-thing-you-can-do-for-your-health-sleep-well

day—all while partying every night and working a twenty-hour-a-week job—put that all in your ideal budget.

List your classes, other major projects, and commitments individually. Budget in fifteen-minute increments—meaning that every activity should be allotted some multiple of fifteen minutes. (It's easiest to do all this on a spreadsheet.)

Some tips:

Be sure to include both professional and personal activities in your budget—and later in your schedule and tracking.

A general rule of thumb is that college professors assign two hours of homework for every hour of classroom time. But be flexible: some of your classes will require more or less time. (If you don't know how much time you should spend on homework ask your professor.)

Since school is currently your professional priority, any "optional" study sessions and test prep sessions should also be priorities. Schedule them in.

Be sure to budget some time for all the Investment Categories listed in Chapter 43.

Be sure to include travel and prep time for each activity. For example, when budgeting for your workout, include the time it takes to travel to and from the gym, change into your workout clothes, and shower and change back after it.

For biweekly, monthly, and other non-weekly commitments, just budget the average weekly time. (A four-hour monthly appointment would be budgeted for an hour a week.) Your schedule won't work out exactly, but doing this works well enough—especially if you underschedule (see below)—and is much easier than trying to work out a budget that accounts for every minute.

When you're done, add up the hours per week. If you're like most people, the total will come in at 150 to 200 hours per week. Time to cut back...

Eliminate as many of your time expenses as you can. I offered some suggestions for this—like quitting unwanted activities, doubling up with friends for chores, cutting back on escapism, and getting frugal—back in Chapter 44. But maybe you can come up with some other ideas. Be ruthless! The goal—which no one ever achieves, but is still worth aiming for—is zero time expenses.

If you can't eliminate an expense entirely, "trim" it. (Recalling that Good Time Managers are optimizers who value small increments of their precious time.) If you can cut fifteen minutes from an expense, you should do that.

When you're done eliminating and trimming expenses, add up all your commitments again. Hopefully, you're now much closer to 119 hours.

***Within each investment category* (Chapter 43), sort your activities into three groups: high-, medium-, and low-priority.** High-priority activities are those you must do or really want to do. Low-priority ones are those you can live without. And the medium-priority ones are somewhere in the middle.

Eliminate as many of the low-priority investment activities as you can. And any that you can't eliminate, trim as much as you can. Just be careful not to entirely eliminate any of the investment categories: it's important to do some self-care, planning and management, etc. every week.

When you're done eliminating and trimming your low-priority investments, add up all your commitments again. Probably, you're now even closer to 119 hours, but still not there. Now it's time to...

Eliminate, or trim, your medium-priority investment activities. This is when budgeting starts to get painful, because now you're cutting back on stuff you want to be doing. You could be asking yourself to give up an exciting extracurricular project or an extra night or two of socializing. But productivity work and Values-Based Time Management are all about getting real, and a major purpose of time management is to make these kinds of difficult decisions consciously and deliberately, instead of impulsively during a scheduling conflict the way Poor Time Managers (PTMs) do.

Postponing can be an option. A friend once tried to write her thesis at the same time she was working full-time and training for a marathon. Needless to say, she wasn't making much progress. "Thesis now, marathon later," I suggested. Presto! Progress on thesis!

You're even closer to your 119 hours now, but probably not quite there. Now it's time to...

Trim your high-priority investment activities. Now budgeting becomes an almost Buddhist discipline, forcing you to acknowledge and accept what may be life's most painful reality: our tragically limited amount of time. It will probably help if you take some time to mourn your losses, as discussed in Chapter 23; also, if you remember you're making these sacrifices for the best possible reason: your personal liberation. Please also remember that, when all is said and done, **you probably will have enough time to do everything you need to do, and even much of what you want to do, if you use your time well.** GTMs derive solace and motivation from that truth, which is often lost on the poor PTMs who remain in stubborn denial about both their time constraints and the potential of time management to mitigate their losses. And so, they struggle on under the delusion that, if they could somehow magically get their act together, they'd be able to "do it all."

GTMs also know the **goal isn't to squeeze every possible activity into our time budget, but rather to eliminate as many of the inessential activities as possible so that we have abundant time for the essentials**. An important time management strategy, in other words, is to not have too many activities to manage in the first place. Sure, you can reclaim little bits of time here and there: say, by walking to class (thus getting in some exercise) or doing schoolwork while you eat lunch. These kinds of habits are worth cultivating, so long as you don't go overboard. (Remember: if it feels stressful or deprivational, you've crossed the line into perfectionism.) You also want to specialize, decline, delegate, and use operating principles as much as possible. While helpful, however, these aren't definitive solutions the way frugality (Chapter 44) and radically emptying your schedule are.

Enjoy the moment. When you arrive at your goal (e.g., 119 hours), take a moment to **appreciate the achievement**. It's a meaningful one.

But you're not quite done yet…

The Genius of Underscheduling

Underscheduling is the GTM's secret weapon. By leaving a few unscheduled hours in your weekly schedule you can accommodate both the irregular (biweekly, etc.) tasks and also the unexpected ones, like when you need to help a friend or stranger.

PTMs resist doing this. Chronically behind in their work and other obligations, perfectionistically attached to suffering and pressure, and grandiosely refusing to accept their time limitations—not to mention, the laws of physics (you can't be in two places at once)—they have a strong compulsion to schedule every moment of their lives.

With all that in mind, let's return to our budgeting process:

Cut and Trim Some More. In particular, see if you've eliminated as many time expenses and low-priority investment activities as possible. A good goal to aim for would be anywhere from three to five unscheduled hours per week.

Finally, we have an important step many people forget...

Show Your Time Budget to Your Professors and Other Mentors. And ask the all-important question, "Am I using my time in the right way to achieve my goals?" This will not only get you some valuable feedback, it will show your mentors you're on the ball.

Sample Time Budget. Table IV, below, shows a sample time budget for a busy undergraduate who goes to school full-time, has a serious extracurricular commitment, and also an active social life. It's also realistic in terms of the human need for down time and escapism.

Table IV: Sample Time Budget for a Full-Time Student

Activity	Hrs/Week*	Notes
Classes	18	16 hours in class, plus 2 hours of travel time.
Homework	32	Rule of thumb: 2 hours of homework per hour of class time.
Extracurricular	12	A job or an arts, athletic, community or other group.
Self-Care	14.5	An hour per day for personal grooming and other personal care, plus 7.5 hours a week for exercise (e.g., three gym sessions or yoga classes).
Meals	14	A half-hour for all breakfasts and lunches, and a full hour for all dinners (includes cooking and cleanup time).
Socializing/ Recreation	7	Two or three recreational events per week (in addition to any recreation you're doing during other activities, such as meals).

Activity	Hrs/Week*	Notes
Escapism	10.5	1.5 hours per day for social media, gaming, television, etc (See Chapter 44.)
Errands	4	Laundry, shopping, cleaning, etc. and Chores
Activism/Comm unity Work	2	Whichever cause you care most about.
Planning & Management	2	Includes research and meetings with mentors; also, reviewing the week's time use—see next chapter.
Total:	116	(Out of 119 hours total = underscheduling!)

*All time estimates include commuting and preparation time.

This schedule provides a decent amount of time for all the investment categories. Still, it's a bit too full, especially since many jobs and extracurricular commitments demand more than twelve hours a week. Budgeting for only one hour of escapism a day—thereby freeing up a valuable 3.5 hours per week—and trimming the Errands category are two possible solutions.

Please let this sample time budget serve as a guide for you as you create your own in Exercise 28.

Exercise 28

Create your own Time Budget using the process outlined in this chapter. Take your time and pay attention to your feelings, especially while cutting and trimming activities. If you feel sad or conflicted about some of your choices, that probably means you're doing it right. Please use the solutions discussed above and in Chapter 23 to process those emotions.

50. Scheduling and Tracking Your Time

After finishing your Time Budget, your next step is to create a weekly schedule. Download a form for this from hillaryrettigproductivity.com or photocopy a page from a daily planner. Then use this process:

1. **Fill in your obligatory commitments**: classes, job, medical/counseling appointments, etc.

2. **Figure out when during the day you're at your highest energy, and schedule your study time then.** Also, if you have any time left over, schedule your exercise and any other priorities you find challenging or might be tempted to skip. Keep this time "sacred" for these activities, doing your best to never, ever schedule anything else during it.

3. As much as possible, **schedule your homework and other important tasks in chunks of an hour or more**. You do this because: (a) interruptions are "expensive" time-wise (as discussed in Chapter 5), (b) it can take a while to immerse ourselves in a task—although nonperfectionism can help reduce that immersion time a lot, and (c) tough creative and intellectual challenges require sustained concentration.

4. **Set up routines**—meaning that, whenever possible, try to do the same thing at the same time and in the same place each day. This sounds boring but, as discussed in Chapter 45, simplifies your life and helps you conserve your precious time, energy, and cognitive capacity.

5. Bonus points, as always, if you **show your schedule to your mentors** and ask for feedback.

Tracking

Once you've developed your schedule, you should start using it. And for a while, at least, you should also track your time use. Tracking helps you to be mindful of your time use, thus making it easier for you to stick to your schedule. Here's how to do it:

1. **Download the tracking form** from hillaryrettigproductivity.com. Or create your own from a spreadsheet. It should be a grid with columns for Monday through Sunday, and a row for each of your activities, including your personal ones. Also, a row to record the amount of procrastination you do each day—Stay cool! No judgments here!—and other rows to record the time you wake up and go to bed each day. Finally, there should be a Total box at the end of every column and row, and a box for recording Notes at the end of each row, after the Total.

2. **Keep the sheet with you**, in either electronic or printed form, as you go through your day.

3. **Every fifteen minutes, put a check mark in the box for the activity you just worked on.** So, if you do two hours of math homework on Monday, you'll have entered eight check marks in the "Monday/Math" box. You track every fifteen minutes for two reasons: (a) it's easy to forget what you've done, even an hour later, and (b) frequent check-ins keep you alert and mindful of your time use, thus helping you stay on schedule.

4. **Record any time you spend procrastinating.** Also, in the Notes box, why you think you did it, and the activity you did instead of your work.

5. **Record your daily wake-up and go-to-bed times.** It's best, from the standpoint of productivity, to wake up and go to bed at the same time most days, so this is how you track that. Also, you can use this data to see how sleep deprivation affects your productivity.

6. On Day 5 of your week, **check for rows with few or no checkmarks**—meaning, tasks you've skimped on or maybe skipped entirely. Be sure to devote some time to those.

7. At the end of the week, **add up all the horizontal and vertical totals** and record those in the appropriate boxes.

8. **Analyze the results** and, if needed, make a plan to do better next week. First, take a moment to appreciate the times you did stick to your schedule and the work you did get done. Then nonperfectionistically (without judgments) look at the times you got derailed and see if you can figure out why. (Maybe do some journaling.) If needed, tweak your budget and schedule so they better fit the realities of your time use. They're living documents you should feel free to change as your needs, situation, and priorities change.

9. **Repeat** the entire process the following week.

Some people track for just a couple of weeks after starting a new schedule, just to get used to it. Others track for their whole career—or beyond, if they're also tracking their personal time. And some track just in a few areas. Do whatever works for you.

Exercise 29

Create a weekly schedule from Exercise 28's Time Budget, then track your time for at least a couple of weeks. Pay particular attention to your stress level and emotions during that time. Hopefully, as you improve at using your time, you'll also get happier, more productive, and less stressed. Paying attention to these kinds of positive changes can help you to stay motivated to continue the practice.

So that's Values-Based Time Management! Like all the work in this book, you want to take it to the max. The harder you rock it, the more benefit you'll receive from it. Don't settle for being a Good Time Manager, in other words, when you can be a Great Time Manager!

Conclusion

Liberating Yourself and the World

Conclusion: Liberating Yourself and the World

A funny thing happens to a lot of people after they graduate from college: they start to settle.

They settle for jobs they don't want but that provide a paycheck.

For relationships that bore or stress them but that they can't bring themselves to end.

For towns they don't like because moving's a hassle.

And for governments and other systems that neglect and exploit them because, "It's always been that way" or, "What can one person do?"

You can watch it happen, and unfortunately probably will. Decade after decade, you'll see more and more of your classmates "settle down" and, in some cases, get stuck.

Please don't let that happen to you.

Don't get me wrong: there's no such thing as a perfect situation, and so, sooner or later, everyone does have to settle. Difficult times, moreover, tend to require more settling than usual—and, as noted in the Introduction, you are graduating at an exceptionally difficult time. (In the midst of a terrible economy and job market, not to mention multiple serious political, ecological, and other crises.) So don't feel bad about any decisions you need to make, even if they're not the ones you'd make if, say, jobs were more plentiful or the political situation less concerning.

At the same time, however, don't settle preemptively or more than you have to. Out there somewhere are a career, place, lifestyle, and relationships that will make you happy—or, at least, happier than the alternatives. These are worth working towards and, if necessary, fighting for. (And as my own story in the Introduction illustrates, even if you happen to be reading this in your 20s, 30s, or 40s—or later—it's not too late to start.)

Your life has value and meaning—and not just to you, but the rest of us. You may be just one small thread in the tapestry we call life, but you matter. If most of the threads in our tapestry shine, then it will be a vibrant work of beauty. But if most don't, then the tapestry, and life itself, will be dull. Best of all, you already have most of what you need to shine. Nonperfectionism, the Joyful Dance, Values-Based Time Management, and the other techniques in this book will take you far. And let's add **authenticity** to your list of foundational values. By that I mean that the trajectory of your life, and of your individual days, should align as much as possible with your true goals, values, needs, and desires. Put another way: you should mostly be doing the things you want to be doing, in the company of those with whom you'd mostly like to be doing them. (As discussed in Chapter 46, if you focus on the things you love, the community often follows.)

Authenticity isn't a goal so much as a path. You walk it by listening to, and then acting on, that quiet inner voice that tells you what's working and not working for you. Also, you want to cherish and nurture your vision of the "ideal" career and life you'd like to have. Sure: you don't want to cling to that vision too tightly or get upset when you fall short of achieving aspects of it. But it should always be there in the background of your thoughts, informing, guiding, and inspiring you.

Do your best to stay on the path, even during—especially during—difficult times. Take bold steps toward your destination when you can, and small steps when you can't. Enjoy the successes and persevere through the setbacks. **And remember that it's your community, more than any other single factor under your control, that determines your success.** Surround yourself with supporters, mentors, and encouragers, and they'll accelerate your progress. But surround yourself with naysayers, cynics, and discouragers, and you'll likely stall.

Similarly, always strive to surround yourself with empowered and effective people, including Good Time Managers, since that will maximize your own empowerment and effectiveness. The goal, really, is to "**live among the wise**," as the Buddha put it—and it's even more important to do that online than off, so you can avoid, as much as possible, social media's rampant perfectionism and other toxicities.

Likewise, be selective in the media you consume. We all have our need for escapism but, as much as possible, your inputs should delight and inspire you, not bore you or drag you down.

Speaking of community, empowered and authentic people seek happiness, health, and success not just for themselves but others. That's partly because they want to pay it forward for help they themselves received or privilege they benefited from, and partly because they know you can't be truly happy or successful while those around you are suffering. And it's also because having your authentic needs met gives you the intellectual and emotional capacity to respond to others' needs with empathy, generosity, and care. Empowered and authentic people, in other words, do their best to see others as the unique and valuable individuals they are—and yes, that includes the precious nonhumans with whom we share the planet.

All of which brings us to my final piece of advice: **trust**.

Trust yourself: your skills, resources, capacities, and commitment. Trust that you are enough and have enough to succeed, especially if you use the techniques in this book to minimize your perfectionism, unmanaged time, and other barriers. (As I've noted earlier, you may not have enough if you are facing poverty, bigotry, violence, or other constraints, but it's even more important, in such situations, to use the techniques I've discussed to reclaim whatever power you can.)

Trust that you can have a satisfying, fulfilling, and often joyful life and career. They may not be exactly the life and career you are envisioning—possibly not even close. But any path built on empowerment and authenticity will have its substantial rewards. Trust the path.

Trust, also, your community. You are surrounded by visionary and powerful teachers, healers, creators, communicators, and seekers after equality and justice in all their forms. Find them, and live and work as much as possible among them.

Trust that, whenever you find yourself needing help, it will be there. (Help is, in fact, abundant.)

Most of all, trust in the possibility of positive growth and change, both for individuals and societies, because—despite the easy, and often loud, pessimism of the doom-mongers—the evidence for that is all around us.

In fact, you're holding a bit of that evidence in your hands right now.

My own journey brought me to writing this book and your own journey brought you to reading it. I am grateful for both of our journeys and wish you well, with all my heart, as you continue on yours.

Hillary Rettig
Kalamazoo, MI
May, 2024

Appendix

Career and Life Strategies

A1. Creating Your Career

Many people will tell you to be realistic when planning your career, but I think you should aim sky high. That's because some people do manage to achieve their dream career—and even if you're not one of the lucky ones, you'll get a better outcome aiming high than if you settle right out of the gate.

Obviously, it's not enough to want a career: you have to plan and prepare for it. "In dreams begin responsibilities," as the poet William Butler Yeats said. The chief requirement for any stellar career is probably connections, and you may feel like you don't have any. But your professors can be your first, and you can use the techniques in this chapter and Chapters A2 and A3 to find others.

Stellar careers also often require money for things like specialized training or to start a small business. If a lack of funds is a barrier for you, look for jobs that offer a tuition-reimbursement benefit. The important things are that you: (a) plan (see below) and (b) consult lots of mentors.

So go for your dream job! Here's a nine-step process to help you get started:

Utilize Your College's Career Center

Along with helping you with your research and planning, these nice professionals also typically offer help with resume-writing and training for interviews. They might even be able to connect you with alumni who can provide advice and referrals. (Also ask your professors for contacts, and see Chapter A3 for suggestions on how to reach out.)

Research

Read at least two years of back issues of your field's main trade magazine—meaning, the magazine most people in your field go to for news. A professor or librarian can tell you what it is, and your school library should have a subscription. Read the new issues as they come out and also follow two or three of your field's leading blogs or other social media accounts. (They'll be mentioned in the magazine.) The goal is to learn your field's history and trends, and also the major problems everyone is trying to solve: information that can help you figure out your entry point and strategy. (If your field is globalizing, for instance, your bilingual/bicultural skills might be an asset.) This research can also help you figure out how best to frame your professional specialty (Chapter 46) for potential employers.

Plan

A few pages ought to do it. (Yeah, you should Joyfully Dance through this project, too. The Joyful Dance isn't just for schoolwork.) Start with where you'd like to be in twenty years and then work backward in five-year intervals (fifteen, ten, and five years). For each of those milestones, list your career goals, the major steps it will take to achieve them, and the major investments (e.g., of time and money) you'll need to make.

When you reach the five-year mark, switch to annual planning (years one through five), still covering the same information.

While doing this, start to problem-solve around your anticipated obstacles—lack of contacts, money, etc.—while, at the same time, figuring out just how much you're willing to work and sacrifice to achieve your goal. Generally speaking, the higher you aim, the more sacrifices you'll need to make. People seeking to be at the top of many fields, for instance, often must move to an area that's a hub for that field. And would-be entrepreneurs often must commit to living on a low income for years while building their business. It's a great sign if you don't see the needed sacrifices as being too big—or as sacrifices at all, compared with the joy of following your dream. Conversely, if the sacrifices seem huge, that might be a sign you should choose a different path.

Because of the sacrifices, or for other reasons entirely, you may decide, in the process of doing all this research and planning, that you don't want to pursue this particular career. That's fine—and an excellent result, really. (Far better to discover this "on paper" than in real life.) Start researching and planning for a career you're more interested in.

Show Your Plan to Your Mentors and Ask for Their Feedback

This should gain you not just useful feedback, but your mentors' respect, because mentors know that a willingness to plan—and, especially, to have one's plan critiqued—is a hallmark of a serious person. Don't forget to ask these two important network-building questions: (1) "Do you know anyone who can help me with task X?," and (2) "Is there anyone else you know who could give me some good feedback on my plan?" (See Chapter A3 for more on finding and cultivating mentors.)

Develop Some Social Media Chops

Employers in all fields crave employees with social media expertise and often hire young people to help with this. So familiarize yourself with the main social media platforms as they are used by successful companies and professionals in your field. Be prepared to discuss your knowledge of this during interviews, along with examples of how social media helped create a success or solved a problem. Also, systematically study—e.g., by taking a class—at least one platform, so you know how to do things on it most users can't. Instead of going with what's trendy, play to your strengths: if you like writing choose a text-based platform, and if you're more visual, a graphics- or video-based one.

Participate

Join your field's main trade association. The trade magazine will tell you what that is, or you can ask a professor. Avoid organizations whose primary focus is lobbying or providing insurance: your goals are professional development and networking, so look for one that offers lots of meetings, classes, networking opportunities, etc. Memberships can be expensive, so ask about a student rate or discount.

Once you've joined, attend whatever local meetings you can, plus, if possible, the annual national or international meeting. (Ask both the organization and your school for a scholarship or travel stipend.) If the organization has a student subgroup, participate in it.

After you graduate, join the main (non-student) group and volunteer in a visible position, like on the association's blog or an event-planning committee.

Apply

When you're ready, start applying for work. If you've followed the above steps, you should be a much stronger candidate, and possibly already on potential employers' radar. Check out my free ebook *It's Not You, It's Your Strategy* for a good job-search strategy. (Download English and Spanish versions at https://hillaryrettigproductivity.com/.)

Grow

Look for jobs that will allow you to grow your skills, get great mentoring, and make great connections. (Title and salary are less important, in other words.) And throughout your career, seek out empowering workplaces that are run on principles of equality, transparency, kindness, compassion, and justice.

Stay Focused

There will be times during your career when you experience a setback, or feel confused or stalled. Try not to let these transient episodes derail you.

Yes, you can change your mind and your plan. Try not to do so impulsively, however, or out of fear or confusion. If you are still committed to your Plan A but can't figure out how to make it work, talk to your mentors.

A2. More Career Advice

Below are short answers to common career-related questions. Remember that, no matter which path you take, Career Task #1 is always nonperfectionism, Career Task #2 is always research and planning, and Career Task #3 is always to work with great mentors.

How Can I Find Work When I'm a Liberal Arts Major?

People are always blathering on about how liberal arts majors can't get jobs, but the truth is that many employers favor them.[71] These employers are looking for candidates with demonstrated communications, teamwork, and leadership skills, so don't just join projects or clubs, lead them.

For an extra advantage, do a bankable minor like marketing or statistics. Fluency in a second language also helps. Also, buff up your social media skills, as described in the previous chapter.

How Can I Become a Professional Artist, Craftsperson, or Performer?

I've taught creative entrepreneurship to hundreds of people, and here is my advice for anyone on that path:

---

[71] See, for example: www.cnbc.com/id/100642178, www.theladders.com/career-advice/liberal-arts-major-hire and www.historians.org/publications-and-directories/perspectives-on-history/april-2017/history-is-not-a-useless-major-fighting-myths-with-data.

1. Take an entrepreneurship class *taught by someone with actual small business experience*. It doesn't have to be geared toward artists: in fact, there are advantages to being in a room full of caterers, locksmiths, hair stylists, and others, and seeing what your business has in common with theirs. If your school happens to offer an excellent entrepreneurship class taught by someone with first-hand knowledge, I'd take it. If not, don't worry: many nonprofits, community colleges, and other venues offer such classes, and you can take one after you graduate.

2. Do an apprenticeship, i.e., work with a successful artist in a position that allows you to observe how they run their business. (By "successful," I mean someone whose business is stable and generates at least a part-time income.) You do this to gain a real-world understanding of what the business entails, and also to gain contacts and learn who the good suppliers, galleries, agents, banks, and other business partners are.

3. Try to get a paid gig, but I wouldn't rule out an unpaid internship with the right person, so long as they are committed to doing a lot of mentoring.

4. Make a business plan. A few pages detailing what you will sell, to whom, and for how much, will be fine. Include three years of profit-and-loss statements showing how the money will flow into and out of your business. (Your entrepreneurship class should teach you how to do all this, and you can also download a Marketing Exercise from hillaryrettigproductivity.com.) When you're done, show your plan to your mentors and ask for feedback.

In my experience, would-be entrepreneurs who skip the above steps almost always fail. By the way, you'll also need exceptional time management skills (Part V) to succeed, because entrepreneurship is a busy, busy gig.

What If I Want to Start a Non-Arts Business?

Entrepreneurship of any kind is a satisfying path. The above advice also applies.

How Do I Build a Career in Community Organizing or Activism?

I am always thrilled when someone wants to pursue this path, both because we need as many organizers as possible, and because social justice work can be incredibly personally rewarding. Paid jobs with top organizations are competitive, but you can boost your odds of being hired by: (1) networking (often via volunteering and attending conferences, as discussed in Chapter A1, above) and (2) being a terrific applicant. (Again, see my downloadable ebook, *It's Not You, It's Your Strategy*.)

A lot of activist learning is experiential, but you should read up on the basics. Some good books are Becky Bond and Zack Exley's *Rules for Revolutionaries*, adrienne maree brown's *Emergent Strategy*, Nick Montgomery and carla bergman's *Joyful Militancy* (a book that's about nonperfectionist activism, although they don't use that phrase), Alexandra Bradbury, Mark Brenner, and Jane Slaughter's *Secrets of a Successful Organizer*, Kelly Hayes and Mariame Kaba's *Let This Radicalize You*, Jane F. McAlevey's *No Shortcuts*, and my own *The Lifelong Activist*. Also read a few sales and marketing books—including Dale Carnegie's classic *How to Win Friends & Influence People*—because the techniques can absolutely be used to promote social good.

Keep in mind, too, that many other types of careers—including in politics, government, medicine, education, and certain industries such as vegan foods or renewable energy—will also allow you to make a great contribution.

What If I Can't Decide What I Want to Do?

There may be many reasons for your ambivalence, so try the solutions in Chapter 24. Especially, ask yourself if you might be self-censoring because you view your desired career as somehow unacceptable or unattainable. "What makes you think you can be a [insert career type]?" someone might have said to you once. Or, "You'll never make a living doing that." Nuts to all the naysayers! The ability to do what you love as your career is a tremendous gift you give yourself over the years and decades of your life, and worth striving for. So, along with the anti-ambivalence work, find some encouraging mentors (see next chapter).

What if you don't have a strong career preference? It's okay to try a few different careers after graduation. (The career equivalent of trial and error.) As mentioned in Chapter 24, a common reason for ambivalence is that we don't have enough information to make a decision. Working for a while in a field you are considering is a good way to get that information. Just be sure that, if you do switch careers, you're doing so because you genuinely want a change and not because you've hit a bump and are afraid to proceed on your current path. (Journal to see whether negativity, dichotomizing, pathology, shortsightedness, or other perfectionist characteristics are contributing to your decision.)

A3. Working with Mentors

The more ambitious you are, the more mentors you need. I once met a woman who said she had hundreds of mentors—her points being that: (a) everyone is a potential mentor, and (b) she had mentors she could call on for help with pretty much any topic.

There are two types of mentors: (1) those who are further along a professional or personal path than you and can advise you on how to proceed, and (2) those who can teach you a useful skill, such as how to ace a job interview, purchase a home, or cook a nutritious meal. You want to have mentors for every important professional and personal endeavor, and it's okay if some of them, like your therapist or personal trainer, are paid.

Obviously, your professors and the other educational staff you've worked with are mentors, and both before and, in some cases, after graduation, you shouldn't hesitate to ask them for advice or support. (If you're reluctant, review Chapter 10's discussion on the importance of getting comfortable asking for help.) You probably also already know a few other people who can mentor you in crucial areas. Sooner or later, however, you'll need to reach out to a stranger. (Perhaps they will be a referral from a professor or a colleague from a professional organization.) Don't be shy about approaching such potential mentors: most people want to help. At the same time, however, successful people get asked for help a lot, including by people who aren't serious. When approaching a potential mentor, therefore, make sure they know you're one of the serious ones by making a knowledgeable, focused, and personalized request for assistance:

- "Knowledgeable" means it's clear that you understand your field, including how to behave professionally within it.
- "Focused" means your request is clear and concise, and the favor you're asking for is obvious and doable. (If the recipient has to puzzle over what exactly you're asking for, that's not good.)
- "Personalized" means it should be obvious why you're asking that person in particular for help.

Below is a sample email from a student to a potential mentor who works at a company they'd like to work for:

Subject: Referred by Dr. Carol Referrer

Dear Dr. Alcantara:

I'm a senior at XYZ College majoring in materials engineering, and my career goal is to work in the field of renewable energy. After graduation, I will be seeking an entry-level scientific position at a leading company in the field, with ABC Company being my top choice. My energy engineering professor, Dr. Carol Referrer, therefore suggested I contact you. Would you be available to talk for a few minutes about opportunities at ABC Company? I am available either by telephone or teleconference at your convenience.

I am attaching my resume and would like to highlight my sophomore and junior summer internships working at LMN Utilities, where I assisted with solar cell efficiency studies. This research has led to a research paper, currently in submission at Prestigious Solar Publication, and I am listed as a coauthor.

Thank you for your time and consideration. I look forward to your reply.

Sincerely,

Trina Salas

Note that Trina does not ask Dr. Alcantara to "be my mentor." What you're asking for is a favor, not a relationship: if the relationship is destined to develop, it will. (In fact, you may never need to use the word "mentor" when interacting with your mentors.)

A note similar to the above should yield a good response from many potential mentors. If you don't get such a response, or any response at all, don't sweat it. This happens to everyone and there could be many reasons for it, including some that have nothing to do with you or your request. (The person could be busy or dealing with some professional or personal problems.) Take another look at your note to see if you can improve it, then reach out to others.

Some final suggestions:

Ace the Meeting. If a mentor agrees to talk with you, that's fantastic. Be prompt, prepared, and professional, and don't go past the agreed-upon time. (Although if the mentor is enjoying the conversation, they might, which is fine.)

Focus on Problem-solving. As opposed to how frustrated or miserable the situation is making you feel. (Save that for your friends or a counselor.)

Thank Them. And not just on the call or with a perfunctory message afterwards. Your thank-you email or note doesn't have to be long, but it should reflect your sincere gratitude and, if possible, include a brief statement of how the advice helped you. (E.g., "Thank you, especially, for suggesting I attend the next XYZ meeting. I'm looking forward to attending and have already applied to my department for a travel grant.")

Follow Through. Meaning, do what your mentor tells you to do. This would seem like a no-brainer, but plenty of people ask others for advice which they then fail to follow. When you do that, you not only waste your mentor's time but discourage them from continuing to work with you. Most mentors are quick to shift their time and energy toward the most productive relationships.

It's not that mentors are infallible or that you have to follow their advice every single time: it's that you should follow it most of the time, and only not follow it when you have a good reason.

Build Your Network. Always ask questions like, "Do you know anyone else whom I should be talking to about this?"

Stay In Touch Even When Everything's Okay. If you just contact your mentors when you need help, they'll feel used. So contact them once or twice a year, just to let them know how things are going. Mentors especially like hearing your good news, which should, of course, include a "thank you" for their ongoing contribution to your success.

Reciprocate. While it can be hard to figure out what you can offer a mentor with more skills, experience, and contacts, most mentors do appreciate receiving articles on topics of mutual interest, and also having their work shared on social media and elsewhere.

Learn to Recognize Mentor Relationships That Aren't Working. This could be because the person isn't a competent mentor or the two of you aren't a good fit.

Be a Mentor. Yes, you should be a mentor! It's a great way to do good, while also growing your skills and network. You can mentor people in any professional or personal specialty (Chapter 46), as well as in nonperfectionism, the Joyful Dance, Values-Based Time Management, and the other techniques in this book. Sharing your hard-won wisdom and skills with others will not only help them but put wings on your own career and life.

Acknowledgments

I gratefully acknowledge the assistance and support of:

James Wilkinson, whose influence in the field of undergraduate education has been immense. I am honored to be among the many people whose work he has supported and encouraged, and even more honored by his friendship.

Lee Busch, who provided yet another fantastic book cover, as well as valuable strategic advice.

Martin Rowe, a brilliant editor whose assistance greatly improved this book.

Christopher Sturr and Eli Massey, for fantastic copy editing.

My diligent manuscript readers: Paul Busch, John Falcone, Julia Falcone, Cristina Florea, Julia Ftacek, Kerry Langdon-Fisher, and Arvind Thomas.

For valuable advice and assistance: Liz Alton, Erin Boydston, Alexis Diller, Cory Doctorow, Lisa Falcone, Joan Frantschuk, Elizabeth McCullough, Michael A. McDonald, Sanjoy Mahajan, Daniel M. Pink, Lauren Rosenthal, Zick Rubin, Karen E. Sprole, and the late Ralph Deal.

My family, and especially my sisters, for walking the path with me, even when it wasn't easy.

Jan Tobochnik, for epic love and support, as well as terrific strategic advice.

My workshop students and coaching clients, for learning, insight, and inspiration.

If This Book Has Helped You...

If this book has helped you, please support my work by:

1. Leaving a review on your favorite online bookseller. (Even a short review is great!)
2. Emailing any comments or suggestions for the next edition to me at hillaryrettig@gmail.com.
3. Signing up for my mailing list at www.hillaryrettigproductivity.com. (You'll find many free articles there, and also information about my workshops.)
4. Inviting me to lead a workshop at your school, arts, community, parenting, or other group. (Email me at hillaryrettig@gmail.com with information about your group, and some possible dates.)

Thank you!

About the Authors

About Hillary Rettig

Along with the book you're holding, Hillary Rettig is also author of *Productivity is Power 2: For Creative and Business Professionals*. Her other books are the bestselling *The 7 Secrets of the Prolific*, *The Journey is the Destination*, and *The Lifelong Activist*. She has taught productivity and time management classes at educational, community, arts, and business organizations throughout the United States and beyond. Her articles have appeared in dozens of publications, including *Wired*, *Working Woman*, *Psychology Today*, *Fortune*, *Time Management Ninja*, *Tomorrow's Professor*, and *The Thesis Whisperer*.

From 2001 – 2012, she worked as a business coach and microlender at two nonprofit agencies in Boston, roles in which she helped hundreds of people from all backgrounds start and grow businesses.

Hillary is also a vegan, a free software/free culture advocate, and a lover of life, dogs, and social justice in all its forms. She is also a living kidney donor and a former foster mother to four teenage South Sudanese refugees, now all adults and living independently.

Hillary was born in the Bronx, NY, has lived in Ithaca, NY, and Boston, MA, and now lives in Kalamazoo, MI, with her partner Jan Tobochnik, a physics professor at Kalamazoo College.

For more information on Hillary and her work, including free ebooks and other downloads, visit https://hillaryrettigproductivity.com/.

About James Wilkinson (Foreword)

Harvard University professor emeritus James Wilkinson is a global leader in the field of undergraduate pedagogy. After receiving his doctorate in history from Harvard in 1974, he taught European history at Boston University and from 1985 – 1988 was founding director of BU's Teaching Center. In 1988 he joined the Harvard faculty, and from then through his retirement in 2007, served as director of Harvard's Derek Bok Center for Teaching and Learning. (He remains affiliated with the Center as a senior associate.)

In 2009, Dr. Wilkinson became the organizer of The International Conference on Improving University Teaching (IUT), the premier international meeting on university teaching. The IUT Conference examines topics relevant to students, faculty, and staff in higher education as well as to representatives of business and organizations concerned with higher education.

Dr. Wilkinson has received fellowships from the Guggenheim Foundation and National Endowment for the Humanities, as well as numerous other honors and awards.

Check out Hillary Rettig's Other Books

Productivity is Power II: For Creative, Business, and Other Professionals (Infinite Art, 2024).

The Journey is the Reward: Fifteen Years of Blogging on Productivity, Love, and Life (Infinite Art, 2023).*

The 7 Secrets of the Prolific: How to Overcome Procrastination, Perfectionism, and Writer's Block (Infinite Art, 2011).

It's Not You, It's Your Strategy: Finding Work in a Tough Job Market (Infinite Art, 2008)**

The Lifelong Activist: How to Change the World Without Losing Your Way (Lantern Books, 2006).

More information on Hillary's books at www.HillaryRettigProductivity.com

*Free download.
**Free download in English and Spanish.